DEADLY DISEASES AND EPIDEMICS

CHICKEN POX

Anthrax, Second Edition

Antibiotic-Resistant
  Bacteria

Avian Flu

Botulism

Campylobacteriosis

Cervical Cancer

Chicken Pox

Cholera, Second Edition

Dengue Fever and Other
  Hemorrhagic Viruses

Diphtheria

Ebola

Encephalitis

Escherichia coli
  Infections

Gonorrhea

Hantavirus Pulmonary
  Syndrome

Helicobacter pylori

Hepatitis

Herpes

HIV/AIDS

Infectious Diseases of
  the Mouth

Infectious Fungi

Influenza,
  Second Edition

Legionnaires' Disease

Leprosy

Lung Cancer

Lyme Disease

Mad Cow Disease

Malaria, Second Edition

Meningitis

Mononucleosis,
  Second Edition

Pelvic Inflammatory
  Disease

Plague, Second Edition

Polio, Second Edition

Prostate Cancer

Rabies

Rocky Mountain
  Spotted Fever

Rubella and Rubeola

Salmonella

SARS, Second Edition

Smallpox

Staphylococcus aureus
  Infections

Streptococcus (Group A)

Streptococcus (Group B)

Syphilis, Second Edition

Tetanus

Toxic Shock Syndrome

Trypanosomiasis

Tuberculosis

Tularemia

Typhoid Fever

West Nile Virus,
  Second Edition

Yellow Fever

DEADLY DISEASES AND EPIDEMICS

CHICKEN POX

Patrick Guilfoile, Ph.D.

CONSULTING EDITOR
Hilary Babcock, M.D., M.P.H.,
Infectious Diseases Division,
Washington University School of Medicine,
Medical Director of Occupational Health (Infectious Diseases),
Barnes-Jewish Hospital and St. Louis Children's Hospital

FOREWORD BY
David Heymann
World Health Organization

CHELSEA HOUSE
P U B L I S H E R S
An imprint of Infobase Publishing

*Thanks to my wife, Audrey, for her support of this project
and my father, Thomas, for his expert proofreading assistance.*

Chicken Pox

Chelsea House
An imprint of Infobase Publishing
132 West 31st Street
New York NY 10001

Library of Congress Cataloging-in-Publication Data
Guilfoile, Patrick.
  Chicken pox / Patrick Guilfoile ; consulting editor, Hilary Babcock ; foreword by David Heymann.
    p. cm. — (Deadly diseases and epidemics)
  Includes bibliographical references and index.
  ISBN-13: 978-1-60413-227-4
  ISBN-10: 1-60413-227-2
  1. Chickenpox—Juvenile literature. I. Title.

  RC125.G85 2009
  616.9'14—dc22
                    2009013076

Series design by Terry Mallon and James Scotto-Lavino
Cover design by Takeshi Takahashi

Printed in the United States of America

Bang EJB 10 9 8 7 6 5 4 3 2 1

This book is printed on acid-free paper.

All links and Web addresses were checked and verified to be correct at the time of publication. Because of the dynamic nature of the Web, some addresses and links may have changed since publication and may no longer be valid.

Table of Contents

Foreword

Communicable diseases kill and cause long-term disability. The microbial agents that cause them are dynamic, changeable, and resilient: They are responsible for more than 14 million deaths each year, mainly in developing countries.

Approximately 46 percent of all deaths in the developing world are due to communicable diseases, and almost 90 percent of these deaths are from AIDS, tuberculosis, malaria, and acute diarrheal and respiratory infections of children. In addition to causing great human suffering, these high-mortality communicable diseases have become major obstacles to economic development. They are a challenge to control either because of the lack of effective vaccines, or because the drugs that are used to treat them are becoming less effective because of antimicrobial drug resistance.

Millions of people, especially those who are poor and living in developing countries, are also at risk from disabling communicable diseases such as polio, leprosy, lymphatic filariasis, and onchocerciasis. In addition to human suffering and permanent disability, these communicable diseases create an economic burden—both on the workforce that handicapped persons are unable to join, and on their families and society, upon which they must often depend for economic support.

Finally, the entire world is at risk of the unexpected communicable diseases, those that are called emerging or re-emerging infections. Infection is often unpredictable because risk factors for transmission are not understood, or because it often results from organisms that cross the species barrier from animals to humans. The cause is often viral, such as Ebola and Marburg hemorrhagic fevers and severe acute respiratory syndrome (SARS). In addition to causing human suffering and death, these infections place health workers at great risk and are costly to economies. Infections such as Bovine Spongiform Encephalopathy (BSE) and the associated new human variant of Creutzfeldt-Jakob Disease (vCJD) in Europe, and avian influenza A (H5N1) in Asia, are reminders of the seriousness of emerging and re-emerging infections. In addition, many of these infections have the potential to cause pandemics, which are a constant threat to our economies and public health security.

Science has given us vaccines and anti-infective drugs that have helped keep infectious diseases under control. Nothing demonstrates the effectiveness of vaccines better than the successful eradication of smallpox, the decrease in polio as the eradication program continues, and the decrease in measles when routine immunization programs are supplemented by mass vaccination campaigns.

Likewise, the effectiveness of anti-infective drugs is clearly demonstrated through prolonged life or better health in those infected with viral diseases such as AIDS, parasitic infections such as malaria, and bacterial infections such as tuberculosis and pneumococcal pneumonia.

But current research and development is not filling the pipeline for new anti-infective drugs as rapidly as resistance is developing, nor is vaccine development providing vaccines for some of the most common and lethal communicable diseases. At the same time providing people with access to existing anti-infective drugs, vaccines, and goods such as condoms or bed nets—necessary for the control of communicable diseases in many developing countries—remains a great challenge.

Education, experimentation, and the discoveries that grow from them are the tools needed to combat high mortality infectious diseases, diseases that cause disability, or emerging and re-emerging infectious diseases. At the same time, partnerships between developing and industrialized countries can overcome many of the challenges of access to goods and technologies. This book may inspire its readers to set out on the path of drug and vaccine development, or on the path to discovering better public health technologies by applying our present understanding of the human genome and those of various infectious agents. Readers may likewise be inspired to help ensure wider access to those protective goods and technologies. Such inspiration, with pragmatic action, will keep us on the winning side of the struggle against communicable diseases.

David L. Heymann
Assistant Director General,
Health Security and Environment
Representative of the Director General for Polio Eradication,
World Health Organization,
Geneva, Switzerland

1

What Is Chicken Pox?

A 27-year-old woman came to the emergency room in a hospital in England with a mild fever, a rash, and breathing difficulty. She was diagnosed with chicken pox that had developed into pneumonia and was rushed to intensive care. During her hospitalization, her breathing difficulty worsened. She was given oxygen, and eventually a tube was placed in her throat and attached to a respirator to aid her breathing. Her fever worsened. After several days, she developed bacterial infections in her lungs and in her bloodstream, both of which were treated with antibiotics. She remained in intensive care for 20 days; finally, she was transferred to a regular hospital room, and was discharged 8 days later. Although she felt better, a week after her discharge from the hospital she still had limited lung function. Aside from being a cigarette smoker, she did not have any risk factors that would have reduced her immunity and made her vulnerable to developing simultaneous infections.[1] In some individuals, as this case shows, chicken pox can lead to serious complications, such as pneumonia.

Chicken pox is a sudden onset, very contagious disease that is characterized by a widespread, blister-like rash. It typically infects children in temperate regions; adults are more frequently infected in tropical areas. Chicken pox is caused by the varicella-zoster virus, a type of **herpesvirus**. Herpesviruses are a group of viruses that include the herpes simplex virus, which causes cold sores, and the Epstein-Barr virus, which causes mononucleosis. Usually chicken pox is relatively mild, although the symptoms can be unpleasant and uncomfortable. However, it can be a serious, sometimes even fatal infection. Before the widespread use of the chicken pox vaccine in the mid-1990s, there were more than 100 deaths per year from complications related to chicken pox infection in the United States.[2]

Chicken pox is of particular concern when it affects individuals over the age of 20, because complications are more likely to occur. Complications of chicken pox, serious enough to require hospitalization, were estimated to occur in about 10 cases out of 10,000 in children 14 years old and younger, but about 127 cases per 10,000 in adults 20 and older.[3] These complications include **pneumonia**, secondary bacterial infections, and damage to the central nervous system. In addition, chicken pox is likely to be more serious in patients who have some type of immune deficiency, including patients with certain types of cancer.

CHARACTERISTICS OF THE VIRUS

The varicella-zoster virus belongs to the herpesvirus family, a group of more than 100 viruses that infect a wide variety of animals including fish, reptiles, birds, and mammals. Herpesviruses share the ability to invade animal tissues, cause infection, and subsequently remain dormant until they reemerge and cause a new infection in the same host.

The varicella-zoster virus is a member of the alpha-herpesvirus subfamily, and the alpha-2 herpesvirus **genus**. The varicella-zoster virus is most closely related to the equine herpesviruses that infect horses, and the pseudorabies virus that infects pigs. Even though the varicella-zoster virus is most similar to animal viruses, the only known host for the varicella-zoster virus is humans, although some laboratory animals can be infected, at least for short periods of time. However, these animals do not develop an infection that mimics all the symptoms of an infection in humans. The varicella-zoster virus is also related, but not as closely, to the human herpes simplex viruses that cause cold sores and genital lesions. Genetic comparison of mammalian herpesviruses suggests they have been evolving from a common ancestor for approximately 75 million years.[4]

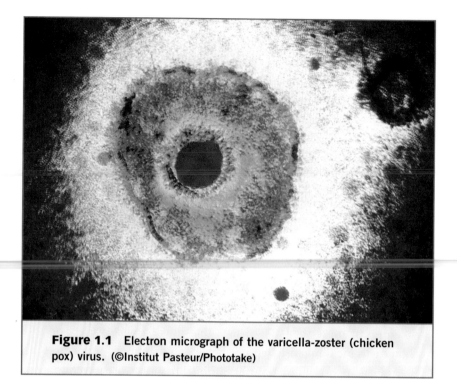

Figure 1.1   Electron micrograph of the varicella-zoster (chicken pox) virus. (©Institut Pasteur/Phototake)

Like other herpesviruses, the varicella-zoster virus contains double-stranded DNA located inside a protein structure called a **capsid**. **Tegument proteins** are also present inside the capsid; these proteins are critical for **replication** (copying) of the viral DNA inside host cells. The capsid is wrapped in an **envelope** made of fats. This envelope comes from membranes manufactured by the infected cell.[5] Embedded in the envelope are several viral proteins required for attachment and entry into human cells, the viral **glycoproteins**. Glycoproteins are proteins that are decorated with sugar molecules. This fatty envelope also means that the virus is less stable in the environment than other viruses that lack an envelope. Once it is outside the body it dries out and can no longer invade human cells, so it is unable to cause infection.

Like most viruses, the varicella-zoster virus is very small (150 to 200 **nanometers**), roughly one-tenth the size of a typical bacterial cell. Also, like most viruses, this microbe can replicate very rapidly, requiring only about 8 to 10 hours between entry into the cell and the appearance of new viruses in that cell, based on studies of infected cells in the laboratory.[6] The infection of a single cell with one virus probably results in the production of hundreds of new varicella-zoster viruses, although the exact number has been difficult to determine experimentally. The virus typically passes from cell to cell when the cell membrane of an infected cell fuses with the membrane of an adjacent, uninfected cell. Consequently, the viruses rarely separate from cells, so they are hard to count.

Unlike many viruses, the varicella-zoster virus does not appear to **mutate** (change its DNA) at a rapid rate. There are no identified subtypes of the virus, and there have not been any identified strains that appear to have enhanced or lower **virulence**. Virulence is associated with the ability to cause disease; more virulent **pathogens** are more readily able to cause disease, or cause a more serious form of the disease.

As noted above, the varicella-zoster virus is related to the herpes simplex Type 1 virus. For example, these viruses share many genes, and the order of genes in the **genomes** of both viruses is similar. However, since the varicella-zoster virus has a smaller genome, it lacks some of the genes found in the herpes simplex Type 1 virus and other herpesviruses.[7] Because of these genetic differences, the life cycle of these two viruses is somewhat different. For example, the varicella-zoster virus normally reactivates once in a person's lifetime, leading to the development of **shingles.** Shingles, which occurs when the original varicella-zoster virus emerges and causes new disease symptoms, often occurs decades after a person is first infected with the varicella-zoster virus. In contrast, herpes simplex Type 1 virus infections are characterized by frequent

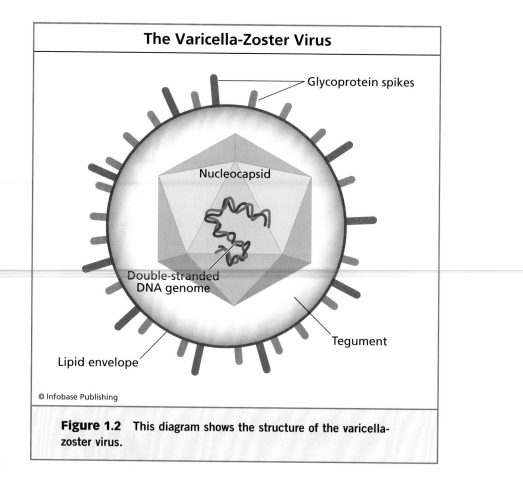

The Varicella-Zoster Virus

Glycoprotein spikes

Nucleocapsid

Double-stranded DNA genome

Tegument

Lipid envelope

© Infobase Publishing

Figure 1.2 This diagram shows the structure of the varicella-zoster virus.

reactivations, seen as the eruption of cold sores. Further research should identify the genes responsible for these differences in life cycle.

TRANSMISSION OF CHICKEN POX

Most commonly, the virus is passed from one person with chicken pox to an uninfected, susceptible person. The virus initially infects the respiratory tract, because the virus is inhaled, or picked up from direct contact with the fluid from the sores of a person with chicken pox. An adult with shingles can also transmit the virus, although rarely, causing chicken pox in a susceptible person.

In many countries, chicken pox is more common during certain seasons. In the Northern Hemisphere for example, the incidence of chicken pox has been highest during the spring (March to June). In several developed countries (e.g., the United States, United Kingdom) the average age of infection has dropped in recent decades, perhaps reflecting a larger proportion of children using day care centers, where they may be exposed to the virus prior to the start of school.

Before the development and widespread use of a chicken pox vaccine, it was estimated that 3 to 4 million cases of chicken pox occurred each year in the United States, and that 90 percent of those cases were in children under 13 years of age. With the widespread use of the vaccine, the number of cases has been reduced approximately 90 percent, to somewhere between 400,000 and 600,000 cases per year.[8]

Close contact with an infected person leads to the development of chicken pox. A second child in a household with one chicken pox case has a 70 to 90 percent risk of contracting the disease. Often the second child develops a more severe case of chicken pox, with more lesions. This is probably because he or she is infected with a higher dose of the virus than the first child, who may have acquired the disease during a brief interaction with an infected child at school. An infected person can transmit the disease for approximately two days before the characteristic rash develops, and a person remains infectious until all the chicken pox sores become crusted over, usually about a week. Normally, a person only gets chicken pox once in his or her lifetime, although there have been a few reports of multiple infections,[9] and one study from California that suggested that upwards of 10 percent of chicken pox infections may be reinfections.[10]

The pattern of transmission is quite different in the tropics. As noted above, in temperate regions, prior to the widespread use of a vaccine, the number of cases approximated the annual birth rate, meaning that relatively few individuals (only about 5 percent) reached adulthood without contracting chicken pox. In contrast, in the tropics, approximately 50 percent of individuals reach adulthood without having chicken pox.[11] There have been a number of possible explanations for the low rates of chicken pox during childhood in the tropics, including limitations on virus transmission at higher temperatures. However, the phenomenon appears to be a consequence of reduced transmission of chicken pox in rural areas. In 1998, researchers from the United Kingdom and India studied about 400 people living in urban and rural areas of India. They found that 96 percent of urban dwellers had evidence of chicken pox infection by age 25. In contrast, only 42 percent of people living in rural areas contracted chicken pox by age 25.[12] In rural areas people live farther apart and may be less likely to come in contact with an infected person.

SYMPTOMS OF CHICKEN POX

The symptoms of chicken pox are variable, depending on the age of the patient and whether the person has an intact immune system. As a rule, the illness is mildest in young children with a normal immune response, and most severe in people who are older, and among those who are immunocompromised. For example, in the 1990s, the mortality rate from chicken pox in the United States was 15 times higher in adults, as compared with children. As another example, patients with leukemia (a cancer that affects the white blood cells that fight infections) are much more susceptible to chicken pox, and more frequently develop serious complications.

In a typical childhood infection, the disease has a substantial **incubation period** (an average of about 14 days) prior to the development of the first symptoms. A mild fever is common, usually less than 102°F (39°C), but occasionally as high as 106°F (41°C). This fever, along with headache, pain in the abdomen, and a general feeling of ill health often are present a day or

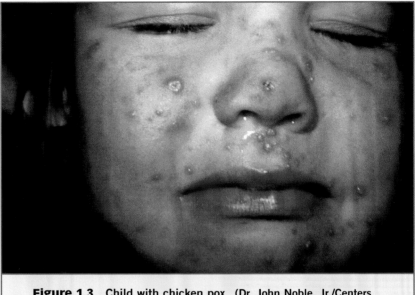

Figure 1.3 Child with chicken pox. (Dr. John Noble, Jr./Centers for Disease Control/ U.S. Department of Health and Human Services)

two in advance of the primary symptom, a widespread rash. The rash is composed of little fluid-filled sacs, which are surrounded by reddened skin. These lesions often first appear on the face or torso and eventually extend to the extremities. In an otherwise healthy child with no previous exposure to the virus, about 100 to 300 of these lesions typically develop, although the range is broad, with as few as 10 lesions and as many as 1,500. New vesicles, or pox, generally develop for 3 to 5 days, until the immune system wins the battle with the virus and new lesions no longer form. Eventually, the pox lesions crust over and fall off. Usually there is not much scarring, although the skin often loses its pigmentation for a time at the site of the lesions.

COMPLICATIONS OF CHICKEN POX
Chicken pox in a young child rarely leads to complications. However, the older a person is when they contract chicken pox,

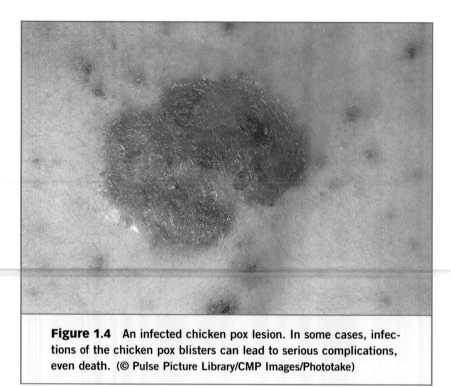

Figure 1.4   An infected chicken pox lesion. In some cases, infections of the chicken pox blisters can lead to serious complications, even death. (© Pulse Picture Library/CMP Images/Phototake)

the greater the chance of serious complications. One example of a complication following chicken pox is a bacterial infection of the skin at the site of a chicken pox vesicle. The most serious infections are caused by *Staphylococcus aureus* and *Streptococcus pyogenes*. These infections can range from local infections of a few chicken pox vesicles to infections that involve tissues throughout the body. The widespread infections can be very serious, even life threatening.

Another potential complication is Reye's syndrome. This illness causes damage to the liver and may cause serious alterations to the nervous system. Reye's syndrome has been linked to cases of chicken pox where a patient took aspirin to treat symptoms of the disease. As a consequence of this connection, since 1980 public health authorities have recommended that children who have viral illnesses such as chicken pox not take aspirin. As physicians and parents became aware of this connection, the number of cases of Reye's syndrome has dropped dramatically in the United States, from 555 cases in 1980, to fewer than 36 cases per year since 1987. This was an important advance in public health, because the death rate, following a diagnosis of Reye's syndrome, was nearly one in three.[13]

In adults, one of the more serious and frequent complications of varicella-zoster infection is chicken pox pneumonia. Pneumonia is associated with fever, cough, wheezing, shortness of breath, and difficulty breathing. As noted in the case study at the beginning of this chapter, this form of pneumonia can lead to serious disturbance of respiratory function and prolonged

VISION CORRECTED BY CHICKEN POX

Typically, an illness does not improve a patient's health. An exception to that rule was a report of a case of chicken pox in an 11-year-old girl from England, who was nearsighted and required glasses for distance vision. The girl initially went to her family doctor with a complaint of pain in her right eye, and hazy vision. Three weeks earlier, she had had chicken pox. She was given a treatment for inflammation of the eye, and sent home. A week later, she went back to the eye clinic, still complaining of hazy vision. An examination showed that the vision in her right eye had suffered as a result of scarring due to chicken pox. However, a year later, her eyesight was rechecked, and the vision in her right eye was found to have markedly improved. Over the year, the scarring in her right eye partially healed. As a result, the surface of her eyeball had become flattened, largely correcting the vision in that eye. This correction was so significant that she no longer needed glasses; she relied on her left eye for near vision, and her right eye for distance vision.[14]

hospitalization. The death rate for healthy adults who contract pneumonia following chicken pox is estimated to be as high as 30 percent.[15]

Complications involving the nervous system occur most commonly in adults or children under five years of age. Usually these disorders begin a few days after the first signs of the typical chicken pox rash. These complications include **encephalitis** (inflammation of the brain), which can result in loss of consciousness and seizures. Another serious neurological complication of chicken pox is **cerebellar ataxia**, a disturbance of the brainstem that causes affected patients to move in an uncoordinated manner, show uncontrolled movements of the eyeballs (nystagmus), and experience a loss of balance.

In adults, another rare complication of varicella virus infection is uncontrolled bleeding. In these very isolated incidents, patients develop bleeding disorders due to a loss of **platelets** following chicken pox. (Platelets are components of the blood that aid in blood clotting.) In severe cases, these bleeding disorders can even be fatal. Most of the time, though, a patient with a bleeding disorder due to chicken pox recovers without any lasting harmful effects.

Kidney damage is another rare complication of chicken pox. It is not clear if this is due to the varicella virus itself, or to subsequent infection with the bacterium *Streptococcus pyogenes* following chicken pox. A few other complications such as arthritis and inflammation of the heart have been reported following chicken pox, but these complications occur so rarely that it is not clear if they are caused by the varicella-zoster virus.

Other serious complications of varicella-zoster infection may occur during pregnancy. If the pregnant woman develops chicken pox during the first 20 weeks of a pregnancy, in about 1 percent of cases, the infection results in severe malformations of the fetus. These deformities frequently include shortened limbs, eye defects, and brain damage. In addition, if the mother develops chicken pox a few days before or after giving birth, there is also a risk of serious harm to the infant. Up to 30 percent of these infections may be fatal to the infant, although there is some question about the accuracy of these figures.[16]

Individuals who are immunocompromised are more likely to develop serious complications, including a varicella-zoster virus infection that spreads throughout the entire body, which can lead to damage to the lungs, liver, and other organs. Prior to the development of effective treatments, one-third to one-half of children with several types of cancer developed these disseminated infections, which were fatal about 10 percent of the time.[17]

In addition, patients who received organ transplants or those who receive steroids for treating arthritis or other conditions are at increased risk for severe varicella infections. This is also true for people with acquired immunodeficiency syndrome (AIDS) or genetic immunodeficiencies. Even in the absence of complications, individuals suffering from immunodeficiences tend to have a longer period of illness, with a more extensive rash and more lesions.

PROBLEMS DIAGNOSING CHICKEN POX

Historically, one of the primary sources of confusion for diagnosing chicken pox was **smallpox**. Both diseases are characterized by raised bumps and rashes that spread across the body, although smallpox was a much more serious illness that caused about one death for every three infections. However, since the eradication of smallpox in 1977, confusing these two diseases is no longer a problem for physicians or their patients.

The remaining illnesses that may sometimes be confused with chicken pox include a variety of diseases that manifest with some type of rash. For example, impetigo is a skin infection caused by bacteria of the genus *Streptococcus,* which sometimes has the appearance of small bumps at and near the place where the bacteria entered the skin. A diagnosis is made by taking some skin scrapings and looking for the presence of ball-like bacteria, strung together in chains, in those wounds. The presence of these bacteria indicates a disease called impetigo, rather than chicken pox. This diagnosis is critical because the treatment of chicken pox and a bacterial skin infection are very different.

Scabies, a skin disease caused by an infestation with a small mite, can cause raised pimples that resemble chicken pox. Rickettsialpox, a bacterial infection transmitted through the bite of a mite, also causes a rash and can sometimes be mistaken for chicken pox. A viral infection called hand-foot-and-mouth disease can produce a rash that may appear to be similar to chicken pox.

Other conditions that may be confused with chicken pox included rashes resulting from some type of allergic reaction, or the bites of midges or mosquitoes which, if prevalent enough, could give an appearance of widespread raised bumps on the skin similar to chicken pox.

CHARACTERISTICS OF SHINGLES

Most viruses have a hit-and-run lifestyle. They get in the body, cause an acute infection, and then are permanently evicted by the immune response. Varicella-zoster virus has a very different natural course. It does cause chicken pox, a short-term, acute infection. However, instead of being completely eliminated from the body as the disease wanes, the virus invades nerve cells, where it lies dormant until the immune defenses break down, perhaps decades after the initial infection. This second outbreak is called shingles (the medical term is Herpes Zoster, or Zoster). Shingles is a painful illness with an outbreak of chicken pox–like sores along the path of a nerve.

Shingles is particularly common in individuals with certain types of cancer such as leukemia, Hodgkin's disease, and non-Hodgkin's lymphoma. It is also common in individuals who are immunosuppressed as a result of receiving an organ transplant, and in patients with HIV infection. However, most people who get shingles do not have an underlying medical condition, although the elderly are most likely to be victims. There is now a Zoster, or shingles, vaccine for people over 60 years old. This manifestation of the varicella-zoster virus will be described in more detail in Chapter 7.

2

The History of Chicken Pox

Chicken pox, like many other infectious diseases, has left its mark on human history. For example, Sayyid Basir Hindi, a key figure in the early years of the Baha'i faith during the mid-1800s, was blind as a consequence of a chicken pox infection at the age of seven. He was considered a mystic, and it is likely that his blindness helped create an aura that contributed to his success as a religious leader.[1]

Chicken pox has likely been a human affliction for thousands of years. For example, there is suggestive evidence of chicken pox in ancient Babylonia more than 2,000 years ago.[2] As a typically mild illness, though, chicken pox did not make it into historical accounts until the 1500s, when Giovanni Filippo, an Italian doctor, provided a description of this disease, and distinguished between chicken pox and scarlet fever. In 1694, Richard Morton, an English doctor, reported on a mild form of smallpox that he called chicken pox. However, many doctors confused smallpox and chicken pox because of the initial similarity of the rashes in both conditions. It was not until 1767 that another English physician, William Heberden, first made a definitive distinction between the two diseases, including a list of criteria that distinguished smallpox and chicken pox.[3]

For a number of years, there was still some confusion about the distinction between chicken pox and smallpox. William Osler, for example, in 1892, had to argue that "there can be no question that varicella [chicken pox] is an affection quite distinct from variola [smallpox] without at

Figure 2.1 In 1767, English physician William Heberden became the first person to make a definitive distinction between chicken pox and smallpox. (National Library of Medicine/U.S. National Institutes of Health)

present any relation whatever to it. An attack of one does not confer immunity from an attack of the other." He then went on to describe a case of a five-year-old boy who was admitted to a hospital with a case of chicken pox. He was on the same floor as smallpox patients and developed smallpox eight days later. The fact that a patient was able to simultaneously get infected with both diseases was strong support that smallpox and chicken pox were entirely different afflictions.[4]

In 1904, Ernest Tyzzer provided further experimental evidence that chicken pox and smallpox were different diseases, while studying a chicken pox outbreak at a prison in the Philippines. Tyzzer noticed that many of the patients with chicken pox had either scars from a previous smallpox infection, or from smallpox vaccination. This made it extremely unlikely that these individuals were suffering from another case of smallpox, because it was well documented that either vaccination or infection normally protected a person from contracting smallpox again. Tyzzer was also aware that smallpox would cause signs of infection in monkeys and in the corneas of rabbits. Consequently, he placed fluid from prisoners with chicken pox into the eyes of rabbits and injected the fluid from chicken pox lesions into monkeys. No signs of infection developed, further affirming the distinction between chicken pox and smallpox. He also studied the lesions microscopically and observed the presence of very large cells in the skin lesions of patients with chicken pox. These cells were not found in cases of smallpox, so this provided a potential means of distinguishing the two ailments.

THE IDENTIFICATION OF THE VARICELLA-ZOSTER VIRUS

A starting point to the identification of the varicella-zoster virus was the work by Johann Steiner, who in 1875 inoculated children with fluid from a patient with chicken pox, after which the children developed the disease; this made it clear that chicken pox was an infectious disease. Investigations by a number of researchers in the 1920s through the 1940s showed that unusual structures were present inside skin cells from patients with chicken pox. Based on investigations with other infectious agents, these unusual structures were identified as the hallmark of a viral infection.

As with all scientific discoveries, many scientists contributed to the final understanding. In the case of any pathogen, the definitive identification normally requires that the pathogen be separated from all other organisms in a culture. This is normally followed by infection of laboratory animals to see if they show symptoms of the disease, and then the re-isolation of the pathogen from the laboratory animals.

THE ORIGIN OF NAMES FOR CHICKEN POX AND SHINGLES

The history of the name "chicken pox" itself is somewhat unclear. Thomas Fuller, in 1730, attributed the name to the type of lesions expected if a chicken pecked the skin. Another explanation was that the lesions look similar to chickpeas (although the term chicken pox was apparently used prior to the origin of the term "chickpeas"). Yet another explanation is that the term chicken pox is derived from the Old English word gican, meaning "itch." There was also a suggestion that chicken pox derived from the name of a coin of small value, the "chequeen." Perhaps the most plausible explanation is that the name came from chicken pox being a minor infection, in comparison with smallpox, which was much more likely to be fatal. This was suggested by Samuel Johnson, in his dictionary, in 1755, and subsequently by other authors.[5]

Similarly, the history of the name varicella is also disputed. Some have claimed that it is derived from a term that means a minor form of smallpox. Others have felt that the term is derived from the word *varus* meaning "pimple."[6]

The origin of the word "shingles" is more generally accepted; it comes from the Latin term *cingulus* for "girdle." The derivation of the synonym for shingles, "zoster," is also generally accepted. The term comes from the Greek, where *zoster* means "belt." Both terms highlight the usually band-like distribution of shingles lesions on the body.[7]

The first attempts to do this, by Ernest Tyzzer, involved laboratory animals and were unsuccessful. Later, in 1944, Ernest Goodpasture and Katherine Anderson tried to grow the virus in cultures in the laboratory. They used skin taken from a woman who had undergone surgery for breast cancer, with the idea of using the tissue as a culture medium for the virus. After the skin was removed from the patient, it was treated with iodine and alcohol to remove contaminating bacteria, cut into small pieces, and placed on blocks of sterile cork for further manipulation. Then, a needle and syringe was used to remove some of the fluid from shingles lesions from a two-and-a-half-year-old child. The skin from the woman was subsequently injected in multiple places with this fluid, and the skin was then grafted to 12 nine-day-old chicken embryos. Finally, these researchers microscopically examined the grafts for the presence of characteristic cells associated with chicken pox. They found those characteristic cells, suggesting that the presumed virus could be grown in culture. This work opened the door for future experiments.[8]

However, it was laborious to graft human skin to chicken embryos, so researchers, most notably Thomas Weller, tested new methods of growing the varicella-zoster virus in the laboratory. His initial attempts to grow the virus using tissues from human embryos or chicken eggs were unsuccessful. Consequently, on the suspicion that the virus had an affinity for human skin, he attempted to grow the virus in samples of fetal skin tissue. Saliva from children with chicken pox was used to inoculate the tissue cultures. This also failed, however. (An explanation came later when it was determined that the virus is rarely found in the saliva.) By 1952, using cells from human embryos and human foreskin, Weller finally had a system that consistently allowed infection of human cells with varicella-zoster virus. For these experiments he used fluid from chicken pox lesions to infect the human cells. The lesions had a much higher concentration of the virus, and were therefore more effective in infecting cells in the laboratory than saliva.[9]

As noted, there was no animal model for the varicella-zoster virus that allowed for growth of the virus and mimicked the symptoms of the human disease. Therefore, to verify the identity of the virus, Weller would have needed to infect human volunteers, something that would be unethical. Instead, Weller did the next best thing and used **antibody** tests to verify that the virus growing in his cultures was the same type of virus that was found in children with chicken pox infections. He did this by taking **serum** (the liquid portion of the blood) from people who had recently recovered from chicken pox. This serum contained specific antibodies against the virus that caused the disease. These antibodies reacted against the virus and therefore demonstrated that the virus, grown in culture, was the same virus that caused chicken pox. This result was first demonstrated in 1954 and subsequently confirmed with additional reports published in 1958.[10]

THE SAME VIRUS CAUSES CHICKEN POX AND SHINGLES

In 1892, James Bokay, a professor in what is now the country of Hungary, studied five cases of people who developed chicken pox after they were exposed to people with shingles. He suggested that the agent that caused shingles might therefore be the same as the agent that causes chicken pox.

About 30 years later, B. Lipschutz showed that when the vesicles from people with chicken pox or shingles were examined with a microscope, the appearance of the cells and other features were similar between the two diseases. In 1925, K. Kundratitz took material from the lesions of patients with shingles and transferred it to children who had never had chicken pox. These individuals developed a disease identical to chicken pox.

Figure 2.2 Dr. Thomas Weller, the first person to grow the varicella-zoster virus in cell culture. (National Library of Medicine/U.S. National Institutes of Health)

During the 1920s and 1930s, antibody tests were used to compare the agents of chicken pox and shingles. People who had chicken pox developed antibodies that reacted against shingles skin lesions. Similarly, people with shingles developed antibodies that reacted against chicken pox skin lesions. By the 1940s, the **electron microscope** was becoming widely used (this was the only microscope powerful enough to view viruses). Seen through the electron microscope, the viral particles in shingles vesicles appeared to be identical to the viral particles in chicken pox vesicles.

More definitive evidence that the virus causing chicken pox and the virus causing shingles were identical came from growth of the viruses in culture. Antibodies from patients with shingles reacted against viruses in culture from patients with both shingles and chicken pox. The converse was also true; antibodies from patients with chicken pox reacted against viruses in culture from patients with both shingles and chicken pox.[11]

Further work focused on whether the virus that causes shingles was the result of a new infection of the varicella-zoster virus, or whether it involved reactivation of virus from the original chicken pox infection. By the 1980s, genetic techniques were becoming powerful enough to address that question. **Enzymes** had been discovered (called **restriction enzymes**) that cut DNA at specific sequences. Individual varicella-zoster viruses that infect different people may have slightly different DNA sequences, and if these sequence alterations affect the sites cut by restriction enzymes, digestion with these restriction enzymes will produce unique patterns from the viral DNA isolated from different individuals. Similarly, if the same virus strain causes chicken pox and then shingles, using this technology it should be possible to determine that the viruses are identical. Researchers did this experiment, isolating DNA from the varicella-zoster viruses from a patient who had chicken pox. They subsequently isolated DNA from varicella-zoster viruses from the same patient when he or she later developed shingles and found that the patterns generated by the restriction enzymes were identical, suggesting that the same exact strain of the virus that first caused chicken pox later became reactivated and caused shingles.[12]

This technique of using restriction enzymes was somewhat crude, in that it only could measure DNA sequence differences that affected sites cut by restriction enzymes; this allowed only a small portion of the viral genome to be scanned. Subsequently, a technique was used to scrutinize each individual portion of a genome (each individual nucleotide). This technique was called **DNA sequencing**. The DNA sequence of the virus used to vaccinate an infant was compared to the DNA isolated from a virus that later caused shingles in the same patient. The viral DNA was very similar, providing confirmation that the virus responsible for chicken pox and shingles in an individual is the same strain, from the original chicken pox infection or vaccination.[13]

In the history of the study of chicken pox and shingles, awareness grew of the potentially serious nature of varicella-zoster infections, at least in some people. This led to research into the development of effective treatments and preventative measures.

3

Chicken Pox in Young Children

A three-year-old boy had a play date with a two-year-old girl. After an after-noon of constructing paper plate masks of monkeys and playing "jungle," the boy went home. The next night, his mother noticed the start of a characteristic chicken pox rash on his left shoulder. Two weeks later, the girl developed the disease as well. Both children had a mild fever and felt lethargic and ill for a week or so, starting around the time the rash first developed. They recovered without any complications or long-term health concerns.

Until the widespread vaccination of children in the United States in the 1990s, it was estimated that 95 percent of all American children developed chicken pox before adulthood.[1] Consequently, the childhood form of chicken pox is widely regarded as the natural form of the disease, at least in temperate regions of the world.

THE CAUSE OF CHICKEN POX SYMPTOMS

Generally, symptoms associated with an illness result either from some factor produced by the pathogen, or the body's response to the pathogen. In the case of chicken pox, it appears that the symptoms result both from viral damage, and from the body's response to infection.

The characteristic pox lesions are the result of viral damage to the skin cells. Infections with the virus start in the bottom layers of the skin (the dermis) and move toward the surface. Initially, skin cells located near the blood vessels show signs of infection, probably as a result of their contact with infected cells of the immune system called **T-cells**. Following infection, these skin cells become swollen. Eventually, these cells degenerate and release virus-filled fluid into the surrounding tissue resulting in the formation of the characteristic chicken pox lesions. The fluid in these vesicles contains a high concentration of the varicella-zoster virus.[2]

Fever is another common symptom of chicken pox. A region of the brain, the hypothalamus, controls body temperature in humans. A variety of substances, either released from pathogens, or from cells in the body in response to infection, can cause fever. In the case of chicken pox, **interferons** are one of the products produced by cells in response to viral infection, and interferons are known to stimulate the production of a fever. Interferons become present at high concentrations in the blood following infection with the varicella-zoster virus. Some of these interferons enter the brain and lead to a change in the biochemistry of the hypothalamus that, in turn, alters the temperature set point for the body. This is an example of an immune system reaction (the production of interferons) leading to symptoms of illness.[3]

THE CELL BIOLOGY OF CHICKEN POX

The molecular details of how the varicella-zoster virus actually causes disease are not entirely clear, largely because of the lack of a simple animal model of chicken pox. Therefore, until quite recently, much of what was known or hypothesized about the ability of the virus to cause disease was based on studies of humans with chicken pox and a study of an animal model for another viral disease. For example, studies of how the mousepox virus causes disease in mice led to inferences about chicken pox in humans. More recently, studies of chicken pox in mice have provided more detailed information. These studies have involved the use of a strain of mouse with a condition called **severe combined immunodeficiency** (SCID).[4] These mice have little natural immune response, so they can readily accept human cells and human tissues, unlike mice with a normal immune system. These mice have had human immune system cells injected into their systems, and human skin grafts attached to their bodies. The result is a mouse with portions of the human immune system, and sections of human skin, to mimic some elements of chicken pox infection in humans. These human tissues and cells allow the varicella-zoster virus to establish an infection in mice and allow for a study (at least in part) of what happens during an infection in humans.

In addition, studies of cases of human infection, where the time between infection and symptoms of the disease were shortened, also provided information about the natural history of the virus in the body. In these cases, patients either had fluid from chicken pox lesions directly transferred to their skin, or infants got chicken pox from their mother right after birth and, being infants, had a poorly developed immune response that allowed the virus to replicate rapidly.

Based on these studies and other information, it appears that the initial infection occurs in the throat or upper respiratory tract. From there, the virus invades the lymph nodes near the site of infection and replicates, likely in the tonsils in the throat. Originally, based on studies of the mousepox virus, it was thought that the virus then spread through the blood to the internal organs, like the liver, and replicated there for some time, before it spread to the skin. This was based, in part, on the long incubation period between infection and symptoms (averaging about 14 days, with a range of 10 to 20 days). Now, based primarily on studies in the SCID mouse containing human skin and immune cells, it appears that the virus infects a type of human immune cell called **memory T-cells**.

T-cells are white blood cells that play several critical roles in the immune response. Memory T-cells are long-lived T-cells that are initially produced in response to a particular infection. These memory T-cells can also shuttle the virus to the skin. Once there, the virus apparently infects skin cells

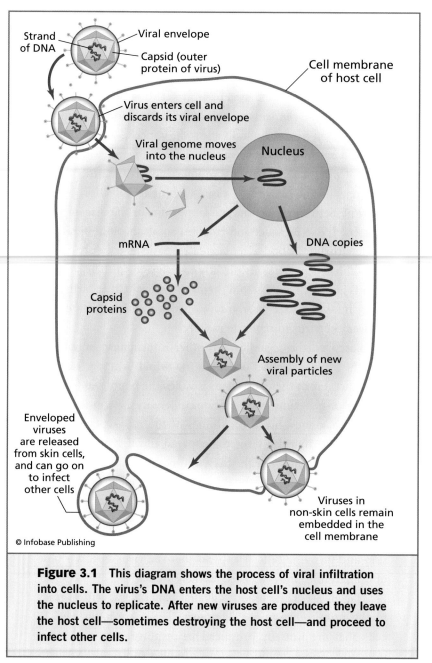

Strand of DNA

Viral envelope

Capsid (outer protein of virus)

Cell membrane of host cell

Virus enters cell and discards its viral envelope

Viral genome moves into the nucleus

Nucleus

mRNA

DNA copies

Capsid proteins

Assembly of new viral particles

Enveloped viruses are released from skin cells, and can go on to infect other cells

Viruses in non-skin cells remain embedded in the cell membrane

© Infobase Publishing

Figure 3.1 This diagram shows the process of viral infiltration into cells. The virus's DNA enters the host cell's nucleus and uses the nucleus to replicate. After new viruses are produced they leave the host cell—sometimes destroying the host cell—and proceed to infect other cells.

and begins replicating. Initially, the virus replicates slowly in the skin cells. This is thought to be in part because of the chemicals the skin cells naturally produce (antiviral molecules like interferon alpha). As the virus infects skin cells, it prevents infected cells from making those antiviral chemicals. Eventually, enough cells are infected, and enough viruses are produced, that skin damage becomes evident in the form of lesions and a rash. The continued formation of additional skin lesions is likely the result of new memory T-cells being infected, traveling to and establishing infections in new sites in the skin, and causing more damage.[5] As noted above, the entire process from infection to the appearance of a skin rash is typically about 14 days. Normally, new lesions develop on the skin for three to five days, and the person remains infectious until all the lesions crust over.

HOW THE VIRUS ESTABLISHES INFECTION

Due to the limitations of animal models of chicken pox, many aspects of the biology of the virus are still somewhat unclear, including some of the details of how the varicella-zoster virus actually causes disease. However, molecular analysis of the virus is beginning to reveal some of these secrets about the natural history of chicken pox infection.

Several of the proteins on the surface of the virus (the viral glycoproteins gE, gI, and gB in particular) are involved in **endo-cytosis**, the process by which the virus enters a host cell. Cell entry is a prerequisite for establishing an infection, because the varicella-zoster virus can only replicate inside human cells. In addition, the entry of the virus through this pathway is apparently essential for proper assembly of the virus, so this is a critical stage in the life cycle of the virus.

These viral glycoproteins interact with a molecule on the surface of the human cell called **heparin sulfate** (a molecule consisting primarily of sugar molecules in chains). As a consequence of this binding, other molecules on the surface of the virus (**mannose-6-phosphate**) interact with the **mannose-6-phosphate receptors** on the host cells, and the viral nucleocapsid enters the cell. Cholesterol in the cell membrane also appears to be essential for viral entry.[6] Along with the nucleocapsid, viral tegument proteins, located in the space between the envelope and the nucleocapsid, are also released into the cell. These tegument proteins then travel to the nucleus, where they will play an important function in the replication of the virus.

Subsequently, this inner region of the virus, the nucleocapsid, migrates to the cell nucleus, where it fuses with the nuclear membrane, releasing the viral DNA into the nucleus. The viral DNA contains ends with sections of single-stranded DNA.

THE MOLECULAR DETAILS OF THE VIRAL LIFE CYCLE

Sophisticated methods have been used to determine how the viral particles are put together inside the host cell during infection. For example, one aspect of the viral life cycle is that the virus acquires an initial envelope, loses it, and then gets a second envelope that contains the viral glycoproteins.

One experiment that helped establish this idea involved monitoring varicella-zoster virus infected cells using electron microscopy. Antibodies that detected the glycosylphosphatidylinositol (gpl) protein were added; this protein is found in the envelope of mature viruses. As the virus left the nucleus, no gpl protein was detected.

However, viruses were identified, by electron microscopy, as acquiring a second envelope when they interacted with the trans-golgi network (a series of membrane-bound compartments responsible for ensuring that different molecules end up in the correct cellular location), and this second envelope did contain the gpl protein.[7]

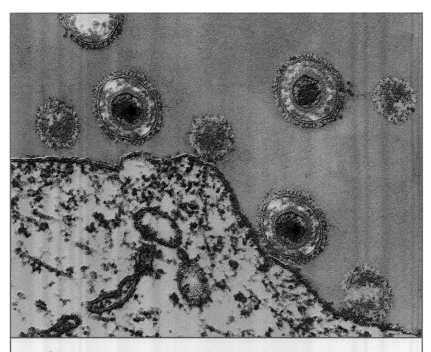

Figure 3.2   Varicella-zoster virus invading human cells. The rounded viruses are sectioned through to show DNA genetic material (red) surrounded by a protein coat (green). At lower left is part of an infected cell (yellow). (© Eye of Science/Photo Researchers, Inc.)

These regions at the end of the viral genome come together, forming a circular viral DNA molecule. The tegument proteins then bind to the viral genome and allow for the production of new viral proteins. The first proteins produced are called the immediate early (IE) proteins, which include **transcriptional activators** and **transcriptional repressors**. Transcriptional activators are proteins that enhance the conversion of the information in the DNA genome into another molecule called RNA. The information in RNA is ultimately converted to proteins. Transcriptional repressors are proteins that inhibit the conversion of the information in DNA to RNA. In particular, IE62, a transcriptional activator, is critical for the production of all other varicella-zoster proteins.

Subsequent stages in the production of the viral proteins are tightly regulated so that the proteins are produced in a specific order. As they accumulate inside the nucleus, the IE proteins then turn off the synthesis of additional IE proteins and facilitate the production of the next group of proteins, the early (E) proteins. These E proteins catalyze the production of the viral DNA through a mechanism called **rolling circle replication**. Rolling circle replication is a process by which DNA molecules are made from a circular DNA template. The DNA is synthesized in a manner somewhat analogous to string being pulled off a spool. Finally, the late (L) proteins are produced, which are the structural proteins required to build the nucleocapsid and the proteins that populate the envelope.[8]

The DNA synthesis by the E proteins results in the production of a long DNA "string"containing a number of genomes. This long DNA molecule is cut into single genomes, which are then ready for packaging into a viral particle. The initial assembly of the varicella-zoster virus occurs in the nucleus of the cell. This involves the capture of the DNA genome by the capsid proteins. The **nucleocapsid** (viral DNA plus the capsid) then exits the nucleus, pulling a portion of the nuclear membrane with it. This nuclear membrane forms a temporary envelope. The capsid is now inside a cellular structure called the **endoplasmic reticulum**, which is part of the transportation system in the cell. The virus envelope then fuses with the endoplasmic reticulum membrane, releasing the virus, lacking an envelope, into the cytoplasm of the cell.

Separately, the glycoproteins that will become embedded in the envelope of the virus are being processed. These proteins are modified though the addition of sugars, including mannose-6-phosphate in the endoplasmic reticulum. Once modified, they are released into a structure called the **trans-golgi network**. The trans-golgi network is part of the transportation system in the cell. It is a series of membrane bound compartments responsible for helping to ensure that different molecules end up in the right cellular location.

It appears, at this point, that the remainder of the life cycle of the virus inside the cell depends on the cell type that is hosting the virus. The virus is only adorned with an envelope in skin cells; in all other cells, the virus ultimately lacks an envelope.

In skin cells, the virus nucleocapsid enters the trans-golgi network compartment, which contains a number of viral proteins, as well as a lipid envelope that is synthesized by the cell. The virus becomes encased in this envelope and is released from the cell. The viruses now have two possible fates: to be released into the environment, where they can go on to infect other people, or to enter into neurons, where the virus can lay dormant for years. It is theorized that only enveloped viruses can enter nerve cells, because they contain the mannose-6-phosphate molecule, which allows them to interact with nerve cells.

In other cells where the virus replicates, it does not end up with an envelope, but this is not essential, because the virus can move directly from cell to cell, thereby infecting new cells even without the envelope.[9] In this case, the viral nucleocapsid again interacts with the trans-golgi network. However, in non-skin cells, once the virus interacts with the trans-golgi network the virus gets targeted for a cellular structure called the endosome. In the endosome, any envelope is removed, and some of the viruses are completely destroyed. Any remaining viable virus is released to the cell surface, but does not exit the cell, limiting the damage caused by runaway viral replication.

Why is the pathway different in skin cells? Skin cells are in the last stage of their life, producing large amounts of **ceramides** (lipids that waterproof the skin) in preparation for their death and transport to the outermost layer of the skin. Therefore, the endosome pathway is largely turned off in skin cells and the enveloped viruses pass directly to the surface of the skin, with the envelope intact.

IMMUNE SYSTEM CELLS AND THE CONTROL OF CHICKEN POX

There are several types of white blood cells that play a role both in spreading the virus and ultimately controlling the virus during infection. T-cells play a role in both the direct destruction of pathogens and the coordination of the other branches of the immune system. During a chicken pox infection, these cells play a role in spreading the virus to the skin, as well as, ultimately, controlling the virus.

During the initial stage of infection in the respiratory tract, T-cells become infected with the varicella-zoster virus. Some of these cells then eventually travel to the skin, where they transfer the virus to the skin cells. In this situation, the virus takes over a normally protective immune system cell and uses it as a shuttle to a site where it can cause infection.

As a specific immune response begins to develop during the course of infection, T-cells play a critical role in eliminating the disease. One type of T-cell, a cytotoxic T-lymphocyte, will target and destroy cells infected with the varicella-zoster virus. Another type of T-cell, the CD4+ T-cell, helps marshal other T-cells and other components of the immune system to fight the infection. Ultimately, some of these T-cells become memory T-cells and provide long-term protection against additional chicken pox infections and outbreaks of shingles.

Another type of immune system cell, the B-cell, plays a less prominent role during chicken pox infections. These cells produce antibodies; during a chicken pox infection, high levels of antibodies are produced against chicken pox. However, these antibodies do not appear to be critical in fighting the infection; for example, patients who lack the ability to produce antibodies as a result of a genetic condition are often able to control a chicken pox infection.

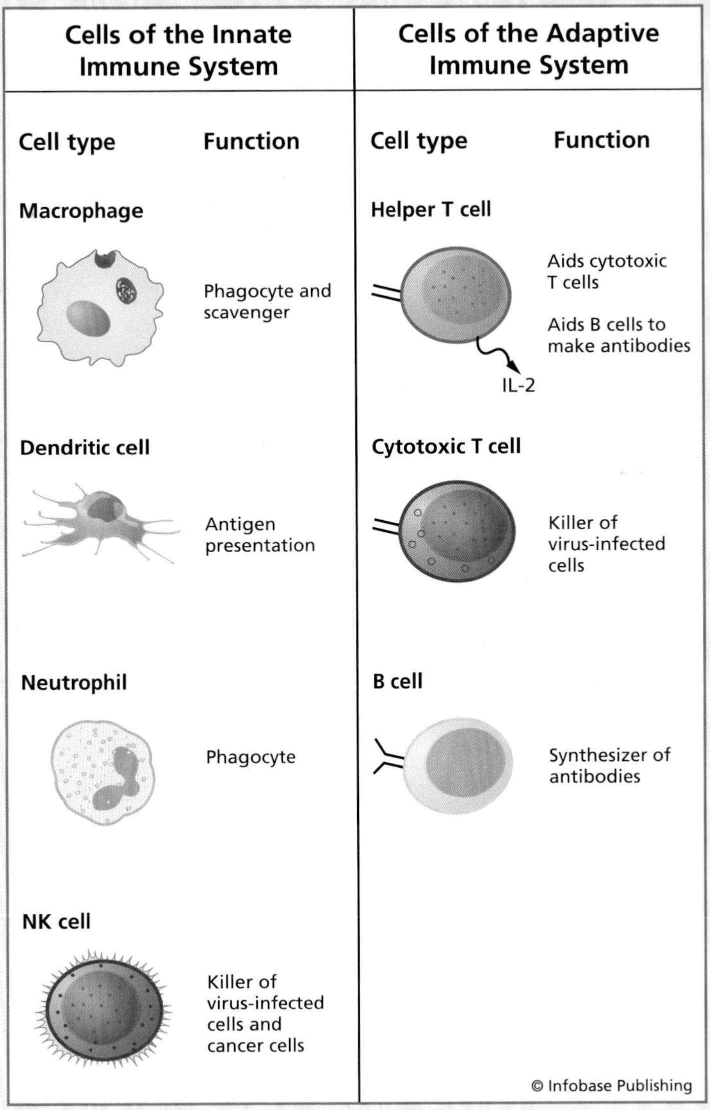

Cells of the Innate Immune System		Cells of the Adaptive Immune System	
Cell type	**Function**	**Cell type**	**Function**
Macrophage		Helper T cell	
	Phagocyte and scavenger		Aids cytotoxic T cells Aids B cells to make antibodies IL-2
Dendritic cell		Cytotoxic T cell	
	Antigen presentation		Killer of virus-infected cells
Neutrophil		B cell	
	Phagocyte		Synthesizer of antibodies
NK cell			
	Killer of virus-infected cells and cancer cells		

© Infobase Publishing

Figure 3.3 The immune system has two arms: the innate immune system and the adaptive immune system.

CELL-TO-CELL SPREAD OF INFECTION

Viruses that are located on the surface of infected cells are capable of fusion with uninfected cells, and this leads to the spread of infection. The glycoproteins on the surface of the virus, particularly gB, gE, gH, and gL, are thought to be critical for the fusion of uninfected cells with infected cells.[10]

IMMUNE SYSTEM RESPONSE TO CHICKEN POX

There are two branches of the immune system that coordinate the response to a chicken pox infection. One branch is called the **innate immune system**; the other branch is called the **adaptive immune system**. The innate immune system has the capability to respond to any pathogen and is always available, so it serves as the first line of defense against infection. However, the adaptive immune responses are more effective at ultimately eliminating pathogens, such as the varicella-zoster virus.

In the case of chicken pox, the innate immune response consists primarily of natural killer cells and a chemical released by immune system cells and skin cells called interferon-alpha. Natural killer cells recognize other cells infected with the varicella-zoster virus and kill the cells and the viruses contained within those cells. These natural killer cells destroy infected cells by releasing a protein called **granulysin**. This protein creates pores in the membrane of the infected cell and these pores lead to a loss of cellular material and, ultimately, death of the cell.

Interferon-alpha is also produced by natural killer cells, another type of white blood cell called a monocyte, and by skin cells. This chemical inhibits the replication of varicella-zoster virus, thereby limiting the growth of viruses in the body.

From studies of immunocompromised children who had an intact innate immune response, but who developed a severe case of chicken pox, it was clear that adaptive immunity was critical for ultimately clearing up a chicken pox infection. The adaptive immune response is primarily through **cell-mediated**

immunity. This means cells of the immune system specifically recognize chicken pox–infected cells and then seek out and destroy these cells. The cells that do the hunting are called **cytotoxic T-lymphocytes** (CTLs). These cells recognize viral proteins that are displayed on the surface of infected cells. The CTLs then bind to the surface of the infected cell and release toxic proteins (like granulysin) that destroy the infected cells and the viruses those cells contain. This dramatically reduces viral replication, and is a critical step in the control of chicken pox infections by the immune system.

Another adaptive immune response that is important in the control of many infections is the production of antibodies. However, antibodies do not appear to play a major role in the control of chicken pox. Individuals with mutations that prevent them from producing antibodies are generally able to control a chicken pox infection. Yet, the administration of antibodies during an early stage of infection can reduce the severity of the disease, so antibody production by immune system cells may play some role in controlling varicella-zoster virus growth and spread in the body.[11]

IMMUNE EVASION

Every successful pathogen has evolved systems for avoiding the host immune response, and the varicella-zoster virus is no exception. This virus, as an internal cellular parasite, automatically avoids some aspects of the immune response, such as antibodies that only affect free pathogens in the bloodstream. This is probably why antibodies are not very important for controlling infection. In addition, this virus has several other strategies for evading other aspects of the host immune response.

For example, one key defense against viruses involves **antigen presentation**, where an infected cell places sections of the virus on the surface of the cell. These virus parts alert immune system cells, such as cytotoxic T-lymphocytes, which then home in on and destroy the infected cells. The varicella-zoster virus is able to suppress the ability of infected cells to display parts of the virus on the cell surface by trapping the display molecules inside the cell. Consequently, these virally infected cells remain invisible to the immune system, and the virus can continue to grow inside these cells.

There is another pathway for infected cells to display "chunks" of the virus on their surface cells. This pathway is enhanced through the production of interferon gamma by T-cells. The varicella-zoster virus has the ability to suppress this display system as well. The suppression only works for infected cells, though, so adjacent cells can produce these display proteins, meaning that once the production of interferon gamma begins, it limits the ability of the virus to infect adjacent cells.[12] The virus also inhibits the activation of another protein in infected cells that would otherwise activate an antiviral response, including the production of interferons.[13]

In addition, the virus takes up residence in nerve cells, and these cells are subject to little scrutiny by the immune system. Consequently, the presence of the varicella-zoster virus inside nerve cells is another important mechanism by which the virus avoids the host immune response.

VARICELLA-ZOSTER VIRUS ENTRY INTO NERVES AND LATENCY

Entry into nerve cells probably plays a critical role in the life cycle of the varicella-zoster virus. It appears that the viruses that enter nerves have an envelope, and enveloped viruses only come from skin cells. These enveloped viruses have mannose-6 phosphate on their surfaces, and nerve cells have a large quantity of mannose-6 phosphate receptors on their surface. So the complementary surfaces of the virus and the nerve cell result in the virus binding to nerve cells. Once bound, the virus enters the nerve cell.

Once inside the nerve cell, a different pattern of gene expression occurs, as compared with the gene expression that occurs in other type of cells. In particular, the only genes that are expressed are ones that, in other cells, are expressed early in the course of infection. None of the genes that are normally expressed later in infection are expressed in nerve cells. This suggests that the varicella-zoster virus, inside nerve cells, is very restricted in terms of the proteins that are produced. As a consequence, the presence of the virus inside these cells probably does not cause much of a perturbation in normal cellular function. This contributes to **latency**, a condition in which the virus can remain inactive for years, until the immune system weakens, rendering the person vulnerable to a flare-up of the viral infection.[14]

4

Chicken Pox in Infants and Adults

A woman in Italy developed chicken pox when she was 15 weeks pregnant, in a case reported in 2003. Subsequent ultrasound examinations showed that the fetus was not developing normally. The infant was delivered by Caesarean section at 37 weeks and was very small (below the tenth percentile in length and weight). The infant had hydrocephalus (an enlarged head) with extensive damage to the brain and one eye. This young boy had breathing difficulty requiring the use of a ventilator, and seizures that were treated with medication. In spite of intensive care, the infant died three days after birth. An autopsy suggested that the child had suffered chicken pox while in the uterus at 15 weeks, and a case of shingles shortly before birth. These bouts with the varicella-zoster virus caused much of the child's brain to be destroyed. Although congenital chicken pox is rare (3 to 4 cases per 100,000 pregnancies) this case shows the potentially devastating nature of chicken pox during pregnancy.[1]

The outcome of any illness is the result of the balance between the virulence of the pathogen and the vigor of the immune response. In the case of chicken pox, individuals who develop more severe cases of chicken pox are not as able to mount a strong immune response against infection. Unlike many other viruses, the varicella-zoster virus strains do not differ in virulence, so the immune system of the patient is the key variable in the outcome of a chicken pox infection.

Infants have an undeveloped immune system. Consequently, they have less ability to fight infections. However, during pregnancy, the mother transfers to the fetus antibodies against diseases she has encountered during her lifetime. These antibodies help the infant fight off any of the diseases his or her mother had previously encountered. This includes chicken pox, if the mother had developed the disease or been vaccinated prior to pregnancy. However, if the mother had not previously developed chicken pox, but came down with a case of chicken pox during pregnancy, the fetus gets a double whammy. On the one hand, the mother has not developed an immune response, so antibodies cannot be transferred. (It normally takes a week or two after infection before an antibody response develops). On the other hand, the virus is present at high levels in the body of both the mother and the fetus, and the fetus lacks many of the innate immune responses normally required to fend off infection.

The result of a maternal chicken pox infection can be, at least in a small number of cases, a condition called **congenital varicella syndrome** (CVS). This can result in the infant's death shortly after birth, or serious damage that can lead to permanent impairment. In one small sample, CVS involved malformation of at least one arm or leg (72 percent of 25 cases), scarring of the skin (72 percent of 25 cases), damage to the eyes (44 percent of 25 cases), and brain damage (48 percent of 25 cases). CVS is most likely to occur if the mother develops a chicken pox infection in the first or second trimester of her pregnancy. Fetuses with significant abnormalities resulting from CVS can be detected in the uterus using ultrasound. The rate of CVS has been reported at about 0.7 percent in women who develop chicken pox during the first stages of pregnancy. (Overall, though, the rate of CVS is very low, taking into account all pregnancies. For example, by one estimate, there are approximately 4 million births per year in the United States, and about 44 cases of CVS, which is a rate of about one-one-thousandth of 1 percent.)[2]

If the mother develops chicken pox in the third trimester of pregnancy, CVS is less likely to develop. However, if the mother contracts chicken pox within five days of giving birth, the child may develop a severe case of chicken pox called disseminated neonatal varicella. Treatments are available for both the fetus and the mother, which may help to reduce the risk of serious side effects from neonatal varicella.[3]

In contrast with chicken pox, the development of shingles during pregnancy does not seem to have adverse consequences for the fetus. One study analyzed 366 mothers who developed shingles early in their pregnancy. None of their infants had any sign of varicella-zoster infection.[4] This is not surprising, because a woman who develops shingles has previously had chicken pox, so she can mount an immune response that would reduce viral growth. In addition, during a shingles attack, the virus has a limited distribution in the body and, therefore, less opportunity to infect the fetus. The fetus also gains protection from antiviral antibodies transferred to the fetus, as a consequence of the mother's previous chicken pox.[5]

CHICKEN POX IN ADULTS

The situation resulting in more serious chicken pox cases in adults is somewhat analogous to that of infants. Compared to the immune response in healthy children, the immune response in older adults, at least the type of immune response that limits chicken pox, is substantially reduced. The immune response continues to tail off with greater age, so the greater the age at the first encounter with chicken pox, the more serious the disease.

In adults, several factors related to the immune response are in play. For example, interferons are key to inhibiting the varicella-zoster virus during early infection.[6] One of these interferons, called interferon alpha, is produced more

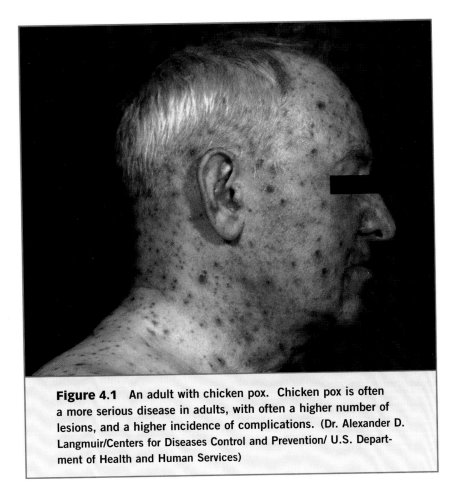

Figure 4.1 An adult with chicken pox. Chicken pox is often a more serious disease in adults, with often a higher number of lesions, and a higher incidence of complications. (Dr. Alexander D. Langmuir/Centers for Diseases Control and Prevention/ U.S. Department of Health and Human Services)

abundantly in children than in adults, who appear to lack sufficient levels of this immunity-fostering agent. This might be one factor in the generally more severe symptoms of chicken pox in adults. Similarly, another critical interferon, interferon gamma, is also found at lower levels in adults than in children. As with interferon alpha, this may help explain the poorer control of chicken pox in adults versus children. In general, interferons prevent the replication of the varicella-zoster virus in infected cells. If interferons are produced at only low levels, the virus can replicate to higher levels, causing a more severe infection in adults.

Another factor relates to cell-mediated immunity. In this process, cells of the immune system recognize virally infected cells and destroy them. This form of immunity also appears to be critical for the control of chicken pox. Adults, as a group, have a reduced ability to produce immune cells that target chicken pox–infected cells. This also contributes to the greater severity of chicken pox symptoms in adults.[7]

All components of the immune system work together. So the effect of lower levels of interferon and the reduced functioning of cell-mediated immunity conspire to make chicken pox in adults with a normal immune system much more serious than chicken pox in children with a normal immune system. In adults, the virus replicates to higher levels and, consequently, more damage is done to organs and tissues in the body, and the risk of complications is substantially greater. In adults, the rate of hospitalization following chicken pox is about 10 times higher than in children who are infected, and the death rate from chicken pox is 15 to 20 times higher in individuals who are older than 20, compared to the death rate in children.[8]

USING ANIMAL MODELS TO BETTER UNDERSTAND CHICKEN POX

One of the longstanding challenges in understanding chicken pox and shingles in any age group has been the lack of an animal model of the disease that reproduces the characteristics of this affliction in humans. During the twentieth century, a variety of animals were tested as possible models for chicken pox and shingles. For example, several nonhuman primates (green monkeys, patas monkeys, macaque monkeys, pygmy marmosets) were infected with the varicella-zoster virus, but none developed the disease, and no evidence of the virus remained in their tissues. However, a six-month-old gorilla in a zoo did contract chicken pox, as confirmed by the symptoms of the illness, DNA analysis of virus isolated from the gorilla, and antibodies that reacted against the chicken pox virus. The source of chicken pox was not clear, as none of the animal handlers had evidence of chicken pox, and the gorilla was separated from the public by glass. It was likely that the illness was contracted from a handler with inapparent illness (for example, a very mild infection with few blisters), although another source, such as the activation of a virus already present in the gorilla, could not be excluded.[9]

As a consequence of these studies and observations, as well as the difficulty and expense of working with these animals, nonhuman primates are not considered a useful animal model for the study of chicken pox and shingles.

One more useful animal model for chicken pox has been the guinea pig, which can be infected with the vaccine strain of the varicella-zoster virus (which had been passaged in guinea pig cells). The virus could be recovered from the guinea pigs for up to three weeks following infection, but the infection did not cause symptoms and did not result in the long-term survival of the virus in nervous system tissue. One potential problem with the use of guinea pigs to study chicken pox is that they have a higher body temperature than humans (102.7°F/39.3°C in guinea pigs versus 98.6°F/37°C in humans), and the virus replicates less well at these higher temperatures. One attempt to overcome these problems involved the use of mutant guinea pigs that lacked hair and consequently had a lower body temperature (100.9°F/38.3°C). Infection of this strain of guinea pigs did result in a rash in almost 90 percent of the animals, although the rash was not identical to that seen in human chicken pox. In addition, there was evidence that the virus does infect cells of the nervous system in these animals. This strain of guinea pigs has subsequently been used to study the immune response in chicken pox, and to test candidate vaccines. Although guinea pigs do model some aspects of chicken pox

Figure 4.2 Mouse with severe combined immunodeficiency (SCID). SCID mice have little natural immune response, so they can readily accept human cells and tissues. Based on research using SCID mice containing human skin and immune cells, researchers have discovered that the varicella-zoster virus infects a type of human immune cell called memory T-cells. (Linda Bartlett /National Cancer Institute/ U.S. National Institutes of Health)

infection, there are limitations, and consequently, additional models have been explored.[10]

Another important model of chicken pox involves the use of SCID mice. Because of a mutation in a gene required for normal development of cells of the immune system, these mice lack immune responses. Consequently, it is possible to graft human tissue to or to inject human cells into these mice and they do not reject the transplants. As a result, human pathogens, which normally do not infect mice, can cause disease in this mouse strain, by infecting the human cells and tissues.

In some experiments, the mice have had human skin grafts attached to their skin, and have had human immune cells injected into their circulatory system. This has provided useful information about the growth of the virus in the skin, and the role of immune system cells in the spread of the virus.

Another important issue that has been addressed with SCID mice has been the study of the interaction of the varicella-zoster virus with nerve cells. In one set of experiments, human embryonic stem cells from the nervous system were injected into the brains of SCID mice. These mice were then infected with the varicella-zoster virus. It was found that the virus did infect the human nerve cells, and it was possible to determine detailed information about which genes are expressed in nerve cells. This information could be useful in better understanding the latency of varicella-zoster virus in nerve cells in the body, and the steps leading to the development of shingles.[11] Collectively, these animal models will likely lead to a better understanding of, and improved treatments for, chicken pox in humans of all ages.

5

How Is Chicken Pox Diagnosed and Treated?

A man in his mid-20s went into the emergency room, complaining of intense chest pain, which had worsened over the previous two days. He was initially examined for a possible heart attack, but his vital signs were normal. The next day, the pain had begun extending to his back. The following day he started to develop a rash along his left, lower chest, which the man attributed to brushing against some shrubbery a few days earlier. Further analysis of his condition led to a diagnosis of shingles. His symptoms persisted for several weeks. Had the drug acyclovir been administered when he first complained of painful symptoms, it is likely that the length of his illness would have been shortened.[1]

One of the keys in proper treatment of chicken pox or shingles is proper diagnosis. In the case of chicken pox, there are several methods for identifying whether a person has this disease. The symptoms, particularly the distinctive rash, which is often accompanied by fever, provide a reasonable basis for assuming that a patient has chicken pox. These symptoms, especially if accompanied by a history of exposure to other individuals with chicken pox, are usually considered a clear indication of chicken pox. For shingles, the rash appears in a narrow band, which only spans one side of the body. The rash is often preceded by pain in that region two or three days prior to the development of a rash. Again, because this pattern of symptoms is so distinctive, additional tests are rarely needed.

However, for definitive diagnosis, there are several laboratory tests available. These tests may be important in cases where a patient has a severe form of the disease, or where there is danger of transmission of chicken pox to susceptible patients. It is therefore critical to verify for certain whether a person has chicken pox.

COLLECTION OF SAMPLES FOR TESTING

Proper collection of the virus is one of the keys to a rapid, proper diagnosis. Skin lesions, particularly those produced early in the course of the disease, are one of the best sources of the virus for laboratory testing. To collect the material, the surface of a chicken pox lesion is cleaned with alcohol to remove contaminating bacteria, and then opened with a sterile needle or other sharp object. Then the material from the lesion is expressed (or squeezed out) with a cotton swab to remove both the liquid and some skin cells. As with all clinical samples, the best results are obtained if they are delivered to the laboratory without delay.[2]

DETECTION OF THE VIRUS USING ANTIBODIES

The most common method for identifying the varicella-zoster virus is an antibody staining method. In this technique, the swab containing material from a chicken pox sore is rolled on to a microscope slide. That material is then chemically fixed to the slide, so it will not wash away in subsequent steps. An antibody, specific for the varicella-zoster virus, is then added to the slide. If the virus is present, the antibody binds very tightly to the material on the slide. This antibody has a dye attached to it. If the virus is present in that sample, it can be detected by visualizing the dye. Typically, the dye is fluorescent. Consequently, if the slide is viewed with a microscope that can visualize fluorescent signals, the virus will be detected as brightly glowing particles on the slide. If the virus is not present, there will be no binding of antibodies, and no glowing particles on the slide. In recent years, this technique has improved, as antibodies have been developed that are very specific to varicella-zoster virus, and which do not react to the presence of other viruses.

DETECTION BY VIRUS ISOLATION

In some cases, varicella-zoster virus can be grown in culture in the laboratory as a way to determine if the virus is the cause of an infection. The virus is added to cells grown in culture; after one to three days, antibody tests are used to determine if the virus is present in cultured cells. These procedures are cumbersome, require the presence of viable virus, and are time consuming, so culture is rarely used as a diagnostic method.

DETECTION OF VIRAL DNA

Increasingly, tests to detect viral RNA or DNA are used for identification of viruses. One of the most common of these tests is called the **polymerase chain reaction** (PCR). This technique is analogous to a molecular copy machine, amplifying a specific bit of DNA from a virus a millionfold or more, to the point where it can be readily detected.

PCR can detect, theoretically, a single DNA molecule. It also can detect both living and dead viruses, which is an advantage in chicken pox, because many of the viruses in lesions are not viable. In addition, by using PCR, researchers can use the small DNA sequence differences to distinguish the virus strains that are used in the vaccine from those circulating in the community.

PCR amplification requires the presence of viral DNA; at least in some cases, clinical specimens can be used directly, without purification. PCR requires a sample for testing, and reagents that can be used to make DNA in a test tube. The PCR itself involves three steps. Initially the PCR reaction mixture is heated to a temperature high enough to cause the two strands of DNA to separate. Next, the reaction is cooled down to the point where small, single-stranded DNA segments called primers bind to the viral DNA if it is present. Primers, as the name suggests, initiate or prime the synthesis of new DNA. In the third and final step, the temperature is raised again, and **DNA polymerase**, an enzyme that makes DNA, begins to operate.

Figure 5.1 A biologist prepares a polymerase chain reaction (PCR) assay, a test that allows researchers to identify viruses by detection of viral DNA. (James Gathany/Centers for Disease Control and Prevention/ U.S. Department of Health and Human Services)

The DNA polymerase uses the primers as starting points for DNA synthesis. The key to this method is the use of primers that uniquely recognize the varicella-zoster virus DNA, and not the DNA from any other virus or other pathogen. The use of proper primers makes this test highly specific for chicken pox. Recent innovations in PCR include the development of methodologies allowing for more rapid detection of the virus and differentiating the strains used for vaccination from those that naturally cause disease in the population.[3]

DETECTION USING MICROSCOPY

Although rarely used now, a variety of other tests had been used in the past to detect chicken pox infections and the varicella-zoster virus. These included electron microscopy, where a very high-powered microscope was used to directly visualize the virus. Another technique involved isolating cells from a chicken pox lesion, and using a light microscope to identify characteristic shapes of cells that are associated with the disease. Although rapid and inexpensive, this method does not distinguish between varicella-zoster virus and herpes simplex virus infections.

DETECTION BASED ON IMMUNE RESPONSES

There are other laboratory tests that detect a reaction to the virus, or the specific effects the virus has on cells or tissues, rather than the virus itself. Most of these tests determine whether a person has specific antibodies to the varicella-zoster virus. These types of tests have two possible applications. One application is to test selected adults, such as health care workers, women who are contemplating pregnancy, and others who are at risk of serious complications from chicken pox. By determining whether or not antibodies are present, it is possible to determine whether the person is likely still susceptible to the disease. If the person does not have antibodies present in their blood, it is a sign they have not been exposed to chicken pox. In these cases, a person may be vaccinated or given medications to reduce the severity of disease if they have been exposed to the virus, but do not yet show symptoms.

Two types of tests for antibodies directed against the varicella-zoster virus are commonly used. In one technique, called an **enzyme-linked immunosorbent assay** (ELISA), proteins from the virus are used to coat small wells in a rectangular plastic plate. A serum sample from a patient is then added to the wells. If antibodies to the varicella-zoster virus are present, they will bind to the proteins in the well and not be washed away in the next step. Following washing, another antibody is added that binds to human antibodies. In some cases, an additional antibody is added that binds to the human-binding

Figure 5.2 A microbiologist uses an enzyme-linked immunosorbent assay (ELISA) test to identify a virus by the detection of antibodies to the virus. (James Gathany/Centers for Disease Control and
Prevention/U.S. Department of Health and Human Services)

antibody. This last antibody contains a molecule that, under the appropriate conditions, produces a signal that can be detected and is used to determine whether antibodies to the varicella-zoster virus are present.

Another method for detecting antibodies to the varicella-zoster virus is called the latex **agglutination** test (agglutination means clumping). This diagnostic method uses viral proteins that are bound to latex beads. To perform the test, a drop of serum from a patient is placed on a glass slide. The latex agglutination reagent is then added. If antibodies to the vari-cella-zoster virus are present on the slide, the latex particles will visibly clump or agglutinate after a few minutes, as the anti-bodies in the serum bind to the latex particles. This clumping is a sign that the patient has had a previous exposure to the varicella-zoster virus and made antibodies.

Tests that provide a more accurate measure of immunity to chicken pox determine the extent of cell-mediated immune response to the virus. These tests are more time consum-ing (requiring several days), more cumbersome, and more expensive, so they are rarely used in normal clinical practice. Examples of these tests include proliferation assays and cyto-toxicity assays.

To perform a proliferation assay, a blood sample is taken from the patient, and the white blood cells are separated. These white blood cells are then grown in an incubator in laboratory culture medium. If the patient has developed a cell-mediated immune response to the varicella-zoster virus, when proteins from the virus are added to the culture, some of the white blood cells in the culture will grow and divide. This can be detected by the ability of these dividing cells to take up a radioactive compound and incorporate this molecule into their DNA. After several days, the amount of radioactivity in cells that were exposed to the virus, and a control group of cells that were not exposed to the virus, are compared. If the cells exposed to the viral proteins are much more highly radioactive, it is an indication that the patient has a strong cell-mediated immune response directed against the virus.

Cytotoxicity assays can also be used to determine if a person has a cell-mediated immune response directed against the virus. These tests are done by taking cells from the patient and infecting them with the varicella-zoster virus. These cells are then incubated with radioactive chromium, which is retained inside the cells unless they are killed. The virus-infected, chromium-laced cells from the patient are then added to white blood cells from the same patient. These white blood cells had been previously exposed to varicella-zoster virus proteins to activate any cells that respond specifically to the varicella-zoster virus. If some of these white blood cells have been produced in response to a previous chicken pox infection, they will attack and kill the virus-infected cells, and radioactivity will be released into the culture medium and be readily detected.

The other application for testing the immune response is to verify that a person does, currently, have a case of chicken pox. By detecting specific antibodies against the virus, and comparing the amount of antibody at the time of initial symptoms and at a later time, it is possible to verify a current infection. This is done either by looking at the change in the amount of antibody, or by looking at the change in the type of antibody. Initially the level of a type of antibody, called IgM, increases in the very early stages of an infection. As an infection progresses, another type of antibody, called IgG, becomes predominant. Therefore, if a patient initially has a high level of chicken pox anti-IgM antibody, and he or she later develops a high level of anti–chicken pox IgG antibody, this change indicates that the person has a current case of chicken pox.[4]

TREATMENT: ANTIVIRAL DRUGS

It is often a challenge to treat viral infections, because viruses must live inside cells in order to replicate. It is difficult to get drugs into cells, but even if that obstacle is overcome, another basic issue in the biology of viruses may pose another obstacle. Viruses use components of human cells to reproduce. Consequently, it is hard to target a virus for destruction without harming the host that harbors the virus. As a result, for many viral infections, there are no drug treatments that have any effect on the course of the illness.

Fortunately, in the case of chicken pox and other diseases caused by herpesviruses, there are several medications available that can reduce the severity and duration of the illness. They include drugs that have been used for a number of years, as well as several drugs that are being tested for use in humans.

Three related drugs—acyclovir, famciclovir, and valacyclovir—are nucleotide analogs. They mimic nucleotides, the building blocks of DNA, but do not function properly, when they are inserted into DNA. In fact, insertion of these nucleotide analogs into DNA prevents the DNA from being further extended, and this stops the virus from making copies of itself.

This is a potential problem, because both human cells and the varicella-zoster virus need to make DNA. However, the virus possesses a gene not found in human cells. This gene codes for an enzyme called thymidine kinase. Thymidine kinase encoded by this gene converts acyclovir and related drugs into an active form. Therefore, the drug will only be active in cells infected with the virus, and will not harm cells that are not infected.

Acyclovir is particularly effective against the herpes simplex viruses. It is not as effective against the varicella-zoster virus, which requires about 12 times more of the drug to inhibit the virus. A related drug, valacyclovir is very similar to acyclovir, but is more easily absorbed by the body when taken orally. Famciclovir is a newer, related drug. It lasts about 10 times longer in the body than acyclovir, but requires a concentration 5 to 10 times higher than acyclovir to inhibit the varicella-zoster virus.

Foscarnet is another drug that has been approved for use to treat varicella-zoster infections. This drug interacts with the enzyme that makes DNA (DNA polymerase) in the

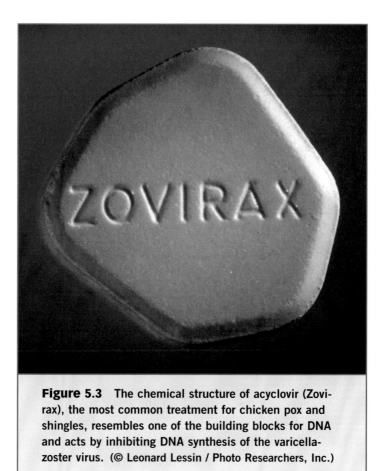

Figure 5.3   The chemical structure of acyclovir (Zovirax), the most common treatment for chicken pox and shingles, resembles one of the building blocks for DNA and acts by inhibiting DNA synthesis of the varicella-zoster virus. (© Leonard Lessin / Photo Researchers, Inc.)

varicella-zoster viruses, preventing the virus from making new DNA. This drug does not have to be acted on by an enzyme in order for it to function. A major benefit of this drug is that viruses that are resistant to acyclovir and related drugs are generally still susceptible to foscarnet. Foscarnet, however, often causes kidney dysfunction and other side effects and so is only used in select cases.

The treatment with these antiviral agents (acyclovir has been studied most intensively) is generally quite effective when given within 24 hours of the first lesions on the skin. Their effectiveness has been demonstrated in studies showing that the number of vesicles is reduced, the number of days where new lesions are produced is reduced, and the symptoms (such as fever) were reduced in intensity.[5] Treatment with acyclovir was also shown to reduce the severity of disease in children who had a compromised immune system, and had value in some cases if taken continuously to prevent infection.[6]

TREATMENT: VARICELLA IMMUNOGLOBULIN

Another treatment available for chicken pox infections is the use of varicella **immunoglobulin**. Immunoglobulins are another name for antibodies, proteins produced by immune system cells that bind to pathogens. The binding of antibodies to the varicella-zoster virus can prevent the virus from entering and infecting cells.

Varicella immunoglobulin consists of blood serum from human donors who had high levels of antibodies to the varicella-zoster virus. It is prepared by taking blood from these donors, removing the red blood cells, and keeping the liquid. The liquid is then treated with ethyl alcohol, which concentrates the antibodies. Solvents and detergents are then added to the preparation to inactivate any blood-borne viruses that could otherwise be transmitted to the patient.

An early study of the effect of varicella immunoglobulin on preventing chicken pox was reported in 1962. Children who were members of a family where one case of chicken pox developed were either treated or left untreated as controls. Of the participants, 242 were given immunoglobulin, and 209 were left untreated. About the same percentage of children (around 87 percent) developed chicken pox whether or not they received the immunoglobulin. Although the attack rate was not reduced, the severity of symptoms was lower in patients who received injections of immunoglobulin, particularly at higher doses.[7]

In a later test of the effectiveness of varicella immuno-globulin, six households with at least three children were studied. In this case, a more potent serum was used, prepared from patients who had recently recovered from an attack of shingles. Within 72 hours of the time one of the children developed chicken pox, one of the children was given the varicella immunoglobulin, and the other a placebo, or inactive infusion (it was not known to the investigators which child had been given which treatment). Subsequently, it was noted that in each of the six families studied, one additional child developed chicken

VARICELLA-ZOSTER RESISTANCE TO ANTIVIRAL DRUGS

Varicella-zoster viruses rarely show resistance to the drugs, like acyclovir, that are used to treat chicken pox or shingles. However, in some patients, especially those who are immuno-compromised, resistance to antiviral drugs has been reported. Typically, these patients are treated for long periods of time with the drug, and this can select for resistant viruses, especially because a defective immune system often leads to exceptionally large numbers of viruses in the body, resulting in a larger pool of viruses that can develop mutations.

For the common drugs, like acyclovir, the mutations that lead to resistance occur either in the thymidine kinase gene, or the DNA polymerase gene. The thymidine kinase enzyme is required to convert the drugs, like acyclovir, to an active form. The DNA polymerase enzyme incorporates acyclovir into a growing DNA chain. Consequently, mutations in either of the genes that encode these proteins can result in resistance to these drugs. Fortunately, for patients with acyclovir-resistant viral infections, there is at least one option. The drug foscarnet is usually active against viruses that are resistant to other drugs, although it can cause significant side effects.

pox. In each case, it was the child who received the placebo. Although this was a small trial, it did help establish the efficacy of the immunoglobulin at preventing chicken pox, if the immunoglobulin contained a high enough concentration of antibodies directed against the varicella-zoster virus.[8]

Early trials in children who had leukemia, and who were therefore susceptible to severe cases of chicken pox due to their suppressed immune systems, suggested that the immunoglobulin did not prevent the development of chicken pox. A later trial was then conducted with more a more potent formulation of immunoglobulin. In this small trial, eight children at risk for more severe chicken pox were treated with a high-potency preparation of immunoglobulin. Three of the children in the study developed a very mild case of chicken pox with 50 or fewer lesions, and the remaining five did not develop the disease, even though they lived in households where another child had developed chicken pox.[9]

Based on these and other studies, patients who are candidates for this treatment have been exposed to chicken pox, are susceptible to it, and are at high risk for severe symptoms following chicken pox infections. These people include mothers and infants who developed chicken pox within five days of delivery, adults without previous exposure to chicken pox, and children or adults who are immunocompromised. The treatment has been found to be effective if administered within 96 hours of exposure to the virus; it is not clear if later administration reduces the symptoms or severity of infection.

Varicella immunoglobulin is injected into the muscle at a rate of approximately 125 units per 20 pounds of patient weight. It can be administered multiple times if a susceptible person has several exposures to the virus. Severe reactions occur in approximately one in every 1,000 treatments. These reactions include **anaphylactic shock**, a serious condition that can normally be treated in a medical setting. Mild reactions are common, including pain and irritation at the site of injection.[10]

While useful in treating some cases of chicken pox, immuno-globulin treatment does not seem to be useful for preventing or reducing the severity of the symptoms of shingles.

TREATMENT-RELATED CONCERNS

The use of aspirin to treat the symptoms of chicken pox is now strongly discouraged. Starting in about 1980, it became clear that there was an association between Reye's syndrome, aspirin, and chicken pox. Reye's syndrome is a serious complication that can follow aspirin use during a viral illness. It often starts with nausea and vomiting, and a loss of mental alertness. The condition can quickly worsen, leading to paralysis and loss of consciousness. The mortality rate can be 30 percent or higher. Prior to an understanding of the cause of Reye's syndrome, there were more than 100 cases per year in the United States associated with the use of aspirin in children with chicken pox. Although the cause of the link between aspirin and Reye's syndrome is not entirely clear, one set of experiments, in 1984, suggested a possible explanation. These experiments showed that the varicella-zoster virus grew in culture to higher numbers in the presence of high concentrations of aspirin. Larger numbers of viruses are likely to cause more severe infections, and that might contribute to the symptoms observed in Reye's syndrome.[11]

There was also a concern about whether treatment with antiviral drugs might limit the growth of viruses to the extent that an insufficient immune response would develop, and the infected person might still be susceptible to a subsequent chicken pox infection. The data available so far does not indicate that this is a problem. This may be due, at least in part, to the fact that the varicella-zoster virus replicates fairly extensively before symptoms develop. Because the drugs are not typically given until symptoms develop, there is adequate time for an immune response to develop before the drugs start to limit further growth of the virus.[12]

6

How Is Chicken Pox Prevented?

Dr. Michiaki Takahashi was a virologist in Japan who had studied a variety of pathogens, including measles virus and polioviruses. In 1964, his three-year-old son developed a severe case of chicken pox, with a high fever and vesicles covering his entire body. This eventually inspired him to start developing a vaccine that could prevent this normally mild, but sometimes very serious, illness. His work on the chicken pox vaccine began in 1972, and two years later he succeeded in developing a vaccine strain of the virus. Another 21 years would elapse before the vaccine was approved for use in the United States, in 1995.

Preventing chicken pox required the development of a vaccine. Because most cases of chicken pox are relatively mild, creating a vaccine had not been a priority among public health officials until fairly recently. However, an increasing awareness of potential complications from chicken pox, along with an expanding pool of immunocompromised people who were vulnerable to severe cases of chicken pox, finally led to the licensing of a commercial vaccine.

The eventual production of the vaccine required a substantial amount of preliminary work in order to determine how best to grow the virus in culture, and to determine conditions for separating the virus from the cells used for growth. Once these problems were surmounted, work on the varicella-zoster vaccine began in earnest in 1972 by the Japanese doctor Michiaki Takahashi.

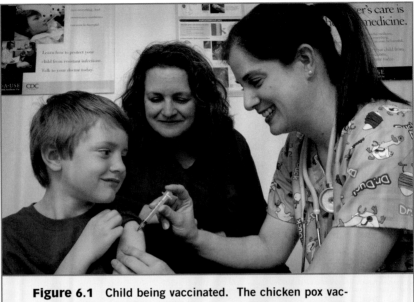

Figure 6.1   Child being vaccinated. The chicken pox vaccine was approved for use in the United States in 1995. (James Gathany/Centers for Disease Control/ U.S. Department of Health and Human Services)

The virus used for vaccine development was isolated from an otherwise healthy three-year-old boy in Japan, who had a case of chicken pox. It was named the Oka strain, based on the name of the boy who contributed the virus to science. Previous work had shown that the virus retained its ability to cause disease for at least a year when held at a low temperature, so the virus was stored in the laboratory at -94°F (-70°C) until it was needed.

From studies of how the body defends itself against chicken pox infection, it was clear that a live virus vaccine would likely be needed. A live vaccine typically stimulates a stronger immune response, as compared to a vaccine that just contains parts of a virus, or an inactivated virus. Specifically, a live vaccine stimulates a cell-mediated immune response as well as an antibody response; a vaccine with an inactivated virus normally only stimulates an antibody response. Consequently, Dr. Takahashi and his group had their work cut out for them. To produce a live virus vaccine, the virus has to be weakened but still be able to grow to a limited extent in the body. Typically, weakening, or attenuating, a virus requires growing it under unusual conditions, and it can be a matter of both good experimental design and good luck to find the right conditions.

In the case of the Oka vaccine strain, the virus was initially grown in culture flasks in human embryonic lung cells, at a lower-than-normal temperature. After several days, when the cells showed definite signs of infection, they were treated with an enzyme that caused them to float off the bottom of the flask. The loose cells, full of the varicella-zoster virus, were then added to a new batch of human embryonic lung cells. This process was repeated 11 times.

After the eleventh passage in human cells, some of the infected human cells were added to another type of cell—guinea pig embryonic fibroblast cells. These cells were one of the few types of nonhuman cells that were known to allow for the growth of the virus. The logic was that, in order for the virus to successfully grow in such an unusual type of cell, it must undergo genetic changes that will make it less harmful to humans. As with the human cells, the same process of waiting a few days until the cells showed some signs of infection was employed, before some of the cells were transferred to new flasks of uninfected cells. This process was repeated six times for the initial vaccine trials. The virus that was eventually used in the vaccine was grown for 12 cycles in guinea pig cells.[1]

At the end of this process, the virus was tested for a lack of virulence in laboratory animals. Not surprisingly, no pathogenicity was observed, because the virus normally does not infect laboratory animals. The next step was to test the virus in human volunteers. Healthy children, with no history of chicken pox, were given various dosages of the vaccine. In almost all cases, the vaccine appeared to promote immunity and did not cause disease.

Next, the vaccine was tested on children in a hospital. Many of the children in this particular hospital had medical conditions that made a chicken pox infection life threatening. Consequently, when the first case of chicken pox was reported in the hospital, the other children were vaccinated. None of the vaccinated children developed chicken pox. These initial trials supported the usefulness of the vaccine and eventually helped lead to the widespread use of this preventative measure.

Before the virus could be produced for mass vaccination, one major problem still had to be addressed. The growth of the virus in the guinea pig cells was relatively poor, meaning that it was difficult to produce the large volumes of the virus required for mass vaccination. Ultimately, several human cell lines were used, instead, for final growth of the virus. This involved five cycles of growth in one of two cell lines.[2]

Additional studies were conducted by Dr. Takahashi and his group to determine the efficacy of the vaccine prepared with this modified method. These studies included vaccination of children in families in Japan where one child developed chicken pox. Normally, chicken pox spreads quickly within a family; however, in this study, none of the vaccinated children developed chicken pox, whereas all the unvaccinated children developed chicken pox. Other studies further supported the efficacy of the vaccine in protecting against chicken pox.

Further analysis of the vaccine included the sequencing of the entire genome of the vaccine strain of the virus, and the parental strain from which it derived. Altogether, 42 mutations were identified in the vaccine strain, as compared to the parental strain. These mutations meant that the vaccine strain and the original parental strain differed by 0.016 percent—a small difference, but enough to turn the virus from a pathogen into a medicine.[3]

The vaccine was first approved in Japan in 1989, and then in the United States in 1995; it has subsequently been approved for use in many countries in Europe. Data from the first randomized trial in the use of the vaccine in the United States was reported in 1984. The study involved children who had not previously been exposed to chicken pox. In this test, children in the same household were randomly given either the vaccine or a placebo. During the first year of follow-up, the vaccine was 100 percent effective; over 7 years, 95 percent of the children who received the vaccine had not developed chicken pox. In another vaccine trial in Europe, those children who received the highest dose of the vaccine had a low rate of chicken pox (3 percent); in contrast, among those children who did not receive a vaccine, 26 percent developed chicken pox. Additional studies have subsequently shown 85 to 90 percent protection against chicken pox, and 90 to 100 percent protection against severe cases of chicken pox.[4]

Since the vaccine became widely used in the United States, the number of cases of chicken pox has dropped dramatically. Prior to the availability of the vaccine, there were more than 4 million cases of chicken pox per year. By 2006, it was estimated that there were about 600,000 cases of chicken pox, about an 85 percent reduction. The number of deaths attributed to chicken pox dropped substantially once vaccination was implemented. In 1994, the year before the United States approved the vaccine, the number of deaths in the United States directly caused by the varicella-zoster virus was 124. By 2001, that number had dropped almost 80 percent, to 26. By 2006, that number was 19, a reduction of 85 percent compared to 1994.[5] A 1994 study suggested that each dollar spent on the vaccine generated $5.40 in savings for medical costs and indirect costs, such as loss of work.[6] In addition, there is evidence that people who are vaccinated are less likely to develop shingles, another important benefit of this medical intervention.

In 2005, a new vaccine formulation was approved called ProQuad. It consists of the varicella vaccine in the same shot along with the measles, mumps, and rubella vaccines (MMRV). It was approved based on a demonstration that the combined vaccine was as effective at promoting immunity as the separate vaccines.[7]

RASHES FOLLOWING VACCINATION

The varicella-zoster virus vaccine consists of a number of closely related viral strains, which differ by a few DNA mutations. The viruses in the vaccine, in general, show a reduced ability to replicate in skin cells and consequently are rarely transmitted from a person receiving the vaccine to another person.

However, about 5 percent of the children who are vaccinated develop a mild rash following vaccination, indicating that the virus, in these children, has some ability to replicate in the skin.

Researchers from the United Kingdom and the United States studied the viruses isolated from patients who developed a rash following vaccination. They found that in each individual vesicle or blister, there was only a single strain of varicella-zoster virus. However, different vesicles on the same person, or from different people, contained genetically distinct strains. This indicated that more than one strain of the genetically mixed strains in the vaccine was responsible for replication in the skin. However, virus strains with at least one of four specific mutations were found much more commonly in a skin rash. This implies that some of the viral variants in the vaccine are more able to replicate in the skin, and the vaccine would be even more useful if some of those variants were eliminated.[8]

SAFETY OF THE VARICELLA-ZOSTER VACCINE

Millions of doses of the vaccine have been administered since its approval in the United States and elsewhere, and the safety record of the vaccine has been very good. The most common side effects are pain at the site of injection and fever. These effects were reported in about 10 percent of the people who received a vaccination. Another common side effect, reported in about 5 percent of healthy children who have been vaccinated, is a mild rash that develops about two weeks after vaccination. There have been relatively few serious side effects from vaccination (such as pneumonia and chicken pox infection that spreads throughout the body). In almost all these cases, the patients had an undiagnosed immune deficiency.[9]

Three groups of people should not receive the vaccine:

1. People who are allergic to a vaccine component.

2. Women who are pregnant.

3. People who are immunocompromised.

However, some immunocompromised people do receive the vaccine with favorable results. For example, there is a compassionate use provision for vaccination of patients with leukemia with the chicken pox vaccine. These individuals have typically had a much lower rate of severe chicken pox, as compared to unvaccinated children with the same underlying disease (approximately 10 percent of vaccinated children get the disease, as compared with 45 percent of unvaccinated children).

This vaccine, like all live virus vaccines, is not recommended for pregnant women, although there have not been reports of harm to the woman or the fetus following vaccination. There have been some cases where women who had received the vaccine decided not continue their pregnancies, however.[10] Currently, no adverse effects associated with this vaccine are eligible for compensation from the National Vaccine Injury Program.

VACCINE SCHEDULE

When the vaccine was first approved in the United States in 1995, it was initially recommended that a single dose be given sometime between 1 year and 12 years of age. Subsequent determination that there was still some spread of chicken pox in the community led to a new recommendation that children be vaccinated twice.[11] It is now recommended that children receive a vaccine for chicken pox between 12 and 15 months of age, and again at the age of 4 to 6 years. For individuals who only received one dose of the vaccine, they should have a second "catch-up" vaccine as soon as possible.[12]

CONCERNS ABOUT VACCINATION

One of the issues raised regarding chicken pox vaccination is ensuring high levels of vaccine coverage. In the years prior to the approval of the vaccine, chicken pox was such a common illness that almost all United States residents developed chicken pox during childhood.

With vaccination, there have been dramatically fewer cases of chicken pox, so the likelihood of encountering chicken pox has decreased significantly. This means that a person who has not been vaccinated is less likely to develop chicken pox during childhood. Because chicken pox is a more serious illness in adults, it is critical to ensure that everyone possible is vaccinated.

7

What Is Shingles?

A 65-year-old man developed a burning sensation on his lower back, just at the waistline. It extended from the right side to the middle of the back. A day or two later, the characteristic rash developed, and was intensely itchy. His physician diagnosed shingles, and prescribed acyclovir. In spite of the treatment, the rash lasted about two weeks, was painful even to light touch, and the gentle pressure of fabric from a shirt caused irritation. The itchiness and pain lasted for several more weeks, but he recovered without further complications. To the best of his knowledge, there was no previous illness, unusual stress or other factors that might have triggered this attack.[1]

Shingles, or zoster, is caused by the reactivation of varicella-zoster virus, which often remains hidden for years in nerve cells in the body. In the United States, approximately 1 million people develop shingles each year, although the number is expected to drop substantially with the use of a recently approved vaccine.

As described previously, the varicella-zoster virus causes both chicken pox and shingles. After the initial chicken pox infection, usually in childhood, almost all the virus is destroyed by the immune system. However, some of the virus retreats to the nerve cells and remains inactive and hidden, but viable, often for decades. The victims of shingles are typically over 60 years old, although shingles can potentially occur in anyone, of any age, who has previously had a case of chicken pox.

Elderly people are at higher risk for shingles because their immunity in general, and their immunity to the varicella-zoster virus in particular, wane with time. In most cases, many years elapse between chicken pox and shingles; however in some select cases (e.g., an infant who developed

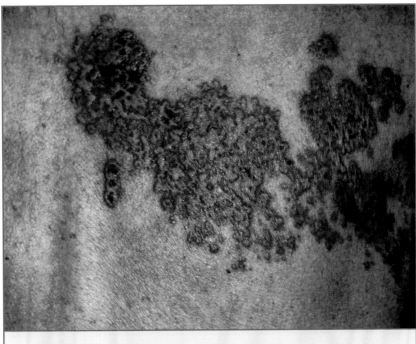

Figure 7.1   **A typical presentation of a shingles rash. (© Dr. Ken Greer/Visuals Unlimited, Inc.)**

chicken pox right after birth), shingles can develop within a year or less of a bout with chicken pox. Based on several studies, about 1 percent of the elderly would be expected to develop shingles in a given year. However, the risk rises with increasing age, probably related to declining immune responses. It has been estimated that 10 to 20 percent of the population will develop shingles at some point in their life if they have not been vaccinated to prevent the disease.[2]

It is not yet clear what causes the varicella-zoster virus to break out of its inactive state and cause disease again. There have been some cases of shingles following an X-ray or surgery, although no clear causal connection has been made between these events. There have also been anecdotal connections between shingles and stress, and a consequently lower immune response. Several studies have addressed this issue. In one study, researchers matched 101 patients with shingles with 101 people who had not developed the disease. Both groups were similar in terms of age, sex, and racial composition. The patients who developed shingles had significantly more stressful life events within six months prior to their illness, compared to the matched group that had not developed shingles. (The connection was even stronger for stressful events within two or three months of their outbreak.) Similarly, another study, reported in 1990, tracked a large group of patients who had not yet developed shingles. The patients who experienced stressful life events were more likely to develop shingles, compared with individuals who did not experience the stressful events, although the association was not very strong.[3]

When individuals develop shingles, they often experience substantial pain prior to the development of the rash. When the rash develops, it is more localized, but also more dense, than a chicken pox rash. The rash is only found on one side of the body, in a narrow band. This band corresponds to the area supplied by a single nerve hub near the spinal cord. When reactivated, the virus travels out from the hub along the nerves to the skin. The affected band of skin is called a **dermatome**. Most shingles episodes affect a single dermatome. In immunocompromised patients, more than one dermatome can be affected. The most frequent sites are the torso or face. In shingles, the entire swath of the rash area can be red, sometimes with a thick network of lesions. As with chicken pox, new vesicles appear for up to seven days. The lesions produce infectious viruses, which can infect people not previously exposed to chicken pox.

For many people, especially those over 60, the rash is very painful. For some, it produces an itching, burning sensation, in others a stabbing or throbbing pain. For some people, the pain is constant, and in others, the pain comes and goes. The pain

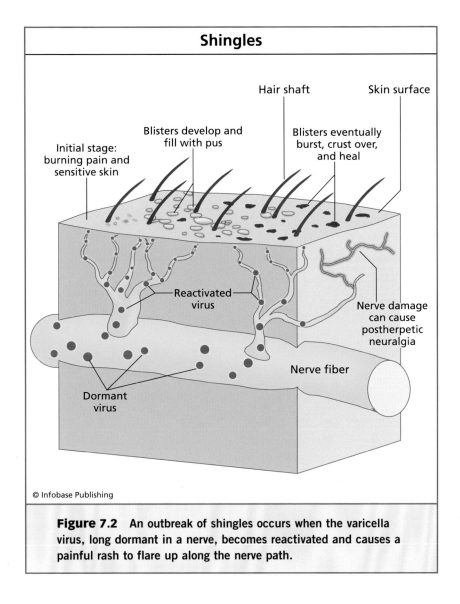

Shingles

Hair shaft

Skin surface

Blisters develop and fill with pus

Blisters eventually burst, crust over, and heal

Initial stage: burning pain and sensitive skin

Reactivated virus

Nerve damage can cause postherpetic neuralgia

Nerve fiber

Dormant virus

© Infobase Publishing

Figure 7.2 An outbreak of shingles occurs when the varicella virus, long dormant in a nerve, becomes reactivated and causes a painful rash to flare up along the nerve path.

results from either damage to the nerves or overstimulation of the sensory nerves. In most cases, after the lesions begin to heal, there are no permanent ill effects. The skin begins to crust over, and the new skin replaces the lesions after about four weeks.

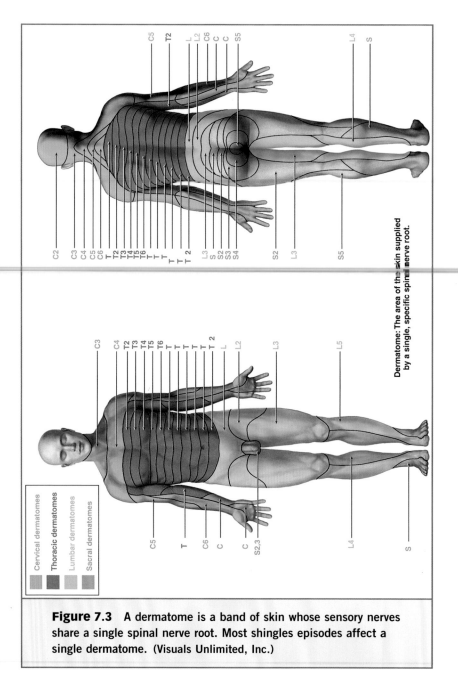

Cervical dermatomes
Thoracic dermatomes
Lumbar dermatomes
Sacral dermatomes

Dermatome: The area of the skin supplied by a single, specific spinal nerve root.

Figure 7.3 A dermatome is a band of skin whose sensory nerves share a single spinal nerve root. Most shingles episodes affect a single dermatome. (Visuals Unlimited, Inc.)

However, some people who develop shingles can develop long-lasting complications. One example is a condition called post-herpetic neuralgia (PHN). It occurs in 10 to 15 percent of patients who develop shingles. In those who are over 60 when they develop shingles, the incidence of PHN is greater than 50 percent. This is a syndrome that results in long-lasting, severe pain following an attack of shingles. The pain is described as a deep, burning pain that is constant; a sharp, stabbing pain that comes and goes; or a dull, blunt pain exacerbated by even a light touch. Some patients with PHN experience all three types of pain—a common description likening the pain to the feeling one gets from chewing aluminum foil, but with the sensation under the skin. In general, PHN occurs because the virus can damage or destroy the nerves where it is replicating. More specifically, the growth of the virus leads to inflammation that can damage the nerves. This inflammation can travel to adjacent nerves, and extend to the spinal cord or brain. This damage can lead to inappropriate signals in the nervous system that are perceived as pain. Also, as some of the damaged nerves regenerate, they become hyperactive and send out abnormal pain signals. This damage can take years for the body to repair, providing an explanation as to why the pain in PHN is often long-lasting.

Many other complications can occur. For example, the patient may lose all feeling in the area where they had an outbreak of shingles. Outbreaks that include the eyes may affect up to 25 percent of patients. Of those patients, 50 percent of the time, eye involvement causes repeat bouts of ocular disease, and in many of those cases, some degree of vision loss. Paralysis, deafness, meningitis, bronchitis, gastritis, colitis, pericarditis, pneumonia, hepatitis, arthritis, and scarring are all reported complications of shingles.

SHINGLES IN PATIENTS WITH IMMUNE DEFICIENCIES

Patients who are immunocompromised are at greater risk for contracting shingles, and for developing serious complications from the illness. For example, several studies have indicated an

THE EVOLUTION OF LATENCY FOR THE VARICELLA-ZOSTER VIRUS

Latency is a condition where a virus (or other pathogen) is kept in check and the net viral population size does not change. Herpesviruses, like the varicella-zoster virus, maintain a static latency during which the virus does not replicate but the viral DNA remains in cells in the body, waiting for a signal to replicate.

A paper from 2002 by researchers from the United Kingdom described some of the factors that might contribute the evolution of viral latency. Essentially, a parasite, like the varicella-zoster virus, needs a strategy that can ensure survival until a new host is available, and the virus can continue to replicate. One potential problem for the varicella-zoster virus is that once a person is infected, he or she is typically immune from a second infection. Because the virus is capable of spreading rapidly within a population, frequently 90 to 95 percent of the population will be immune by virtue of having contracted a case of chicken pox. Consequently, viruses that infect a person late in an epidemic will frequently not be able to find new, susceptible hosts to infect.

These researchers calculated that in populations with few susceptible hosts, viruses with a long latent period have a selective advantage over viruses without the ability to become latent. In these situations, a virus that can wait for years, until a new cohort of susceptible children is born, is more likely to survive and continue to be an effective pathogen.[4]

increased incidence of shingles in patients with systemic lupus erythematosus (SLE). SLE is a disorder of the immune system, where patients produce antibodies that attack their own cells and tissues. This derangement of immune function apparently creates an opening for latent varicella-zoster virus to replicate and produce symptomatic disease.

In patients who are infected with HIV, the risk of developing shingles is 15 to 25 times higher than the risk for individuals who are not infected with HIV. The risk for HIV-infected individuals developing shingles increases with age. HIV patients younger than 50 years of age have a risk for developing the disease of about 4 percent per year; HIV patients over 50 have a risk of about 25 percent per year for developing shingles. In addition, individuals with HIV infection are also prone to develop complications from shingles at higher rates than the general population. For example, HIV patients have a risk of developing severe complications of the nervous system at a rate of about 7 percent, as compared with a rate about 3 percent in the general population.[5] In addition, these patients are prone to unusually severe side effects that are rarely, if ever, seen in patients with normal immunity. For example, some HIV infected patients with AIDS develop progressive outer retinal necrosis, a condition that can lead to blindness following a shingles attack. Other HIV/AIDS patients have developed progressive multifocal leukoencephalopathy, a neurological disorder that damages the brain to the point where death normally follows within a month to a year from onset. HIV/AIDS patients were also likely to have repeated recurrences of shingles, something that occurs very rarely in people with an intact immune system.

There has been a strong association of shingles with certain types of cancers. Patients with Hodgkin's disease, non-Hodgkin's lymphoma, and leukemia had some of the highest shingles attack rates. For example, in one analysis of patients at a comprehensive cancer center in Ontario, Canada, published in 1988, 14 percent of patients with Hodgkin's disease developed shingles; rates were also high for leukemia (10 percent) and non-Hodgkin's lymphoma (5 percent).[6] It is not entirely clear to what extent the elevation of the shingles incidence is due to the disease itself, or to the chemotherapy and radiation treatments that are often used to treat these diseases. As with patients with AIDS, individuals with these types of cancers often develop a severe case of shingles, and complications are common.

Although the data are sparse, there is also evidence that organ transplant recipients develop shingles at higher rates than the general population. These high rates of shingles are likely attributed to the immunosuppressive drugs taken to prevent rejection of the donated organ or tissue, and for bone marrow transplants, the radiation treatment required to destroy the recipient's bone marrow cells. For example, about one-third of patients receiving bone marrow transplants developed shingles within a year of receiving the transplant.[7] Elevated rates of shingles have also been reported in patients receiving kidney and heart transplants.

SHINGLES AS A MARKER FOR UNDERLYING DISEASE

Because shingles occurs at a higher rate, and with more complications, in patients with conditions that weaken the immune response, this raises the question of whether shingles may be a sign of a more serious underlying disease, such as cancer or diabetes. The information available suggests that is not the case, at least for these two diseases. In one large analysis of patients from Rochester, Minnesota, reported in 1982, there was no difference in cancer or diabetes rates for patients who developed shingles, versus those who did not. However, severe or recurrent cases of shingles, as described above, are likely a sign of an underlying immune deficiency like AIDS, because individuals with a normally functioning immune system typically get shingles no more than once.[8]

SHINGLES TREATMENTS

Because of the potential seriousness of the complications from shingles, attempts have been made to treat or prevent this disease. As with chicken pox, treatment for shingles consists of acyclovir, or similar drugs that prevent the virus from replicating, and these can reduce the seriousness of a shingles attack, if taken early enough.

Because PHN is so common in the elderly, a number of studies have been conducted to test various treatments for this condition. In general, a graded approach is used. Initially, patients are treated with a nonsteroidal anti-inflammatory drug, such as acetaminophen or aspirin. If those drugs do not sufficiently reduce pain, then an additional drug is added. One example is the tricyclic antidepressants such as amitriptyline. In addition to their antidepressant effects, these drugs also reduce the uptake of **neurotransmitters**, thereby reducing the transmission of pain signals. (Neurotransmitters are chemicals that relay signals to nerve cells.) However, there are a number of side effects of these drugs, such as confusion and drowsiness, which limits their usefulness.

If the tricyclic antidepressants are ineffective, or cause too many side effects, another option is a drug like gabapentin, which is one of several drugs used for preventing epilepsy. Limited trials have suggested a reduction in pain in patients suffering from PHN, compared to a placebo, and fewer side effects, compared to the tricyclic antidepressants. It is not clear how gabapentin works to reduce pain, but it may act on nerves in the spinal cord to prevent the transmission of pain signals.

If the combination of a nonsteroidal anti-inflammatory drug and one of these other drugs is not effective at reducing pain, then a physician may prescribe an opioid like codeine or oxycondone (oxycontin). Although side effects such as respiratory problems and drowsiness are common, and there is potential for addiction, these risks can often be managed.

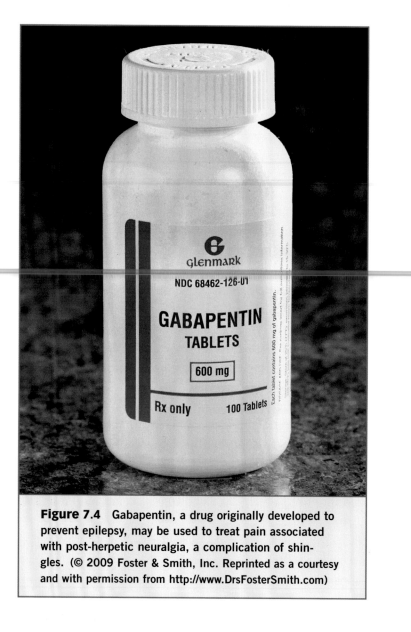

Figure 7.4 Gabapentin, a drug originally developed to prevent epilepsy, may be used to treat pain associated with post-herpetic neuralgia, a complication of shingles. (© 2009 Foster & Smith, Inc. Reprinted as a courtesy and with permission from http://www.DrsFosterSmith.com)

Patients who still do not have pain relief following these treatments have a few other options. There are topical treatments, such as lidocaine, an anesthetic that can be applied to areas of the skin where a patient is experiencing intense pain. Capsaicin (the active ingredient in hot peppers) can also be applied to the skin. Over time, it can reduce pain, but it does cause a burning sensation that can be intolerable to some people with PHN. There are also surgical interventions, methods of electrical stimulation, and other measures that have sometimes been helpful in treating cases of severe, unrelieved PHN. These techniques may involve cutting some nerves to reduce transmission of pain signals or strong electrical stimulation to alter the sensory input to the brain.[9]

PREVENTING SHINGLES

Prevention has become a more critical component in the medical care for shingles. In 2006, a shingles vaccine was approved for use in the United States for people over the age of 60. The vaccine has a much higher dose of the virus, compared to the vaccine used to prevent chicken pox. This high dose is used because older individuals tend to have a weakened immune response, so greater exposure to the virus is needed in order to stimulate a strong enough reaction to protect against shingles. The vaccine was shown to be safe in clinical studies. In a large-scale study, reported in 2005, nearly 40,000 volunteers, aged 60 to 69, were included. Those who were vaccinated had about 50 percent fewer cases of shingles. Those who were vaccinated and did develop shingles had less painful cases, and were less likely to develop complications.[10]

It is likely that, as the number of chicken pox cases continues to decline in the United States, vaccination for shingles will become more important. When chicken pox was common, people at risk for shingles would be exposed to the varicella-zoster virus whenever they encountered someone with chicken pox. This exposure would boost their immunity to the virus, and possibly prevent an attack of shingles. As chicken pox becomes rare, the likelihood of boosting the response to the virus decreases, and the risk of an attack of shingles

TAI CHI AND SHINGLES

Researchers have also studied some less conventional therapies to prevent or treat shingles. One report from researchers
in California analyzed a study of the effect of tai chi on immunity to shingles. Tai chi is an oriental exercise that involves
the slow repetition of martial arts movements. They studied
a small group of 36 people over the age of 60, 18 of whom
took tai chi three times per week, and 18 of whom did not.
The study ran for 15 weeks. During this time, the participants'
immune response to the varicella-zoster virus was determined.
Those seniors taking tai chi had significant increases in their
response to the virus compared to those not participating,
suggesting they might be less susceptible to the development
of shingles.[11]

Figure 7.5   Senior citizens practicing tai chi. (© Anne Clark/
iStockphoto)

will likely increase. This phenomenon was reported from a study in Massachusetts, where the incidence of chicken pox declined following vaccination, but the incidence of shingles increased. Further study will be needed, though, to verify this association between chicken pox vaccination and shingles.[12] The shingles vaccine will likely be increasingly important as a means of providing a boost to the immune response, thereby reducing the risk of shingles in an individual. The vaccine is now recommended by the Centers for Disease Control for all adults over the age of 60, unless they are significantly immunocompromised.

8

The Future of Chicken Pox and Shingles

In the United States, with the widespread implementation of the chicken pox vaccine and the recent introduction of the shingles vaccine, it is expected that the number of cases of chicken pox and shingles will continue to decline. Vaccination has already substantially reduced the number of deaths and the associated medical costs for treating chicken pox in the United States.

As mentioned previously, one of the unanswered questions is what will happen to patients who do not receive the vaccine. Until recently in the United States, most people got chicken pox during childhood. In general, chicken pox becomes more serious the older one is when one contracts it. Therefore, it appears likely that unvaccinated people will be less likely to contract chicken pox in childhood, and may be more likely to get it later in life, when it will be a more serious disease. Consequently, it will be critical that public health authorities work to ensure that the vaccination rate is very high. Doing this would ensure that any chicken pox outbreak would not spread, because the virus cannot spread to vaccinated people, a phenomenon called herd immunity.

Another unanswered question is how long the vaccination protects against infection. So far, the protection from the vaccine seems durable, although the vaccine has not been available for a long enough period to document that the vaccination protects for 40 to 50 years. In the United States, there are also some unanswered questions about the incidence of shingles in future years. As the elderly population is expected to grow substantially in the next decades, one would expect a substantial increase in the number of shingles cases. However, the approval of the shingles vaccine should help people maintain their immunity, and reduce the incidence and severity of the disease. In addition, those who received the chicken pox vaccine are less likely to develop shingles, based on early studies. Over time, this will likely reduce the overall number of shingles cases.

It will not be known for some time how long immunity from the shingles vaccine will last. The vaccine is approved for people over 60, but with a larger number of people living into their 80s and beyond, it is not yet clear if the vaccine will provide protection for 20 years or more.

In other parts of the world, the future of chicken pox and shingles is even less clear. Many other developed countries have not adopted the universal vaccination for chicken pox that has been put in place in the United States. In these countries, it would be expected that the incidence of chicken pox and shingles would not decrease as much as in the United States. In the less developed countries, where there is little or no vaccination, the long-term patterns of infection are likely to continue. In many of these countries, there is a higher rate of chicken pox in adults, when the disease is likely to be more serious. That is not likely to change in the near future.

Some general aspects of the biology of the varicella-zoster virus suggest hope for continued reduction of the incidence of the disease. The virus has a relatively low mutation rate, so it is unlikely that mutations will lead to the vaccine becoming ineffective.

As described in previous chapters, advances in molecular biology have led to a greatly enhanced knowledge of the natural history of the varicella-zoster virus. The sequencing of the

Figure 8.1 The Centers for Disease Control now recommends shingles vaccination for all adults over 60, unless they are significantly immunocomprimised. (Judy Schmidt/Centers for Disease Control and Prevention/ U.S. Department of Health and Human Services)

entire genome of the vaccine strain, the parental viral strain, and other isolates of the virus have aided in understanding how the virus causes disease.[1] The ability to use polymerase chain reaction and other techniques to identify the location of the virus during latency in the body has provided a better understanding of strategies the virus uses to remain hidden in the body, and should aid in the development of improved therapies and preventative measures for dealing with shingles.

One of the continuing limitations in understanding the biology of the varicella-zoster virus is the lack of an animal model that reproduces all aspects of the disease in humans. The SCID mouse model of chicken pox has been an important development, but still lacks some elements of natural infections in humans (for example, the lack of a clear latent phase of infection). Consequently, additional tools for understanding all aspects of the biology of this pathogen will continue to be important. If the pace of recent advances continues, there is reason to hope for a continued reduction in the number of deaths, and the pain and suffering caused by chicken pox and shingles.

Notes

Chapter 1

1. P. Nee and P. Edrich, "Chickenpox Pneumonia: Case Report and Literature Review," *Journal of Accident and Emergency Medicine* 16 (1999): 147–150.
2. G. Mandell, J. Bennett, and R. Dolin, eds., *Mendel, Douglas, and Bennett's Principles and Practices of Infectious Diseases*, 4th Ed (New York: Churchill Livingstone, 1995); H. Nguyen, A. Jumaan, and J. Seward, "Decline in Mortality Due to Varicella after Implementation of Varicella Vaccination in the United States," *New England Journal of Medicine* 352 (2005): 450–458.
3. H. Guess, D. Broughton, L. Melton, and L. Kurland, "Population-based Studies of Varicella Complications," *Pediatrics* 78 (1986): 723–7.
4. A. Davison. "Molecular Evolution of Alphaherpesviruses" in *Varicella-Zoster Virus: Virology and Clinical Management*, eds. A. Arvin and A. Gershon, (Cambridge, UK: Cambridge University Press, 2000).
5. G. Mandell, J. Bennett, and R. Dolin, eds., *Mendel, Douglas, and Bennett's Principles and Practices of Infectious Diseases*, 4th Ed. (New York: Churchill Livingstone, 1995).
6. Ibid.
7. A. Arvin, "Varicella-Zoster Virus." *Clinical Microbiology Reviews* 9, 3 (1996): 361–381.
8. M. Marin, H. C. Meissner, and J. Seward, "Varicella Prevention in the United States: A Review of Successes and Challenges." *Pediatrics* 122 (2008): e744–e751
9. C-H Ku, Y-T Liu, and D. Christiani, "Case Report: Occupationally Related Recurrent Varicella (Chickenpox) in a Hospital Nurse," *Environmental Health Perspectives* 113, 10 (2005): 1373–1375.
10. S. Hall, T. Maupin, J. Seward, A. Jumaan, C. Peterson, G. Goldman, L. Mascola, and M. Wharton, "Second Varicella Infections: Are They More Common Than Previously Thought?" *Pediatrics* 109 (2002): 1068–1073.
11. A. Arvin, "Varicella-Zoster Virus." *Clinical Microbiology Reviews*. 9, 3 (1996): 361–381.
12. B. Mandal, P. Mukherjee, C. Murphy, R. Mukherjee, and T. Naik, "Adult Susceptibility to Varicella in the Tropics Is a Rural Phenomenon due to the Lack of Previous Exposure." *Journal of Infectious Diseases* 178 (Suppl 1) (1998): S52–54.
13. E. Belay, J. Bresee, R. Holman, Ali Khan, A. Shahriari, and L. Schonberger, "Reye's Syndrome in the United States from 1981 through 1997," *New England Journal of Medicine* 340, 18 (1999): 1377–1382.
14. Y. Choong and N. Hawksworth, "Spontaneous Reduction in Myopic Correction Following Varicella Disciform Stromal Keratitis," *British Journal of Ophthamology* 86 (2002): 939-940.
15. P. LaRussa, "Clinical Manifestations of Varicella," in *Varicella-Zoster Virus: Virology and Clinical Management*. eds. A. Arvin and A. Gershon (Cambridge, UK: Cambridge University Press, 2000).
16. G. Gilbert, "Chickenpox During Pregnancy," *British Medical Journal* 306 (1993): 1079–1080.
17. A. Arvin, "Varicella-Zoster Virus." *Clinical Microbiology Reviews* 9, 3 (1996) 361–381.

Chapter 2

1. S. Manuchehri, "Historical Accounts of Two Indian Babis: Sa'in Hindi and Sayyid Basir Hindi. Research Notes in Shaykhi, Babi and Baha'i Studies," 5, 2 (2001), http://www.h-net.org/~bahai/notes/vol5/hunud.htm. Accessed on August 17, 2008.
2. P. Adamson, "The 'Bubu'tu' Lesion in Antiquity," *Medical History* 3 (1970): 313–318.
3. "History of Chickenpox," TheChickenPox.com, http://www.thechicken pox.com/history-of-chicken-pox.php (accessed August 16, 2008); T. Weller, "Historical Perspective," in *Varicella-Zoster Virus: Virology and*

Clinical Management. eds. A. Arvin and
A. Gershon (Cambridge, UK: Cambridge
University Press, 2000).

4. W. Osler, *The Principles and Practice of
Medicine,* 6th ed. (New York D. Appleton
Company, 1905), 128–129.

5. J. Aronson, "When I Use a Word:
Chickenpox," *British Medical Journal* 321
(2000) 682.

6. A. Arvin and A. Gershon, eds.,
*Varicella-Zoster Virus: Virology and
Clinical Management* (Cambridge, UK:
Cambridge University Press, 2000).

7. Ibid.

8. E. Goodpasture and K. Anderson,
"Infection of Human Skin, Grafted
on Chorioallantois of Chick Embryo,
with Virus of Herpes Zoster," *American
Journal of Pathology* 20 (1944): 447–455.

9. T. Weller, "Historical Perspective,"
*Varicella-Zoster Virus: Virology and
Clinical Management.* A. Arvin and
A. Gershon, eds. (Cambridge, UK:
Cambridge University Press, 2000).

10. T. Weller, H. Witton, and E.J. Bell,
"The Etiologic Agents of Varicella and
Herpes Zoster. Isolation, Propagation,
and Cultural Characteristics In Vitro,"
Journal of Experimental Medicine 108
(1958): 869–890.

11. T. Weller and H. Witton, "The Etiologic
Agents of Varicella and Herpes Zoster.
Serological Studies of the Viruses
Propagated In Vitro," *Journal of
Experimental Medicine* 108 (1958):
869–890.

12. S. E. Straus, W. Reinhold, H. Smith, W.
Ruyechan, D. Henderson, R. Blaese, and
J. Hay, "Endonuclease Analysis of Viral
DNA from Varicella and Subsequent
Zoster Infections in the Same Patient,"
New England Journal of Medicine 311, 21
(1984): 1362–1364.

13. A. Sauerbrei, E. Rubtcova, P. Wutzler,
D. S. Schmid, and V. Loparev, "Genetic
Profile of an Oka Varicella Vaccine Virus
Variant Isolated from an Infant with
Zoster," *Journal of Clinical Microbiology,*
42, 12 (2004): 5604–5608.

Chapter 3

1. C. Sadzot-Delvaux and B. Rentier,
"Virology and Clinical Management,"
in *Varicella-Zoster Virus,* eds. A. Arvin
and A. Gershon (Cambridge, U.K.:
Cambridge University Press, 2000).

2. M. Quinlivan and J. Breuer, "Molecular
and Therapeutic Aspects of Varicella-
Zoster Virus Infection," *Expert Reviews
in Molecular Medicine* 7, 15 (2005) 1-24.

3. C. Dinarello, H. Bernheim, G. Duff, H.
Le, T. L. Nagabhushan, N. Hamilton,
and F. Cocean, "Mechanisms of Fever
Induced by Recombinant Human
Interferon," *Journal of Clinical
Investigation* 74 (1984): 906–913.

4. C-C Ku, J. Besser, A. Abendroth, C.
Grose, and A. Arvin, "Varicella-Zoster
Virus Pathogenesis and Immunobiology:
New Concepts Emerging from
Investigations with the SCIDhu Mouse
Model," *Journal of Virology* 79, 5 (2005):
2651–2658.

5. Ibid.

6. S. Hambleton, S. P. Steinberg, M.
D. Gershon, and A. A. Gershon,
"Cholesterol Dependence of Varicella-
Zoster Virion Entry into Target Cells,"
Journal of Virology 81, 14 (2007): 7548–
7558.

7. A. Gershon, Z. Zhu, D. L. Sherman,
C. A. Gabel, R. T. Ambron, and M. D.
Gershon, "Intracellular Transport of
Newly Synthesized Varicella-Zoster
Virus: Final Envelopment in the Trans-
Golgi Network," *Journal of Virology* 68
(1994): 6372–6390.

8. M. Quinlivan and J. Breuer, "Molecular
and Therapeutic Aspects of Varicella-
Zoster Virus Infection," *Expert Reviews
of Molecular Medicine* 7, 15 (2005);
M. Rahaus, N. Desloges, M. Yang, W.
Ruyechan, and M. Wolff, "Transcription
Factor USF, Expressed during the Entire
Phase of Varicella-Zoster Virus Infection,
Interacts Physically with the Major
Viral Transactivator IE62 and Plays a
Significant Role in Virus Replication,"
Journal of General Virology 84 (2003):
2957–2967.

9. M. Dougherty, "From Chickenpox to Shingles," *News from Columbia Health Sciences* 1, 7, (2002), http://cpmcnet.columbia.edu/news/in-vivo/Vol1_no7_apr15_02/varicella.html. Accessed September 28, 2008; J. Chen, Z. Zhu, A. Gershon, and M. Gershon, "Mannose 6-Phosphate Receptor Dependence of Varicella Zoster Virus Infection In Vitro and in the Epidermis during Varicella and Zoster," *Cell* 119 (2004): 915–926.

10. M. Quinlivan and J. Breuer, "Molecular and Therapeutic Aspects of Varicella-Zoster Virus Infection," *Expert Reviews of Molecular Medicine* 7, 15 (2005).

11. P. Brunell, "Passive Antibody Prophylaxis," in *Varicella-Zoster Virus: Virology and Clinical Management*, eds. Arvin and A. Gershon (Cambridge, U.K.: Cambridge University Press, 2000).

12. A. Abendroth and A. Arvin, "Host Response to Primary Infection," in *Varicella-Zoster Virus. Virology and Clinical Management*, eds. A. Arvin and A. Gershon (Cambridge, U.K.: Cambridge University Press, 2000), 150-151.

13. J. Jones and A. Arvin, "Inhibition of the NF-κB Pathway by Varicella-Zoster Virus In Vitro and in Human Epidermal Cells In Vivo," *Journal of Virology* 80, 11 (2006): 5113–5124.

14. J. Chen, Z. Zhu, A. Gershon, and M. Gershon, "Mannose 6-Phosphate Receptor Dependence of Varicella Zoster Virus Infection In Vitro and in the Epidermis during Varicella and Zoster," *Cell* 119 (2004): 915–926.

Chapter 4

1. M. Mazzella, C. Arioni, C. Bellini, A. Allegri, C. Savioli, and G. Serra, "Severe Hydrocephalus Associated with Congenital Varicella Syndrome," *Canadian Medical Association Journal* 168, 5 (2003): 561-563.

2. G. Enders and E. Miller, "Varicella and Herpes Zoster in Pregnancy and the Newborn," in *Varicella-Zoster Virus: Virology and Clinical Management*, eds.

A. Arvin and A. Gershon (Cambridge, U.K.: Cambridge University Press, 2000).

3. G. Koren, "Risk of Varicella Infection during Late Pregnancy," *Canadian Family Physician* 49 (2003): 1445–1446.

4. G. Enders, I. Bolley, E. Miller, J. Cradock-Watson, and M. Ridehalgh, "Consequences of Varicella and Herpes Zoster in Pregnancy: Prospective Study of 1739 Cases," *Lancet* 343, 8912, (1994): 1548-1551.

5. G. Enders and E. Miller, "Varicella and Herpes Zoster in Pregnancy and the Newborn," in *Varicella-Zoster Virus: Virology and Clinical Management*, eds. A. Arvin and A. Gershon (Cambridge, U.K.: Cambridge University Press, 2000).

6. A. Abendroth and A. Arvin, "Host Response to Primary Infection," in *Varicella-Zoster Virus: Virology and Clinical Management*, eds. A. Arvin and A. Gershon (Cambridge, U.K.: Cambridge University Press, 2000), 144.

7. A. Abendroth and A. Arvin, "Host Response to Primary Infection," in *Varicella-Zoster Virus: Virology and Clinical Management*, eds. A. Arvin and A. Gershon (Cambridge, U.K.: Cambridge University Press, 2000), 147.

8. J. Seward, K. Galil, and M. Wharton, "Epidemiology of Varicella," in *Varicella-Zoster Virus: Virology and Clinical Management*, eds. A. Arvin and A. Gershon (Cambridge, U.K.: Cambridge University Press, 2000).

9. M. Myers, L. Kramer, and L. Stanberry, "Varicella in a Gorilla," *Journal of Medical Virology* 23 (1987): 317–322.

10. C. Sadzot-Delvaux and B. Rentier, "Animal Models of Infection," in *Varicella-Zoster Virus: Virology and Clinical Management*, eds. A. Arvin and A. Gershon (Cambridge, U.K.: Cambridge University Press, 2000).

11. A. Baiker, K. Fabel, A. Cozzio, L. Zerboni, K. Fabel, M. Sommer, N. Uchida, D. He, I. Weissman, and A. Arvin, "Varicella-Zoster Virus Infection of Human Neural Cells In Vivo," *Proceedings of the National*

Academy of Sciences 101, 29 (2004)L: 10792–10797.

Chapter 5

1. J. Willis and J. Wiese, "This Rash Hurts!" *Journal of General Internal Medicine* 19, supplement 1(2004): 77.
2. B. Forghani, "Laboratory Diagnosis of Infection," in *Varicella-Zoster Virus: Virology and Clinical Management*, eds. A. Arvin and A. Gershon (Cambridge, U.K.: Cambridge University Press, 2000).
3. J.P. Campsall, N. Au, J. Prendiville, D. Speert, R. Tan, and E. Thomas, "Detection and Genotyping of Varicella-Zoster Virus by TaqMan Allelic Discrimination Real-Time PCR," *Journal of Clinical Microbiology* 42, 4 (2004): 1409–1413.
4. B. Forghani, "Laboratory Diagnosis of Infection," in *Varicella-Zoster Virus: Virology and Clinical Management*, eds. A. Arvin and A. Gershon (Cambridge, U.K.: Cambridge University Press, 2000).
5. T. Klassen, E. Belseck, N. Wiebe, and L. Hartling, "Acyclovir for Treating Varicella in Otherwise Healthy Children and Adolescents: A Systematic Review of Randomised Controlled Trials," *BMC Pediatrics* 2 (2002): 9.
6. M. Boeckh, H. Kim, M. Flowers, J. Meyers, and R. Bowden, "Long-term Acyclovir for Prevention of Varicella Zoster Virus Disease after Allogeneic Hematopoietic Cell Transplantation—A Randomized Double-blind Placebo-Controlled Study," *Blood* 107, 5 (2006): 1800–1805.
7. A. Ross, "Modification of Chicken Pox in Family Contacts by Administration of Gamma Globulin," *New England Journal of Medicine* 267 (1962): 369–376.
8. P. Brunell, A. Ross, L. Miller, and B. Kuo, "Prevention of Varicella by Zoster Immune Globulin," *New England Journal of Medicine* 280 (1969): 1191.
9. P. Brunell, A. Gershon, A. Hughes, W. Riley, and I. Smith, "Prevention of Varicella in High Risk Children: A Collaborative Study," *Pediatrics* 50 (1972): 718–722.
10. Food and Drug Administration, "Varicella-Zoster Immune Globulin (Human)," http://www.fda.gov/CbER/label/mphvzig0400LB.pdf (accessed October 11, 2008).
11. T. Weller, "Varicella and Herpes Zoster: A Perspective and Overview," *Journal of Infectious Diseases* 166, Suppl 1 (1992): S1–S6.
12. J. Englund, A. Arvin, and H. Balfour, "Acyclovir Treatment for Varicella Does Not Lower gpI and IE-62 Antibody Responses to Varicella-Zoster Virus in Normal Children," *Journal of Clinical Microbiology* 28 (10): 2327–2330.

Chapter 6

1. M. Takahashi and S. Plotkin, "Development of the Oka Vaccine," in *Varicella-Zoster Virus: Virology and Clinical Management*, eds. A. Arvin and A. Gershon (Cambridge, U.K.: Cambridge University Press, 2000): 442–459.
2. M. Takahashi and S. Plotkin, "Development of the Oka Vaccine," in *Varicella-Zoster Virus: Virology and Clinical Management*, eds. A. Arvin and A. Gershon (Cambridge, U.K.: Cambridge University Press, 2000): 442–459.
3. Y. Gomi, H. Sunamachi, Y. Mori, K. Nagaike, M. Takahashi, and K. Yamanishi. "Comparison of the Complete DNA Sequences of the Oka Varicella Vaccine and Its Parental Virus," *Journal of Virology* 76, 22 (2002): 11447–11459.
4. A. Gershon and P. Annunziato, "Primary Immunization against Varicella," in *Varicella-Zoster Virus: Virology and Clinical Management*, eds. A. Arvin and A. Gershon (Cambridge, U.K.: Cambridge University Press, 2000), 460–476.
5. S. Roush, T. Murphy, and the Vaccine-Preventable Disease Table Working Group, "Historical Comparisons of Morbidity and Mortality for

Notes

Vaccine-Preventable Diseases in the United States," *Journal of the American Medical Association* 298, 18 (2007): 2155–2163; H. Nguyen, A. Jumaan, and Jane F. Seward, "Decline in Mortality Due to Varicella after Implementation of Varicella Vaccination in the United States," *New England Journal of Medicine* 352 (2005): 450–8.

6. Centers for Disease Control, "Prevention of Varicella: Recommendations of the Advisory Committee on Immunization Practices (ACIP)," *Morbidity and Mortality Weekly Report* 45, RR1 (1996): 1–25.

7. M. Marin, D. Güris, S. Chaves, S. Schmid, and J. Seward, "Prevention of Varicella Recommendations of the Advisory Committee on Immunization Practices (ACIP)," *Morbidity and Mortality Weekly Report* 56, RR04 (2007): 1–40.

8. Quinlivan, M., A. Gershon, M. Al Bassam, S. Steinberg, P. LaRussa, R. Nichols, and J. Breuer, "Natural Selection for Rash-Forming Genotypes of the Varicella-Zoster Vaccine Virus Detected within Immunized Human Hosts," *Proceedings of National Academy of Sciences* 104, 1 (2007): 208–212.

9. M. Marin, H. C. Meissner, and J. Seward, "Varicella Prevention in the United States: A Review of Successes and Challenges," *Pediatrics* 122 (2008): e744–e751.

10. S. Chang, R. Ball, and M. M. Braun, "Elective Termination of Pregnancy after Vaccination Reported to the Vaccine Adverse Event Reporting System (VAERS): 1990–2006," *Vaccine* 26 (2008): 2428–2432.

11. M. Marin, H. C. Meissner, and J. Seward, "Varicella Prevention in the United States: A Review of Successes and Challenges," *Pediatrics* 122 (2008): e744–e751

12. Centers for Disease Control, "Recommended Immunization Schedule for Persons Aged 0–6 Years," http://www.cdc.gov/vaccines/recs/schedules/downloads/child/2008/08_0-6yrs_schedule_bw_pr.pdf (accessed October 10, 2008).

Chapter 7

1. Personal communication to the author from a relative.

2. A. Arvin and A. Gershon, eds., *Varicella-Zoster Virus: Virology and Clinical Management* (Cambridge, UK: Cambridge University Press, 2000).

3. K. Schamader, E. Studenski, and J. MacMillan, "Are Stressful Life Events Risk Factors for Herpes Zoster?" *Journal of the American Geriatric Society* 38 (1990): 1188–1195.

4. M. Stumpf, Z. Laidlaw, and V. Jansen, "Herpes Viruses Hedge their Bets," *Proceedings of the National Academy of Sciences* 99, 23 (2002): 15234–15237.

5. B. Yawn, P. Saddier, P. Wollan, J. St. Sauver, M. Kurland, and L. Sy, "A Population-Based Study of the Incidence and Complication Rates of Herpes Zoster Before Zoster Vaccine Introduction," *Mayo Clinic Proceedings* 82, 11 (2007): 1341–1349.

6. J. Rusthoven, P. Ahlgren, T. Elhakin, P. Pinfold, J. Reid, L. Stewart, and R. Feld, "Varicella-Zoster Infection in Adult Cancer Patients," *Archives of Internal Medicine* 148 (1988): 1561–1566.

7. M. Boeckh, H. Kim, M. Flowers, J. Meyers, and R. Bowden, "Long-term Acyclovir for Prevention of Varicella Zoster Virus Disease after Allogeneic Hematopoietic Cell Transplantation—A Randomized Double-Blind Placebo-Controlled Study," *Blood* 107, 5 (2006): 1800–1805.

8. K. Schmader, "Epidemiology of Herpes Zoster" in *Varicella-Zoster Virus: Virology and Clinical Management*, eds. A. Arvin and A. Gershon (Cambridge, U.K.: Cambridge University Press, 2000).

9. K. Elliot, "Management of Postherpetic Pain." in *Varicella-Zoster Virus: Virology and Clinical Management*, eds. A. Arvin and A. Gershon (Cambridge, U.K.: Cambridge University Press, 2000).

10. D. Quan, R. Cohrs, R. Mahalingam, and D. Gilden, "Prevention of Shingles: Safety and Efficacy of Live Zoster Vaccine," *Therapeutics and Clinical Risk Management* 3, 4 (2007): 633–639.

11. M. Irwin, J. Pike, and M. Oxman, "Shingles Immunity and Health Functioning in the Elderly:Tai Chi Chih as a Behavioral Treatment Evidence-based Complementary and Alternative Medicine," *Evidence-based Complementary and Alternative Medicine* 1, 3 (2004): 223–232.

12. W.K. Yih, D. Brooks, S. Lett, A. Jumaan, Z. Zhang, K. Clements, and J. Seward, "The Incidence of Varicella and Herpes Zoster in Massachusetts as Measured by the Behavioral Risk Factor Surveillance System (BRFSS) during a Period of Increasing Varicella Vaccine Coverage, 1998–2003," *BMC Public Health* 5 (2005): 68-77.

Chapter 8

1. Y. Gomi, H. Sunamachi, Y. Mori, K. Nagaike, M. Takahashi, and K. Yamanishi, "Comparison of the Complete DNA Sequences of the Oka Varicella Vaccine and Its Parental Virus," *Journal of Virology* 76, 2 (2002): 11447–11459.

Glossary

adaptive immune system   A branch of the immune system that develops in response to a particular pathogen. It consists of both cell-mediated immunity and antibody production. This response is generally very effective, but it takes a week or more to develop, so the innate immune response is critical early in an infection.

agglutination   A reaction that results in clumping. One method for detecting the varicella-zoster virus involves an agglutination reaction.

anaphylactic shock   An allergic reaction where the blood vessels suddenly dilate, causing the blood pressure to drop and the bronchial tubes to close off, resulting in breathing difficulty. It can occur following exposure to an allergen and can result in death if not treated quickly.

antibody   Proteins in the blood that are involved in responding to an infection. Antibodies can also be used to identify specific pathogens, such as the varicella-zoster virus. *See also* **immunoglobulins**.

antigen presentation   A mechanism by which cells of the immune system recognize cells that are infected with a virus (or other pathogen). In this process, the infected cell places some parts of the virus on the cell surface. These viral fragments, in the context of a host molecule (the MHC), activate cytotoxic T-lymphocytes, which then destroy the infected cells.

B-cells   A type of circulating white blood cell that produces antibodies. While apparently not a critical factor in the immunity to chicken pox, antibodies may play some role in control of the disease.

capsid   A portion of the varicella-zoster virus. The capsid consists of proteins that completely surround and protect the DNA genome of the virus.

CD4+ T-cell   A type of white blood cell that regulates the function of other components of the immune system. These cells play at least two roles during an infection of the varicella-zoster virus. Initially, they become infected with the virus and help transport the virus to the skin. As a specific immune response develops, these cells help coordinate the immune response that clears the virus from the skin.

cell-mediated immunity   A type of specific immune response where cells of the immune system (cytotoxic T-lymphocytes) recognize cells infected with viruses or other intracellular pathogens and destroy those infected cells as a means of limiting infection.

ceramides   Lipids produced by skin cells that provide a waterproofing coating for the skin.

cerebellar ataxia   A potential complication of chicken pox in the cerebellum of the brain that results in disturbances in balance and gait and other critical functions.

chicken pox An illness characterized by a widespread rash. Chicken pox is caused by the varicella-zoster virus.

congenital varicella syndrome (CVS) A group of symptoms that may occur in the fetus following a maternal chicken pox infection during early pregnancy. Although rare, CVS can result in death or serious malformations of the fetus.

cytotoxic T-lymphocytes (CTLs) Cells that form a critical part of the specific immune response to chicken pox (and other viral infections). CTLs are a type of white blood cell that can recognize cells that are infected with a particular virus and target and destroy those cells to limit viral replication.

dermatome A band of skin whose sensory nerves share a single spinal nerve root.

DNA polymerase An enzyme that is used to make DNA.

DNA sequencing A technique for determining each letter of the genetic code in a gene, a virus, or an organism. This provides the most definitive method for comparing genetic information between, for example, different isolates of a virus.

electron microscope A microscope that uses an electron beam (rather than visible light) to visualize objects. Electron microscopes are powerful enough to visualize tiny objects (such as the varicella-zoster virus).

encephalitis A complication of chicken pox that involves inflammation of the brain

endocytosis A process by which cells take up materials from their environment. Some viruses, like the varicella-zoster virus, take advantage of this process and use it to enter the cells.

endoplasmic reticulum A channel-like structure inside human cells that is involved in the transport of materials to their proper location in the cell. In the life cycle of the varicella-zoster virus, the newly formed viral particles transit from the nucleus through the endoplasmic reticulum.

envelope A membrane that provides the very outer coat of the varicella-zoster virus. The envelope consists of lipids that come from the nuclear membrane of the infected host cell.

enzyme-linked immunosorbent assay (ELISA) A laboratory technique for detecting antigens or antibodies. For example, to detect antibodies to the varicella-zoster virus, a lab can manufacture a plastic plate that contains small wells coated with varicella-zoster virus proteins. Patient serum samples are added to the wells, and, if antibodies to the virus are present, those antibodies will bind, and can be detected through the addition of other chemicals.

enzymes Proteins that catalyze a particular chemical reaction.

genome The entire set of genetic instructions for a virus or an organism. In the case of the varicella-zoster virus, the genome is a double-stranded DNA that consists of approximately 125,000 individual pieces of information (nucleotide base pairs).

genus A category in the classification of viruses that includes the most closely related members of a virus family or subfamily.

glycoproteins Proteins that have sugars attached to them. In the case of the varicella-zoster virus, glycoproteins on the surface of the virus play a critical role in the viral entry into cells, and in the human immune response that ultimately curtails the infection.

granulysin A protein produced by immune system cells that kills other cells that are infected with intracellular pathogens like viruses.

heparin sulfate A molecule on the surface of many human cells. It is composed of a chain of sugar molecules, which have sulfur attached. Heparin sulfate is a molecule that the varicella-zoster virus uses for binding to host cells and entering them.

herpesviruses A family of viruses that includes a number of human pathogens, including the varicella-zoster virus that causes chicken pox. These viruses contain a double-stranded DNA genome, which contains information that specifies 100 to 200 proteins. The DNA is encased in a protein capsid, which in turn is surrounded with an envelope made of lipids. The name *Herpes* comes from a Greek word meaning "to creep," describing the repeated cycles of infection that are typical of most illnesses caused by this group of viruses.

immunoglobulins Also known as antibodies. Proteins made by cells of the immune system that bind to and inactivate pathogens. Immunoglobulins are selected, in the body, in response to specific pathogens.

incubation period The time from infection or exposure to a virus until disease symptoms appear.

innate immune system A branch of the immune system that is always available to fight infection. It includes the chemical interferon-alpha, which is an important factor in reducing the ability of the virus to replicate. Although the innate immune response is the first line of defense, it is not as effective as the immune response that develops specifically to fight a particular infection.

interferons Chemicals produced by cells in the body in response to viral infection that reduce the ability of the virus to replicate. The name of these compounds derived from the fact that they interfere with viral replication.

latency A condition where a virus remains viable but is inactive. The varicella-zoster virus can remain inactive for years in nerve cells.

mannose-6-phosphate A sugar with an attached phosphate. In cells, mannose-6-phosphate is a targeting signal that sends proteins (or the varicella-zoster virus) to a cellular compartment called the golgi apparatus.

mannose-6-phosphate receptor A protein on the surface of cells that binds to mannose-6-phosphate. In relation to the varicella-zoster virus, this receptor aids in the uptake of the virus into nerve cells, establishing a latent infection.

memory T-cells A type of T-cell that is long lasting and retains the ability to react to the chemical signature of a specific pathogen, such as the varicella-zoster virus.

mutate To change. In a biological context, mutation generally describes a change in the genetic material, the DNA.

nanometer A measure of length, corresponding to one-billionth of a meter. This is the size range of most viruses, including the varicella-zoster virus, which is approximately 175 nanometers in size.

neurotransmitters Chemicals (like serotonin) that relay signals to nerve cells.

nucleocapsid A viral particle consisting of the protein capsid, which contains the viral DNA. In the case of the varicella-zoster virus, the nucleocapsid is an intermediate in the synthesis of the final viral particle.

pathogen A microbe, usually a bacterium or virus, that causes disease.

platelets Components of the blood that facilitate clotting. Chicken pox complications rarely include disruption of platelet function.

pneumonia An infection of the lungs or a portion of the lungs by a pathogen. This can be a serious complication, particularly in adults, following a bout of chicken pox.

polymerase chain reaction (PCR) A method for amplifying sections of DNA. Polymerase chain reaction tests can be used to determine whether the varicella-zoster virus is present in a patient sample.

replication Copying, reproducing. The replication of the varicella-zoster virus means that the virus is producing many copies of itself inside human cells.

restriction enzymes A type of enzyme that recognizes and cuts a particular DNA sequence. These enzymes have been used for many purposes, including the comparison of viruses isolated from the same person, or different people, to see if the viruses are similar or different.

rolling circle replication A process of DNA replication in which a circular DNA molecule acts as a template for the production of linear DNA. The process begins with one strand of the circular DNA being cut and used as a template for the other DNA strand. The mechanism is somewhat like the unspooling of string, with a second strand of string being made and attached to the first strand of string, as it is pulled off the spool.

serum The liquid portion of the blood that contains antibodies. These antibodies can be used to identify pathogens and, in some cases, even treat diseases like chicken pox.

severe combined immunodeficiency (SCID) A strain of SCID mice has been used to study chicken pox. These mice lack almost all normal immune responses, and consequently, they do not reject transplants of human tissue. The human tissue in the mice is infected with the varicella-zoster virus, and the development of stages of infection can be studied in detail.

shingles Herpes zoster. A disease, usually characterized by a localized, banded, painful rash. It is caused by the varicella-zoster virus, the same virus that causes chicken pox. In the case of shingles, the same virus that originally caused chicken pox in a person reactivates in the person's nerve cells and travels to the skin, producing shingles.

smallpox A serious, frequently fatal disease caused by the variola virus. Prior to the eradication of this disease by a worldwide vaccine campaign, it could sometimes be confused, in its initial stages, with chicken pox.

T-cells White blood cells that play a number of critical roles in the immune response. During the early stages of a chicken pox infection, the varicella-zoster virus infects T-cells, which eventually travel to the skin.

tegument proteins These are proteins located between the viral nucleocapsid and envelope. They are critical for early stages in replication of the varicella-zoster virus.

transcriptional activator A protein that enhances the production of RNA from a DNA template in a cell.

transcriptional repressor A protein that inhibits the production of RNA from a DNA template in a cell.

trans-golgi network Part of a cellular system for sorting molecules in the cell. In the case of the varicella-zoster virus, the trans-golgi network is the place where the virus acquires an envelope studded with viral glycoproteins.

virulence A property of a pathogen that makes it more likely to cause disease, or to cause a more serious disease

Books

Arvin, Ann, and Anne Gershon, eds. *Varicella-zoster virus: Virology and clinical management.* Cambridge, Mass.: Cambridge University Press, 2000.

Royston, Angela. *Chickenpox (It's Catching).* Chicago: Heinemann Library, 2002.

Web Sites

Centers for Disease Control and Prevention
http://www.cdc.gov

eMedicine
http://www.emedicinehealth.com/chickenpox/article_em.htm

KidsHealth
http://kidshealth.org/parent/infections/skin/chicken_pox.html

Mayo Clinic
http://www.mayoclinic.com/health/chickenpox/DS00053

VSV Research Foundation
http://www.vzvfoundation.org

Index

Page numbers in *italics* indicate illustrations.

deaths, 8–9, 14, 72
dendritic cells, *41*
dermatome, 78, *80,* 101
diagnosis
  chicken pox, 19–20,
    54–61
  shingles, 54
differential diagnosis, 19–20
disseminated neonatal
  varicella, 48
DNA, viral, detection of,
  55–56
DNA polymerase, 55–56,
  62–64, 65, 101
DNA sequencing, 30,
  101
dormancy, 38

early proteins, 38
elderly
  shingles in, 76–77, 85, 88
  tai chi for, 88, *88*
electron microscope, *10,* 29,
  36, 58, 101
ELISA. *See* enzyme-linked
  immunosorbent assay
eMedicine (Web site), 105
emerging infections, 6
encephalitis, 18, 101
endocytosis, 35, 101
endoplasmic reticulum,
  38, 101
endosome, 39
entry and invasion, viral,
  33–39, *34, 37,* 44–45
envelope, viral, *10, 12,* 36,
  45, 101
enzyme(s), 29
  definition of, 102
  restriction, 29, 103
enzyme-linked immuno-
  sorbent assay (ELISA),
  58–60, *59,* 101

famciclovir, for chicken
  pox, 62–64
fetal malformation, 18–19,
  46–48

fever
  chicken pox and, 14–15,
    32, 54
  vaccine and, 74
Filippo, Giovanni, 22
foscarnet, 62–63
Fuller, Thomas, 25
future issues, 90–93

gabapentin, for shingles,
  85, *86*
genetic testing, 29–30
genome, 11, 38, 91–92, 102
genus, 9, 102
glossary, 100–104
glycoproteins, 10, *12,* 36,
  42, 102
glycosylphosphatidylinositol (gpl) protein, 36
Goodpasture, Ernest, 26
gpl. *See* glycosylphosphatidylinositol protein
granulysin, 42, 102
guinea pig embryonic fibroblast cells, 70–71
guinea pig models, 51–52

hand-foot-and-mouth
  disease, 20
headache, 14–15
heart, inflammation of, 18
Heberden, William, 22, *23*
helper T-cells, *41*
heparin sulfate, 35, 102
herpes simplex virus, 8, 9,
  11–12
herpesvirus, 8–12, 102
herpes zoster. *See* shingles
Hindi, Sayyid Basir, 22
history of chicken pox,
  22–30
HIV/AIDS, 19, 83, 84
Hodgkin's disease, 20,
  83–84
human immune deficiency
  virus. *See* HIV/AIDS

IE proteins. *See* immediate
  early proteins
IgG. *See* immunoglobulin G
IgM. *See* immunoglobulin
  M
immediate early (IE)
  proteins, 37–38
immune evasion, 43–44
immune response, 31–32,
  40, *41,* 42–43
  adaptive, *41,* 42–43, 100
  in adults, 48–50
  cell-mediated, 42–43, 50,
    60, 100
  detection of, 58–61
  in infants, 47
  innate, *41,* 42, 102
  as key variable, 46
immunocompromise
  and chicken pox, 14, 19,
    42, 68
  and mouse model, 32–33,
    52, 52–53, 92–93
  and shingles, 20–21, 78,
    82–84
  and vaccination, 68, 74
  and varicella immuno-
    globulin, 66
immunoglobulin
  definition of, 102
  varicella, 64–67
immunoglobulin G (IgG),
  61
immunoglobulin M (IgM),
  61
impetigo, 19–20
incubation period, 14, 102
infants, chicken pox in,
  46–48
infection, chicken pox
  cell biology of, 32–35, *34*
  cell-to-cell spread of, 42
  establishing, 35–39, *37*
  immune response to,
    31–32, 40, *41,* 42–43,
    58–61
  reactivation of. *See*
    shingles

Index

Index

variola. *See* smallpox
vesicles, 14–15, *15*
viral culture, 56
viral damage, 31–32
viral DNA, detection of, 55–56
viral entry and invasion, 33–39, *34, 37*
viral envelope, 10, *12,* 36, 45, 101

viral life cycle, 11–12, 35–39
virulence, 11, 46, 104
virus. *See* varicella-zoster virus
vision, 17
VSV Research Foundation, 105

Web sites, 105
Weller, Thomas, 26–27, *28*

young children, chicken pox in, 31–45

zoster. *See* shingles
Zovirax. *See* acyclovir

About the Author

Patrick Guilfoile earned his Ph.D. in bacteriology at the University of Wisconsin–Madison. He subsequently did postdoctoral research at that institution, as well as at the Whitehead Institute for Biomedical Research at the Massachusetts Institute of Technology. He is a professor of biology at Bemidji State University in northern Minnesota. Currently on leave from his faculty position, he is serving as an associate dean at the University. His most recent research has focused on the molecular genetics of ticks and other parasites. He has authored or coauthored more than 20 papers in scientific and biology education journals. He has also written three other books in this series, along with a molecular biology laboratory manual, and a book on controlling ticks that transmit Lyme disease.

About the Consulting Editor

Hilary Babcock, M.D., M.P.H., is an assistant professor of medicine at Washington University School of Medicine and the medical director of occupational health for Barnes-Jewish Hospital and St. Louis Children's Hospital. She received her undergraduate degree from Brown University and her M.D. from the University of Texas Southwestern Medical Center at Dallas. After completing her residency, chief residency, and Infectious Disease fellowship at Barnes-Jewish Hospital, she joined the faculty of the Infectious Disease division. She completed an M.P.H. in Public Health from St. Louis University School of Public Health in 2006. She has lectured, taught, and written extensively about infectious diseases, their treatment, and their prevention. She is a member of numerous medical associations and is board certified in infectious disease. She lives in St. Louis, Missouri.

God's Presence in My Life

JOURNEYS IN FAITH

Creative Dislocation—The Movement of Grace
Robert McAfee Brown

Speech, Silence, Action! The Cycle of Faith
Virginia Ramey Mollenkott

Hope Is an Open Door
Mary Luke Tobin

By Way of Response
Martin E. Marty

Ten Commandments for the Long Haul
Daniel Berrigan

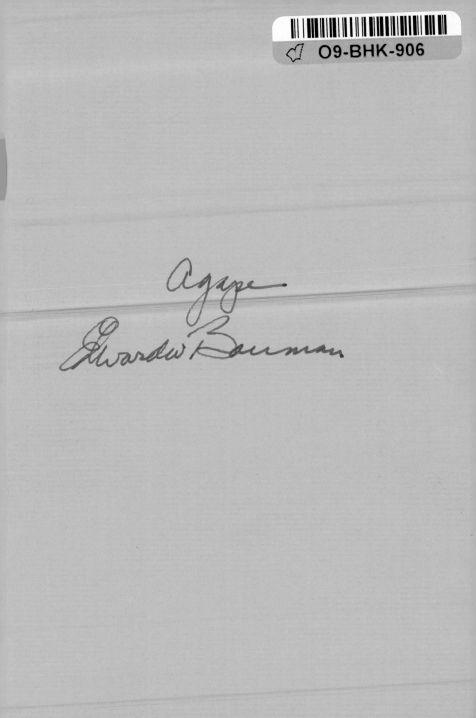

agape

Edward Bauman

God's Presence in My Life

Edward W. Bauman

Journeys in Faith
Robert A. Raines, Editor

ABINGDON
Nashville

GOD'S PRESENCE IN MY LIFE

Copyright © 1981 by Abingdon

Library of Congress Cataloging in Publication Data

BAUMAN, EDWARD W.
  God's presence in my life.
  (Journeys in faith)
  1. Christian life—Methodist authors. 2. Bauman, Edward W.
  I. Title. II. Series.
  BV4501.2.B38452   287'.6'0924   81-3600   AACR2

ISBN 0-687-15444-8

Scripture quotations unless otherwise noted are from the Revised Standard
Version of the Bible, copyrighted 1946, 1952, 1971, © 1973, by the Division of
Christian Education of the National Council of the Churches of Christ in the
U.S.A., and used by permission.

Scripture quotations noted JB are from The Jerusalem Bible, copyright ©
1966 by Darton, Longman & Todd, Ltd. and Doubleday & Company, Inc.
Used by permission of the publisher.

The quotation on page 130 is from *Songs of Kabir*, Rabindranath Tagore,
translator (New York: Macmillan, 1915).

MANUFACTURED BY THE PARTHENON PRESS AT
NASHVILLE, TENNESSEE, UNITED STATES OF AMERICA

FOR

Audree

Deborah

Kathleen

and

Mark

Contents

Editor's Foreword

People inside and outside the church today are engaged in a profound revisioning of the faith journey. Wanting to honor our own heritage and to be nourished by our roots, we also want to discern the signs of the kingdom now, and to move through the 1980s with a lean, biblical, ecumenical, and human faith perspective.

The Journeys in Faith book series is offered to facilitate this revisioning of faith. Reflecting on the social justice openings of the 1960s and the inward searching of the 1970s, these books articulate a fresh integration of the faith journey for the years ahead. They are personal and social. Authors have been invited to share what has been happening to them in their faith and life in recent years, and then to focus on issues which have become primary for them in this time.

We believe that these lucidly written books will be widely

9

used by study groups in congregations, seminaries, colleges, renewal centers, orders, and denominations, as well as for personal study and reflection.

Our distinguished authors embody a diversity of experience and perspective which will provide many points of identification and enrichment for readers. As we enter into the pilgrimages shared in these books we will find resonance, encouragement, and insight for a fresh appropriation of our faith, toward personal and social transformation.

Edward W. Bauman offers an engaging portrait of the struggle of his own faith journey. Trained to try to please others, "duty bound" by nature and profession, uncomfortable in conflict and confrontation, he suffered his way through ill health toward a responsible autonomy. Warm personal faith abounds in these pages, both in the experiences of the author and in the moving and colorful quotations from letters written to him. Bauman's story is one of maintaining, developing, and celebrating the continuities of marriage, ministry, and faith. He deals with the question of "closed" and "open" marriage, the "unexplored territory" in many marriages, in the light of his own journey and biblical perspectives. Above all, he is a clergy person. He struggles with his self and his role, seeking, through a workaholic profession and personality, wholeness of life and vocation.

There is integrity here, and impressive congruence between Bauman's United Methodist heritage and his own way of being a Christian human being. He is a good example of what John Wesley sought in a Methodist preacher, ". . . a preacher whom you know to live as he speaks, speaking the genuine gospel of present salvation through faith, wrought in the heart by the Holy Ghost."

Especially notable is this story's setting in a particular congregation. Bauman's story is reflected and refracted in the story of his faith community. He and they learn and develop together. Feedback and shared searching are elements in the author's growth. A remarkable television ministry and a developing healing ministry are described. The congregation deals in its own way with the civil rights movement and the emergence of homosexuality as an issue in church and society. Clergy and laity will find this story of one congregation's journey useful for reflecting on their own. Clergy will see some of their own self-role tensions in their brother minister's struggle, and will find insight and comfort. The book is salted with often humorous and touching anecdotes which serve as connectors to the reader's own experience. Bauman writes, as he teaches and preaches, in a clear, clean style.

This is a hopeful book from a hopeful man, whose hope is based on his own continuing personal experience of God's grace in his own life and the life of the congregation he serves, through Jesus Christ. Amen!

Robert A. Raines

God's Presence in My Life

BAUMAN

Dr. EDWARD W. BAUMAN, JR.

Dr. Edward W. Bauman, Jr, 94, passed away on November 26, 2021, at his home in Bethesda, Maryland after a period of declining health. He was born in East St. Louis, Illinois, on January 22, 1927, to Edward and Dorothy (Woodruff) Bauman. He was predeceased by his parents, his sister Ruth Price, and his first wife Audree. He is survived by his wife Karen Jones, her children Adam and Sarah Jones, his children Deborah, Kathleen and Mark Bauman (Debbie), four grandchildren and two great grandchildren.

Edward earned a PhD in Systemic Theology from Boston University in 1954 and began his ministry at Utica Methodist Church in Utica, Ohio. In 1956, he taught Philosophy and Religion at American University in Washington, DC and later became a professor of Christian Ethics at Wesley Theological Seminary. While teaching at American University, and in conjunction with the DC Council of Churches and WJLA-TV, he began a weekly television series that ran for 34 years. Bauman Bible Telecasts was formed to distribute the Emmy winning series to television stations, churches and other organizations across the United States and around the world, including US Navy and Coast Guard ships and bases. He authored five books and was a weekly presenter on WMAL-AM radio for 25 years.

In 1964, at the age of 37, Edward became senior minister at Foundry United Methodist Church in Washington, DC. In his 28 years at Foundry, he guided the large, inner city church through many societal changes and historical events with love, hope and faith.

A Time Magazine article published in 1979 titled "American Preaching: A Dying Art?" named Edward Bauman as one of "seven star preachers" in America. In the article, Edward said, "Someone once told me I always preach on tiptoe. I consider that the greatest compliment I ever received."

In 1993, Edward traveled to India to work with Mother Teresa in her Home for the Dying in Khaligat. He kept a journal of his time there and upon returning became a volunteer at Hospice of Washington.

After his retirement from Foundry, he served for eight years as associate rector at St. Paul's Rock Creek Episcopal Church in DC and then as part-time chaplain at the Virginia Hospital Center in Arlington, VA, retiring at the age of 91.

Edward summered in Cape Porpoise, Maine where mornings were spent outlining his sermons for the year and writing the study guide that would accompany his television program. Afternoons were spent walking the beaches, boating with family, and enjoying the beauty of Maine. His love of Maine continued throughout his life.

A service to celebrate Edward's life will be held at St. John's Norwood Episcopal Church in Chevy Chase, Maryland on January 7, 2022 at 10 a.m. The internment of his ashes at Rock Creek Cemetery will be private.

Memorial contributions may be made to Madison Fields or a charity that is special to you. (Madison Fields 19300 Mouth of Monocacy Rd. Dickerson, MD 20842. Please put Edward's name in the memo line.)

JOHNSON

GLADYS ABELL JOHNSON (Age 93)

Of Springfield, VA passed away on Sunday, November 21, 2021.

She is survived by her children Ralph A. Johnson (Beth) of Midland, TX, Stephen A. Johnson of San Francisco, CA, Lawrence M. Johnson (Beverly) of Centreville VA, Marian J. Wasem (Steve) of Fairfax VA; and four grandsons. She is predeceased by her husband of 49 years, Dr. Lester D. Johnson, Jr.; and son Lester D. Johnson, III.

Family and friends may pay their respects at Fairfax Memorial Funeral Home, 9902 Braddock Road, Fairfax, VA on Thursday, December 9 from 2 p.m. to 4 p.m. and 6 p.m. to 8 p.m. A Mass of Christian Burial will be celebrated in memory of Gladys on Friday, December 10 at 10:30 a.m. at St. Anthony of Padua Catholic Church, Falls Church, VA. In lieu of flowers, donations in memory of Gladys may be made to Catholic Charities USA.

JOHNSON

The Rev.
WILLIAM PEGRAM JOHNSON III
(Age 82)

Of Richmond, VA, died on November 25, 20 A Burial (Memorial) Eucharist is scheduled f p.m. on January 2, 2022, at St. Paul's Episco Church, 815 E. Grace St., Richmond, VA w a reception following the service. Please flowers; instead, memorial gifts may be m to Episcopal Relief and Development, P.O. 7058, Merrifield, VA 22116 or the Virg Historical Society, P.O. Box 7311, Richmo VA 23221. Arrangements are being handle Richmond Cremation.

GARERI

DAN JAMES GARERI (Age 99)
Col., USAF (Ret.)

Wright-Patterson AFB, Ohio, and rose Chief, Foreign Technology Programs Divisio HQ Air Force Systems Command. As a engineer skilled in R&D and evaluating S& data and foreign technology, Dan specialize in Soviet propulsion and weapon system electronic warfare, command and contr operations, and strategic planning. He serve with the Air Technical Liaison Office whe he developed and conducted field collectio activities; exploited the first Soviet-built Mi -15 and Yak-23 aircraft flown to the Wes directed a tactical intelligence unit in Sout east Asia during the Vietnam War; was program manager for Directorate of S& Defense Intelligence Agency; and headed tri-military team in Israel analyzing foreig weapons used in the 1973 Yom Kippur War.

In addition to NASIC's Major General Harc E. Watson Award in 1994, Dan's USAF meda and decorations totaled 14, with the Legic of Merit awarded at his 1974 retireme from active military service. Civilian hono include Who's Who in Technology, 198 Who's Who in Aviation & Aerospace, 198 Dictionary of International Biography, 197

Beloved father, grandfather, great-grandfather, and uncle, passed away after a brief illness on November 21, 2021. Born in Bovey, Minnesota, Dan was the only son of Italian immigrants, the late Vincenzo Gareri and

1
Father

The presence of God is the thread that holds my life together, the constant reality that has given my life its meaning. This has always been true. The beauty of the last few years comes from knowing that it is true.

Growing up in a middle-class family in the suburbs of Cleveland, I'm sure I did not project the image of "religiosity." In fact, the friends I had grown up with were surprised when I later headed for the ministry. In those early years two of my greatest ambitions were to play second base better than anyone else on our neighborhood team and to make model airplanes that would stay in the air longer than any others. How many hours did I spend laboriously creating rubber-band powered planes of balsa wood and tissue paper?

Otherwise I spent my early years suffering growing pains and projecting my anxieties onto others, especially

15

my parents, my younger sister, and my teachers. One of my most painful memories is a flagrant lie I told in order to avoid losing a teacher's approval.

In the fifth grade, I fell in love with a girl named Gypsy. She was my first love, and for a while she was even more important to me than baseball and model airplanes. One of the notes I wrote to her in class was intercepted by the teacher who recognized my handwriting and called me to the front of the room. When she asked me if I had written the note, I lied. She had specifically warned us not to write notes in class, and I was afraid of losing her approval. She knew I was lying, and her way of letting me know was to award a coveted position on the safety patrol, for which I was a top candidate, to someone else. I don't remember how my romance with Gypsy ended. But the memory of the lie still causes pain.

In the midst of these normal childhood experiences of pain and pleasure, my awareness of God's presence was born. One of the gifts my parents bestowed on me was their insistence on regular church attendance. After I joined the local Methodist church, it became the center of my social life and my place of meeting with God. I didn't understand it then, and I can't explain it now. But whenever I attended a worship service I had a feeling of being "home" in the presence of a power which I did not feel in other places.

There were times when manifestations of the power made a lasting impression on me. On one occasion, for example, I had a factoring problem in my algebra homework. My friends and I tried all weekend to solve it, without success. On Sunday morning I took my homework paper with me to church and began to work on it during the sermon. Within a short time the problem miraculously opened up and I immediately saw the answer. What further evidence did I need of the existence of a merciful God?

I never talked with anyone about these first stirrings of spiritual awareness. I'm not sure whether I thought everyone had them and therefore wouldn't be interested, or whether I thought no one else had them and would therefore think me strange. But all through these early years God continued to be a vague and undefined, but real, presence in my life.

At seventeen I enlisted in the United States Navy. The Second World War was winding down and, like most young men at the time, I wanted to be part of the action. As it turned out, the war ended a few months later and my military career ended. But not before I had made a decision to enter the ministry.

I will never be able to write a book about my military exploits. I never met the enemy. I never even got on board a real ship! But I found myself in the same radar training unit with a former high-school friend who was headed for the Baptist ministry. We talked a lot about religion and became active in a Methodist church near the military base in Biloxi, Mississippi. One Sunday evening after the worship service I found myself kneeling at the altar, giving my life to God and declaring my intention to become a minister. Had God led me into a military life just long enough to make this crucial decision about my life with him?

I wish I could report that the experience at the church altar was dramatic. Others who tell about life-shattering conversions and decisions to enter the ministry "after a life of sin" arouse my envy. Their stories are so much more interesting. My experience that night was very quiet and undramatic. I simply *knew* that this was the right thing for me to do. What I did not know was how much the ministry would dominate my life from that time on. An elderly man, a Sunday school teacher in that church, who knelt at the altar with me that night arose with tears streaming down his face. The love in his tears was all the confirmation I needed in that quiet moment of dedication.

Only once did I have serious doubts about the decision, and they were so serious I began to make other plans for my life. While I was in the Navy stationed near Washington, D.C. I met Audree. Audree was not another Gypsy, fading in and out of my life. She came to stay, as my best friend, wife, and lover.

But the first months of our relationship were painful because of separation. I had made the decision to go to DePauw University in the Midwest; she would remain in Washington. I arrived on campus in a state of depression because I had left Audree. I didn't know anyone, and I was assigned a Jewish roommate from Long Island. Later we became good friends, but at the time we seemed to be coming from two different worlds and this compounded my loneliness. For several days I lived in misery thinking about the years of college and seminary ahead of me. Then I began to make plans. I would give up the idea of being a minister, return to Washington, get a job, marry Audree, and live happily ever after. The only thing that prevented immediate action was the lack of train fare for the return trip.

Then God intervened. Others will find logical explanations for what happened. I'm sure the explanations contain elements of truth, but for me God's presence was the important truth. I was out walking late at night because I could not sleep. Without thinking much about where I was going, I made my way out to the football stadium at the edge of town. A full moon was shining and everything was very quiet. But my mind was in turmoil. Should I leave college? Should I try to figure out a way to stay in college and get married? How could I get money to leave? Should I give up the idea of the ministry? What should I do? I walked up into the upper level of seats in the stadium, turned around, and there was my answer—the shadow of a cross nearly a hundred yards long!

The press box across the stadium was built in the shape of a cross. The moon, shining behind it, was casting the shadow almost the full length of the playing field. This is the simple explanation of what I saw. What I *saw* at a deeper level is more difficult to put into words. For a few moments I felt overcome by a sense of presence that was telling me not to give up the ministry. It was a confirmation of my earlier decision, a sign pointing out the way I should go. From that moment I have never doubted that the ministry is the right place for me to be and I have been grateful to a God who would go to so much trouble to tell me so!

I married Audree and spent the next eight years making my way through college, seminary, and graduate school, working toward a doctorate in theology. Audree used her unusual administrative skills in several jobs along the way to provide the financial resources for the long academic program. These were good years, in spite of the hard work, but I was always restless. Part of the problem was the eagerness to reach the goal and get on with the work of the ministry. Since then I have often reflected on how few persons seem to enjoy what they are doing while they are doing it. If I had it to do over, I would do exactly what I did but I would try to enjoy it more!

My restlessness was also caused by the nature of seminary education. Theology is the attempt to interpret our experience of God. Theological education, by definition, deals mostly with the interpretation and very little with the experience. I kept wanting my teachers to help me find God. Without understanding it at the time, I was hungering for the immediate presence of God. My training gave me valuable knowledge about the way other persons, including the early disciples, interpreted their experience of God. But it did not satisfy my hunger, which has driven me to a lifetime of searching.

With the passing of the years, I have been able to teach in college and seminary and to minister in local church parishes. The years at Foundry United Methodist Church, an active parish in downtown Washington, D.C., have been especially rewarding and demanding. Because of my love of preaching, teaching, and pastoral care, I know the parish is where I belong. The story of my life has been the story of living my way ever more deeply into the faith community and sharing with others my own hunger for God through my gifts of ministry. There have been times of fatigue, anger, depression, and stress-induced illness. But I have never doubted that the parish is where I belong.

Confirmation has come from many sources, including a letter from a young woman describing what our church meant to her in her struggle with alcoholism.

> Without preamble, I want you to know that I hit the lowest point of my life about three weeks ago. If it had not been for the acceptance and love I have been experiencing in the Foundry community, I simply do not know what horrible consequences might have resulted.
>
> I want to tell you that I am so deeply grateful to a patient and redeeming God who has let me find my "place of repentance" with you and your wonderful Easter people.
>
> I know that I have a long way to go—and knowing my history, it will be an erratic journey—but I can never again say,

as I have so often said in the past, that I have no HOPE! I have
found out that forgiveness, acceptance, peace, health, and
hope are possible even for me.

I love you all so much.

I am deeply grateful and excited about ministering in a
community of Easter people. I also know that the love
and support I have received there have made so many
things possible: a television program that has been on the
air for more than twenty years, a radio program,
continued seminary teaching, a ministry of healing,
Bible-study groups and prayer groups, growth toward a
more inclusive congregation, mission groups formed,
books written, worship services shared, and countless
opportunities to be with others in their times of greatest
joy and sorrow.

The thread that has held it all together has been the
presence of God. In recent years I have come to
understand the fact of God's presence so much better
than before. I have come to see Jesus Christ as the one
who made God's presence immediate and the Holy Spirit
as one way the community of Christ has described that
immediate presence. I am eager for this pearl of great
price, this treasure hidden in the field, this one thing
needful. And all of this in the midst of my full share of
selfishness, laziness, and insensitivity!

Perhaps this is why I am so grateful to Jesus for helping
me think of God as a gracious Father. I know God is not
literally a father and I know he is not literally masculine.
But having had a caring father in my childhood and
having experienced a father's love for his own children, I
like to think of myself as being loved by the fatherlike
(and motherlike) God. One of my happiest childhood
memories is sitting on my father's lap at night and falling
asleep while he told me stories and sang to me. One of my

happiest adult memories is doing the same thing for our children.

God loves each one of us. He cares for each of us individually and is continually working to call us into a relationship with himself through which we experience wholeness of life. This is part of what the New Testament means by the word *grace*. Unconditional, unexpected, unlimited, undeserved, overflowing, superabundant love for each one of us. Grace is one of the words I use most often when talking about God, because it describes my experience of God.

As a gracious Father, God welcomes the prodigals when we come home from riotous living in the far country. He also loves the older brothers and sisters who have never wandered very far from home, especially when we come in from the hard work in the fields and learn to dance! (Cf. Luke 15.) The elder brother's story is not nearly as dramatic or attractive as the prodigal's. It will not sell as many books or movie rights. But it can be just as authentic, just as life-transforming, and just as much of a born-again conversion.

God loves each of us in the way that is uniquely right for us. He does not expect us to come home by imitating another person's way, dramatic and appealing as it may appear. His way for me has been through the continuous and growing awareness of his life-giving presence.

2
Son

We were attending a performance at the Kennedy Center in which Julie Harris was portraying the life of Emily Dickinson, the poet. Suddenly I heard Emily talking about religion—about her father's strict Puritan moralism, about the preachers of her childhood who made her feel "guilty, guilty, guilty," and about her growing disenchantment with organized religion. But I also heard her talk about Jesus Christ and about her love for him. "I do believe," she said, "that no person can be truly happy until that person can say, 'I love Christ.'"

That struck a chord deep in my spirit, because I feel the same way about Jesus Christ. He is the one in whom and through whom the presence of God is revealed most clearly and most completely. I love Jesus Christ as the "way" to truth about life with God.

But in recent years I have learned to be more careful in

differentiating between Jesus and the Christ. A thought-provoking letter triggered much of my growth in this direction.

> I enjoyed last Sunday's sermon so very much that I felt impelled to write and complain that you didn't do better. Now, have you ever heard such a reason for complaint?
>
> In recent years, it grates on my ears to hear the name of "Jesus" (which connotes the physical man of Nazareth) used when the present-day Spirit of Christ or the indwelling Christ is intended. I am very partial to the term "Christ-consciousness," but I realize that it is not commonly used or recognized and that maybe other terms will serve as well.
>
> In any event, it not only seems a contradiction of terms to speak of the indwelling Christ as "Jesus," but seems to undercut your wonderful analogy and to smack of fundamentalist mishmash by relating back two thousand years to a historical figure instead of emphasizing the here and now of the Christ-consciousness. I can keep substituting words for you as you talk and I get the point—beautifully, and I am thrilled by it—but I wonder if the point gets through to the average church member who got his or her Sunday schooling years ago.
>
> But don't worry—I'll be back.

As I thought about his complaint I realized that John, in the first chapter of his Gospel, and Paul, in the first chapter of Colossians, are talking about a universal Christ Spirit which has existed "from the beginning"—long before Jesus came—as a part of God's own being. This Christ Spirit "was with God, and . . . was God." All things were created through him. This means that from the beginning of time, everywhere in the created order, God has been revealing himself as the Christ! The Christ Spirit has been present at the center of life from the beginning, in all persons and everywhere in the world of nature.

Then, at a certain time and place in history this Christ Spirit became fully "embodied" in one human being. "The

Word became flesh," John said, "and dwelt among us, full of grace and truth" (John 1:14). Paul said the same thing when he talked about Jesus in whom "all the fulness of God was pleased to dwell" (Col. 1:19). The author of the Book of Wisdom in the Apocrypha joyfully anticipated this incarnation: "When peaceful silence lay over all, / and night had run the half of her swift course, / down from the heavens, from the royal throne, leapt your all-powerful Word" (Wis. of Sol. 18:14-15a JB).

The all-powerful Word, the Christ Spirit, which has been present at the center of life from the beginning, became fully embodied in Jesus of Nazareth. As a result, the life of Jesus is the model of what all human life is intended to be. He is the model of the faith relationship with God through which each one of us experiences wholeness of life. A little girl who lost her birth certificate on the way to school told her teacher she had lost her "excuse for being born." As the model for my life, Jesus has shown me how my relationship with God is my excuse for being born.

At every moment in his life, Jesus responded to God's loving presence with absolute trust, and he demonstrated the authenticity of that trust through his obedience. He "became obedient unto death." It has been very helpful and liberating for me to learn that his obedience was not a heavy burden of legalism aimed at earning the favor of God. It was the obedience of faith resulting in joy, freedom, and love.

One thing that has added to my appreciation for the life of Jesus as the model of human life has been the opportunity to travel to the Holy Land. On several occasions I have escorted groups of people in order to talk about the life and teaching of Jesus where it happened. This travel ministry, as I have come to think of it, is full of surprises. Once we lost a man for four days! On another occasion I found myself playing a good Samaritan role on the Jericho Road to one of our group members who had suffered a heart attack. Once I walked along the shores of the Sea of Galilee with a woman named Maria Magdalena who was tearfully talking about her need to be forgiven.

For me, on-site lectures and discussions about the life and teaching of Jesus have brought him much closer to me. Looking out over the shepherds' fields in Bethlehem, we sang Christmas carols and talked about his birth. Seated in a garden on a hillside overlooking the Sea of Galilee, we were able to experience the Sermon on the Mount in a new way. Gathered on the Mount of Olives, we experienced "the benefits of his passion" as we thought about how his crucifixion reconciles us with God. And in Emmaus we had a love feast and experienced the resurrection in the breaking of the bread. By getting close to Jesus in these and other ways, I have gained a new appreciation for his life as the model for my own.

But the same Christ Spirit that was fully embodied in Jesus is also present in each of us and in our world today. The gradual unfolding of this truth has had a profound effect on my life in recent years. Once, while visiting Capernaum, I experienced it in a vivid and memorable way. I had talked with the group about the ministry of Jesus around Capernaum, and we had dispersed to enjoy some time alone in this place where Jesus had walked. It was an unbearably hot summer day without a breath of air stirring. For relief, I sat down in the shade of one of the stone columns still standing on the site of the first-century synagogue where Jesus preached while in Capernaum. Suddenly I became aware of a gentle breeze fresh from the sea, blowing across my parched face. At the same time, I became aware of a "breath" stirring within me, at the center of my being. I sat very quietly and received this gift of presence which brought relief and healing to my parched spirit. It was a time of healing made possible by the presence of the Christ Spirit within me.

This is an example of what Paul meant when he spoke of "Christ in us" as our hope of glory. It is what he meant when he said, "God has sent the Spirit of his Son into our hearts." New power has been released in my life and ministry by recognizing this difference between Jesus as the incarnational model for our human life and the universal Christ Spirit as a continuing source of God's living presence.

One consequence of this has been my increasing use of the Jesus Prayer. This is a prayer with a long history, especially in the Orthodox tradition of the church. It is a composite of words taken from the Gospels, "Lord Jesus Christ, Son of God, have mercy on me." Many saints and teachers have written about the benefits of continuous repetition of this prayer. In my theological studies, I learned about the prayer, but it made no great impression on me. In recent years I find myself using it more and more as a way of positioning myself to receive the gift of the Christ presence. I am not asking for the historical figure of Jesus to come into my heart when I use this prayer. I am asking for the living Christ Spirit, the Christ presence, the Christ-consciousness.

Another benefit of the Jesus Prayer is the protection it affords against the powers of evil. In contrast to my earlier years, I have become a "reality-of-evil person." Age and experience have taught me all too clearly about the principalities and powers of darkness that are

present in our world, working to destroy goodness,
truth, and beauty. I have also become painfully aware of
the abyss within, the powers of darkness within my own
being which often cause me to do the very thing I do not
want to do. I easily identify with Paul in Romans. "I find it
to be a law that when I want to do right, evil lies close at
hand. For I delight in the law of God, in my inmost self,
but I see in my members another law at war with the law
of my mind and making me captive to the law of sin
which dwells in my members. Wretched man that I am!
Who will deliver me from this body of death?" (Rom.
7:21-24). There have been times when I have felt the
weight of evil as real as a physical presence riding on my
back, trying to pull me down.

I also know what the members of the early church
meant when they talked and sang about power in the
name of Jesus Christ. By calling on the Name, we ask for
the protecting presence of the Christ Spirit, a power
greater than all the forces of evil, a light that will never be
overcome by the darkness. When I become aware of the
presence of evil and darkness in my life, I use the Jesus
Prayer for protection. It is especially valuable in those
times when I am most vulnerable, such as fatigue and
illness. I have also found that the powers of evil are very
active when I am getting close to something vital in my
search for God or in my ministry to others. At times I
have worked very hard on a sermon, for example, or
invested myself in a counseling session, only to find
myself assailed by temptation and evil thoughts. At such
times I turn to God for protection, using the Jesus Prayer
as a way of releasing the power of the Christ presence.

Another consequence of recognizing the difference
between Jesus as a historical figure and the Christ Spirit
as a continuing presence has been a whole new

understanding of the relationship between Christians and non-Christians. Do non-Christians have to accept Jesus Christ in order to be saved? This is one of the most perplexing questions we face. If we answer no, then we seem to be denying the uniqueness of Jesus Christ and ignoring the Scripture, "No one comes to the Father, but by me." If we answer yes, then we seem to be cutting off countless persons from the love of God. What about those who lived before Jesus came? What about those who have never heard of Jesus? What about those driven away from Jesus by the selfishness of so-called Christians? Would the loving Father deny salvation to so many?

On one of our trips to the Greek Islands to study the life and letters of Paul, we also visited the city of Istanbul. After returning to our ship, I said to the group, "We have just seen thousands of Muslims in the busy streets of this city. Do you believe that all these persons must become Christians before they can be saved? In a few minutes we are going to take a vote on this." The question threw the group into turmoil. It is one thing to talk about this in an abstract academic way. It is quite another to spend time with living human beings and then think about them being eternally lost because they haven't accepted Jesus.

Several members of our group became very angry with me for raising this question. Others left the room before the vote was taken. Weeks after the trip I was still receiving letters from persons struggling with the issue. When the vote was finally taken, it revealed how ambivalent many of us are on this issue. This same ambivalence was displayed by the prominent evangelist Billy Graham who said in the January, 1978, issue of *McCalls:* "I used to believe that pagans in far-off countries were lost—were going to hell—if they did not have the Gospel of Jesus Christ preached to them. I no longer believe that. I believe that there are other ways of recognizing the existence of God—through nature, for instance—and plenty of other opportunities, therefore, of saying 'yes' to God." A short time later he called a press conference and said, "Contrary to what the article says, I do believe that non-Christians are lost, whether they live in far-off countries or in America."

As the ship sailed from Istanbul toward Philippi where we would share Paul's surpassing joy in Christ, I tried to explain to our group how a recognition of the universality of the Christ Spirit has resolved the dilemma for me. God has been acting everywhere among all people from the beginning of time as the Christ presence. Many persons who have not heard of Jesus come to know God at least to some degree. They learn how to say yes to God. Whenever they come to him, it is through the Christ presence that is within them. They may not understand it this way. They may not know the name. But they are coming to the Father through Christ. The gift that the Christian has to offer non-Christians is to tell them the Name and to share with them the fullness of the Christ presence in Jesus. After talking for a long time with a young Christian who had been telling him about Jesus, an elderly Hindu said, "I have known him all my life. Now you have told me his name."

A young minister's wife wrote to me after the trip about the acute spiritual crisis which my question triggered in her. Back in Istanbul her small group of fifteen persons had voted fourteen to one that the Muslims did not have to become Christians to be saved. She was the "one." It was a crushing experience. "I would certainly have felt more comfortable," she said, "if the vote had been eight and seven or even ten and five, but fourteen to one! I had the dreadful feeling that I had just been convicted of a crime, and actually I had. Christ had just convicted me of rejecting millions of his children. The guilt overcame me."

She then described the terrible struggle she had for days, experiencing emotions that almost spoiled the rest of her trip. She kept struggling to fight back the tears, feeling that something profound was happening to her, but she was afraid. Then one evening, after a long period of prayer and Bible reading, she felt the guilt and sorrow leaving her. "I realized that a wonderful thing had happened. You see, Christ was convicting me so that I might begin to realize the depth of God's love, the vastness of his outreach. He was actually pulling me up out of myself, bringing me nearer to the source of himself, and showing me what he is really like."

In another letter she talked about some of the implications of this insight. "What does this mean to Christians in regard to evangelizing and converting others? Someone explained to me that we don't need to take Christ to other people; rather we must go out to others to meet the Christ who lives in others already. Our task is to help them see and respond to the Christ living in themselves and us. I am so thankful for this new understanding which God gave me."

The apostle Paul has helped me understand how this emphasis on the universality of the Christ Spirit in no way undermines the uniqueness of Jesus. Twice in Colossians Paul speaks about the *plērōma* of God in Jesus (1:19; 2:9). *Plērōma* is difficult to translate, but it means complete fullness. Even though the Christ Spirit is present in others and has been especially evident in some great religious leaders of history, only Jesus has embodied the *plērōma,* the "whole fulness" of God. He brings to light that which is only partially revealed in others. This is why we who bear his name are so eager to share him, in a spirit of love, with the rest of the world.

The other consequence for me of acknowledging the reality of the continuing Christ Spirit has been a new appreciation for the mystery of the cross. I have never fully understood what the church has meant by saying that "Christ died for us" and that we are "saved by the blood of Jesus." But I have spent a great deal of time in recent years thinking about the immensity of this sacrifice. This reached a climax when I immersed myself in a series of lectures on the meaning of the crucifixion for our travel group as we made our way through Austria toward the Oberammergau Passion Play. Strangely enough, the moment in the six-hour drama which moved me most deeply was not Golgotha but Gethsemane, when Jesus cried out in pain and anguish, "Father, it is your Son. Listen to him!" I immediately felt the suffering of Jesus in a new way. Reflecting on that moment afterward, I better understood how this suffering has made a difference in the way every person can now be related to God. The Christ Spirit, identifying totally with us in our estrangement from God, makes himself totally available to us through this sacrifice to reconcile us to God. In other words, the gift of Christ's presence which I can experience in my present life is a costly gift! In recent years I find myself approaching it with greater reverence and accepting it with deeper thanksgiving.

The presence of God is the thread that holds my life together, the constant reality that has given my life its meaning. But Jesus Christ is the one who most clearly embodies and reveals that presence. As this becomes more clear to me with the passing years, I find myself reaching more and more for the "unsearchable riches of Christ." He is the joy of my desiring. He is the Son of God, the way to God, and my window to God. In the light of my new understanding of the universality of the Christ Spirit, I find myself agreeing strongly with Emily. "I do believe that no person can be truly happy until that person can say, 'I love Christ.'"

3
Spirit

The Holy Spirit is the immediate presence of God. For years I did not understand this. I did not know that the Holy Spirit is the answer to the hunger for God I have felt as long as I can remember. But now I understand.

Part of the problem was that I misunderstood the experience of several friends who had been "baptized in the Holy Spirit" and occasionally "spoke in tongues." I assumed from what they told me that speaking in tongues would be the only way I would know that I had received the Holy Spirit. Their whole experience pointed to a different God than the one I knew, and their exclusive emphasis on ecstatic utterance did not ring true for me. After talking with them I often felt judged, excluded, and unloved.

Now I know that the coming of the Spirit is like the wind. Jesus said, "The wind blows where it wills, and you hear the sound of it, but you do not know whence it comes or whither it goes; so it is with every one who is born of the Spirit" (John 3:8). In the New Testament the same Greek word *(pneuma)* means both wind and spirit. For some it comes with gale force and stirs up an ecstatic emotional response. For others it comes as a gentle breeze filled with peace and healing. This is the way it came to me.

Reflection on the New Testament experience of the Spirit has had a strong influence on me. In the fourteenth chapter of John's Gospel, Jesus promised the disciples that the Father would send the Spirit. This promise was made in an atmosphere of "peace and love." "The Counselor, the Holy Spirit, whom the Father will send in my name, . . . will teach you all things, and bring to your remembrance all that I have said to you. Peace I leave with you; my peace I give to you" (14:26-27). Then, in the twentieth chapter, God kept his promise! The risen Christ appeared to the disciples and said to them, "Peace be with you. As the Father has sent me, even so I send you." And when he had said this he breathed on them, and said to them, "Receive the Holy Spirit" (20:21-22). No mention is made of ecstatic utterance. Later, on the day of Pentecost, a larger group of disciples received the Holy Spirit. This time, according to the second chapter of Acts, the Spirit came like a mighty wind and fire. "And they were all filled with the Holy Spirit and began to speak in other tongues, as the Spirit gave them utterance" (2:4). In the remainder of the New Testament there are references to the gift of the Spirit, some accompanied by "tongues" and some not.

I am convinced that the gift of the Holy Spirit is the gift of God's immediate living presence. To be filled with the Holy Spirit is to be filled with God's presence. To be baptized in the Holy Spirit is to be immersed in the presence of God. Part of the good news of the gospel is that God is eager to give himself to us as the Spirit, to deepen and fulfill our relationship with him in this way. But it is necessary for us to "receive the Holy Spirit," to be open to the Spirit's coming, to acknowledge our hunger for it, to long for it as an essential part of our Christian life. It is also important to know that the coming of the Spirit and the fruit of the Spirit will be different for each one of us.

A crucial step in my own pilgrimage has been the opportunity to "retreat" from my busy schedule and open up inner space for God. My life is full of appointments, meetings, deadlines, and activities from early in the morning to late at night. Most of the things I do are creative and I enjoy doing them, but without time set aside to be with God in this special way the whole enterprise begins to fall apart. Retreat is one way I have found of taking this time.

Dayspring, The Church of The Saviour retreat center near Washington, D.C., has been the scene of many spiritual milestones for me. I have also been spiritually refreshed at Kirkridge in the Pocono Mountains of Pennsylvania, at the Benedictine Priory at Weston in the Green Mountains of Vermont, and at the Trappist Abbey of St. Joseph in central Massachusetts. Another highlight has been a week at a Jesuit retreat center in New England, working with a spiritual director on centering prayer.

A few years ago I passed a major spiritual milestone on one of the retreats while listening to a Carmelite priest talk about union with God. So many of the things I had known intellectually for many years suddenly fell into place, and I knew them in a completely different way. It is very difficult to put into words. On the surface it seems so simple, but my life has never been the same since that weekend. It was easy for me to identify with a woman who wrote about a similar experience which occurred while she was watching one of our television programs.

> For many months I have intended to write you of the tremendous impact your telecasts have had upon my life over the years.
>
> It was just six years ago, while sitting in front of my television set during one of your lectures on the meaning of life, that God opened my mind to the astounding truth that a right relationship to him is, literally, what gives meaning to life. You cannot imagine how real this revelation was to me.
>
> From this "moment of truth" came genuine surrender, something I had never before experienced. I have learned through trial and error that changed attitudes come from a yielded, open life before God and not from futile human efforts. I have also learned that God does guide us, step by step, if we will but let him.

"You cannot imagine how real this revelation was to me," she said. This was the feeling I had after my own moment of truth on this retreat.

On another occasion I spent ten days living as a hermit in the Arizona desert. The Nova Nada Community near Sedona, founded by a Carmelite priest who understands the importance of the wilderness in our journey to God, provides hermitages and spiritual support for those who want to be with God in desert solitude. My fantasies and wish dreams about the hermit's life were quickly shattered by this experience. I had made plans to go in early spring, looking forward to the warmth and wild flowers of the desert after a cold winter. Unfortunately, I didn't know the difference between the lower desert and the upper desert. In the upper desert, where the hermitage is located, it was still winter. The snow that was falling on the day of my arrival was the first real sign of trouble. Would the light clothes I had brought for my desert vacation be adequate for the days ahead? As it turned out, I had very little time for prayer the first few days because of the struggle to survive.

First there was the pervading cold of the desert. Next there was the problem of food. For ten days I lived on oatmeal and peanut butter. Actually I don't mind oatmeal and peanut butter, but after three days I felt like the Hebrews in the wilderness who started remembering the slavery of Egypt with nostalgia. There was also the problem of sleep. I got used to the springless bunk after a while, but the first morning when I woke up I discovered that a lizard had been sleeping with me. When I picked him up to put him out, his tail broke off in my hand and kept wiggling long after the lizard (minus a tail) had buried himself in the covers. From then on I felt nervous getting into bed.

This was a great learning experience for me. I understand now that the wilderness experience is not fun and games. The People of Israel in the wilderness, Elijah in the desert, Jesus on the Mount of Temptation, Paul in Arabia—all of these were experiencing real suffering and deprivation. But the suffering made them aware of their dependence on God, and the deprivation opened up space for the presence of God. I was glad for the opportunity to make myself available to God in this way and I was sorry to leave when my days in the Arizona desert came to an end. Since then I often think of God's word to Hosea: "I will espouse you, lead you into the desert, and there I will speak to your heart" (2:14, Father William McNamara's version).

What I didn't know was that these retreats were preparing me in a special way to receive the gift of the

Holy Spirit on a Pentecost weekend at the Dayspring retreat center. I arrived Friday night very fatigued, looking forward to a weekend of walking in the sunshine and breathing fresh air. It rained the entire weekend. This was a blessing in disguise, however, because it gave me an opportunity for some refreshing sleep and also left me in an introspective state of mind. The retreat leader spoke on the first night about God's love as the Father. The next morning he spoke about God's love in the Son. Saturday night he spoke about the Holy Spirit. When I went to bed I knew that something important was happening because I felt myself completely surrounded by a healing presence. The next morning, Pentecost Sunday, we sat around the table for our closing Communion Service. I was aware of the spirit of love we were all feeling, of the steady rain falling outside, and of the mystery of the sacrament we were about to receive. While receiving the bread and wine I felt that I was literally filled with God. I don't know any other way to describe it. My whole being was permeated with this feeling and by the sense of peace which accompanied it. I have often thought since about how Jesus received the Holy Spirit at the time of his baptism, not like wind and fire, but with gentleness, like a dove.

This experience of the Holy Spirit has made a profound difference in the way I think about my life, my ministry, and the world around me. It has also made a difference in the way I think about the Holy Spirit. Such an experience is a "second blessing" that God is eager to give to everyone who has come to know and love him through Christ. This second blessing is the gift of his immediate presence, a healing and empowering presence. It is experienced as an "infilling" and a welling up of life from our own deepest center, making us aware of

God's life-giving presence in the world around us. It is accompanied by "gifts" to be shared with the community of faith "for the common good," and the end result is the "fruit" of "love, joy, peace, patience, kindness, goodness, faithfulness, gentleness, self-control" (Gal. 5:22-23a). This is not an esoteric experience intended for a select group, but the natural result of the Christian disciple's expanding love for God. Jesus "breathes on us" and tells each of us to receive the Holy Spirit.

During one period of time when several friends were pressuring me on the matter of tongues, I tried it. There were at last two occasions while I was in prayer (and once while jogging!) that I found it very easy to let go and express my love for God in unintelligible sounds. This seemed to be an authentic expression of love and joy, welling up from within. It was a good experience. But I do not regard speaking in tongues as an essential gift of the Spirit, and in my case it does not seem to be of great interest or importance. I find it much more desirable to sit in the profound silence of contemplative prayer and allow the love of God to wash over me, or to identify with another person's pain and become involved with him or her in dealing with the pain. Silence and service make me feel much closer to God than tongues. Or I would rather preach a good sermon that helps someone in his or her pilgrimage toward union with God. Paul would agree: "I would rather speak five words with my mind, in order to instruct others, than ten thousand words in a tongue" (I Cor. 14:19).

My experience with the Holy Spirit has further convinced me that God is full of surprises! I did not expect to be learning about the "femininity" of God in connection with the Holy Spirit, but this is the direction in which "he" is leading me. I have so much to learn about this! To talk about the feminine qualities of God, for example, and immediately use masculine pronouns to refer to "him" creates problems for which I have no satisfying solution. But I feel like a whole new world is opening up around me here.

I have never considered myself a sexist. Imagine my dismay when some of my female seminary students pointed out how I had consistently used masculine pronouns throughout my previous books not only in reference to God but also to other persons. When I protested that I used masculine pronouns in a generic sense, referring to humans in general, they let me know how excluded this practice made them feel. This and other experiences have made me conscious of the widespread use of sexist language. I am trying very hard now to use inclusive terms when referring to other persons. I also find an alarm sounding in my head when I perceive another speaker or writer blithely excluding half the human race through the careless use of language. This is not without lighter moments. With tongue in cheek, a friend suggested that I change my last name to "Bauperson." I can laugh at the suggestion, but I want to make sure I do not use my laughter as a way of hiding from the real issue. I am working hard on changing my use of language when referring to other persons.

The language I use in referring to God is another matter. A major problem arises out of our exclusive use of masculine terms and images in reference to God. Even though we might deny it in a theological discussion, most of us think of God as literally masculine—a Father, a Son, a King. The result has been the unconscious (and conscious!) oppression of women and the impoverishment of our conception of God.

What to do about the language problem I simply do not know. It is too awkward to refer to God as "him/her" and there are no inclusive pronouns available in English. But there is a great deal I can do about perceiving God in a more inclusive way, and about communicating that perception to others. The Psalmist helps by using the image of a mother and her child when talking about the way God comforts and cares for us (Ps. 131). Jesus helps when he compares himself with a mother hen concerned about her chicks, and when he uses the joy of a woman finding a lost coin to help us understand the love of God (Luke 15). But the greatest help for me has come through the discovery that the Hebrew word for spirit, *ruach*, is feminine in gender.

Father and Son are distinctively masculine terms, and we would lose too much in giving them up as ways of thinking about God. But why not think of the Holy Spirit in more feminine terms? This is a way to include in our perception of God the best of masculine and feminine qualities as we have experienced them. Actually, of course, God is neither masculine nor feminine. Why not think of "him" as both? Jesus referred to the Holy Spirit as Comforter or Healer. Both comfort and help, in my experience, have often been associated with women, and it is enriching my life to think more often of God in this way.

Help has also come from an unexpected source. In all my years in the ministry I had never read the books of the Apocrypha until recently. These books, included in the Roman Catholic Bible, are unknown to most Protestants. Several of the books speak about Wisdom in a way that anticipates the Christian experience of the Holy Spirit, and Wisdom is always feminine.

God of our ancestors, Lord of mercy. . . .
With you is Wisdom, she who knows your works,
she who was present when you made the world;
she understands what is pleasing in your eyes
and what agrees with your commandments.
Despatch her from the holy heavens,
send her forth from your throne of glory
to help me and to toil with me
and teach me what is pleasing to you,
since she knows and understands everything.
She will guide me prudently in my undertakings
and protect me by her glory. . . .
As for your intention, who could have learnt it, had you not
   granted Wisdom
and sent your holy spirit from above?

                               (Wisd. 9 JB)

This practice of referring to Wisdom in the feminine gender is also anticipated in the eighth chapter of Proverbs. Meditating on words like these and attributing feminine, as well as masculine, qualities to the Holy Spirit is enriching my life in many ways.

It should be noted in passing that Carl Jung, the Christian psychotherapist, has helped me also at this point. In his writings, he insisted that there is a masculine quality (animus) in every woman and a feminine quality (anima) in every man. Recognizing and coming to terms with this opposite within our own nature is essential in our movement toward wholeness of life. But if human persons, created in the image of God, are both male and female, why not think of God in the same way?

It has also been helpful for me to learn that the terms Holy Spirit, Spirit of God, Spirit of Christ, and Spirit are all used interchangeably in the New Testament. This happened because the writers were not trying to construct an elaborate and carefully integrated doctrine of the Holy Spirit. They were simply describing their experience of God's immediate presence. They were filled, led, guided, and empowered by that presence. They came to believe that the Holy Spirit, like God's Word, has always been. As the Nicene Creed says, the Holy Spirit "spake through the prophets." But their experience of the fullness of God's presence in Jesus sensitized them to the presence of the Spirit and enabled them to receive it in a new and life-enhancing way. The Holy Spirit was communicated to them as the fullness of God in his most immediate form.

I have said that the presence of God is the thread that holds my life together. I have also said that this has always been true, but that my joy in recent years has been in knowing that it is true. Another way of putting this would be to say that my joy in recent years has been this growing awareness of the reality of the Holy Spirit.

4
Community

One of the most important things in my life in recent years has been my discovery of the church. For as long as I can remember I have been involved one way or another in the institutional church, but it has only recently become clear to me that the institution is not what the church is all about.

Several years ago three little boys came in from their home on the farm to attend the circus. They were so impressed by the colored posters advertising the circus and by the crowd milling around on the midway that they never got inside the big tent to see the show. They went home thinking they had seen the circus, and it wasn't until years later they discovered they had missed out on the "real thing."

It has become clear to me that the institutional church is not the real thing. Confusion on this point leads to the kind of widespread frustration and hostility reflected in a recent nationwide poll in which only 4 percent of those participating thought of their church as a major factor in their lives. A man told me his church was nothing but a "hymn-singing Rotary Club"; a woman expressed anger because all they talk about in her church is money; and many young adults have stopped going to church because they "never get anything out of it." One minister who was asked to say something good about the church replied, "That would be like telling a man who has leukemia that his tonsils are healthy."

Once I spoke in Indianapolis to a group of people who had been watching our television program for a number of years. During the question-and-answer period, a woman made a speech. She said she had been very active in her church, working on committees, helping with the budget campaign, and serving at church dinners. But she was angry because she was convinced that all this church activity was "killing her spiritual life." The memorable thing about the incident is the way the whole group broke into loud applause at this point, expressing similar feelings of anger and frustration.

I can identify with this because I have spent more than my share of time supporting the institution. But now I am seeing things differently. The union with God made possible by the coming of Jesus Christ is essentially a one-on-one relationship between ourselves and God. But to our amazement we discover this I-Thou encounter drawing us into a new relationship with other persons. When we are born again as individuals we are born into a new family, a new fellowship of sharing, a new community of love, and the more we allow ourselves to be drawn into this family, the more we discover the joy of God's presence. Here we find a place where rebellion is accepted and forgiven, where selfishness is conquered by love, where hidden guilt is brought into the light and healed, and where anxiety is examined and overcome. All this is possible because God makes his presence known in powerful and life-transforming ways in the faith community. The deeper we enter into this fellowship of life-sharing, the more we become aware of God's presence and the more opportunities we have to respond to him.

This life in community is a gift of grace. It is the means God has provided to nourish us in our new life with him and the means he uses to call others into relationship with himself. A husband and wife who had withdrawn from the church were having serious problems in their marriage. They wrote to me and shared their gratitude for the way in which they had experienced God's healing presence when they returned to the church.

> We have found a new concept of Christian community. How I have longed for someone to discuss our problem with, but it is tremendously difficult to share one's deepest feelings. However, it becomes so much easier in a group of people who are seriously searching for closeness with God.

By searching *together* for closeness with God, we position ourselves to experience the reality of his presence and the fullness of his love.

Recent emphasis on psychosomatic medicine provides an analogy that helps me understand the relationship between the church as community and the church as institution. The word *psychosomatic* is taken from the Greek words *psyche* (soul) and *soma* (body) and indicates the close relationship between our inner being and the physical organism which embodies it. The biblical writers insisted that we cannot separate the soul and body, but they also recognized the different functions of these two fundamental parts of our being.

More and more I find myself thinking about the psychosomatic nature of the church. The soul of the church is the community. This is where the true life of the church is centered, the place where lasting values are created and communicated. The body of the church is the institutional structure. The building, the budget, the committees, and other institutional forms are necessary and important, but they are valid only when they express the true life of the community of faith. They are to be treated as means to an end and never as ends in themselves. We can discover how God offers us his love even in the midst of our business agenda when we gather as a Spirit-filled community, using the institutional structures as the physical means of supporting and communicating our spiritual life rather than meeting for the sole purpose of supporting an institution.

Many of the most profound changes in my life and ministry have occurred in recent years because of this new understanding of the nature of the church. Something deep inside of me identifies with the movement away from the contemporary emphasis on individuality in our search for wholeness and away from an emphasis on the church as institution into an awareness of what it means to experience God's presence in the community of Christ. When others come to me, sharing their personal problems or burdened with the world's pain, I find myself offering them an invitation into the "family" as one of the most loving and healing things I can do for them. When we think of the church as our "extended family" and enter deeply into its life, soul and body, we position ourselves to experience the love of God in special ways.

I can't help wondering why it has taken me so long to discover the power of the church as community. From beginning to end, the biblical story is about God's revelation of himself to individuals through their participation in community. The Old Testament, for example, is more the story of the people of God and of God's presence in their life together than it is the story of individuals. Together they are the people of God, the holy nation, the community of Israel. The escape from Pharaoh, the wandering in the wilderness, the golden age of David, and similar milestone events are included to show how God called and shaped the life of the community.

A similar emphasis is found in the New Testament. One of the first things Jesus did was to create a community by calling disciples to be with him (Mark 1:16-20). According to the Gospels, these disciples were with him most of the time during his ministry in Galilee and Jerusalem. In times of unusual stress, such as the retreats to the Mount of Transfiguration and the Garden of Gethsemane, he made a special point of taking members of the community with him (Mark 9:2-8; 14:32-42). "Where two or three are gathered in my name," he said on another occasion, "there am I in the midst of them" (Matt. 18:20).

This biblical emphasis on God's revelation of himself through community reaches a climax in the second volume of Luke's comprehensive work on the birth and growth of Christianity, usually called the Acts of the Apostles. The title is somewhat misleading because the book is mainly concerned with Peter and Paul and with only a few of their acts. The author's main purpose is to describe the life of the early church in Jerusalem and the expansion of Christianity from Jerusalem to Rome. It would be difficult to overestimate the historical value of this record. No comparable narrative covering the early life of the Christian community has survived. While Luke's Gospel is one of the richest sources of our knowledge about Jesus, we do have other Gospels that cover much of the same ground. This is not true of the story that unfolds in the book of Acts.

From the beginning, the emphasis in this primary history of Christian community is upon what happens to the early Christians "when they had come together" (Acts 1:6). This is especially true in the second chapter where God gave himself to the community in a way which forever changed the history of the church and of the world. According to the opening statement of the second chapter, the disciples were "all together in one place" on the day of Pentecost. Pentecost was originally a Jewish harvest festival, but for Luke and the early Christian community the gift of the Holy Spirit on this occasion changed its meaning completely, marking the beginning of a new order and a new age.

On the day of Pentecost, God's power was experienced by the community as an immediate presence. The Spirit came like the breath or *pneuma* (spirit, breath, wind) of God, moving in a tangible and powerful way. The mighty wind and tongues of flame in Luke's description are symbolic of the *shekinah* (divine presence) which is experienced at crucial points in the biblical story. On this occasion the Spirit's presence made possible the breaking down of barriers, such as nationality and language, which had divided the community and threatened its unity.

The experience of God's presence on Pentecost marked an important stage in the creation of the Christian community. Different answers have been given to the question, When did the church begin? Some trace it to the calling of the first disciples (Mark 1:16-20). Others believe it began with the experience of the disciples on the road to Caesarea Philippi when Jesus asked them who he was (Matt. 16:13-20). Others think the church began during the resurrection appearance of Jesus when he said to the disciples, "Receive the Holy Spirit" (John 20:22). Most persons, however, celebrate Pentecost as the birthday of the church. The Pentecost experience is especially important, because from this time on the disciples had a vivid awareness of their life together as the people of God. This was the beginning of a self-conscious awareness by the disciples that they were "the church."

The summary at the end of the second chapter of Acts reveals how important the community was to the disciples. "They devoted themselves to the apostles' teaching and [koinōnia], to the breaking of bread and the prayers" (Acts 2:42). The word koinōnia means fellowship, but this English word fails to convey the richness of life-sharing intended by the New Testament writers. "All who believed were together and had all things in common. . . . And day by day, attending the temple together and breaking bread in their homes, they partook of food with glad and generous hearts, praising God and having favor with all the people" (Acts 2:44, 46-47).

Part of my problem through the years has been my association of the word *fellowship* with many of the superficial activities of the organized church. How often I have attended fellowship committees planning fellowship dinners to be held in a Fellowship Hall! The koinōnia, the fellowship created by the presence of the Holy Spirit, is completely different from mere social gatherings or associations of people. It is a community of life-sharing at the deepest levels, a community whose life together is grounded in the redemptive love revealed by Jesus Christ. Each member of the community performs his or her own particular function, but needs the others in order to live. As Paul points out, the members of the "body" are so closely joined together that "if one member suffers, all suffer together; if one member is honored, all rejoice together" (I Cor. 12:26). There is ample evidence throughout all the New Testament writings of the joy experienced by the early Christians as they entered into the life-transforming presence of God in this *koinōnia* of the Holy Spirit.

After reading the results of several nationwide polls on religion, I did a lot of thinking about the church. Why do so few persons think of the church as having an important influence on their lives? What could restore the power experienced by the early disciples when the church was young? What is the purpose of the church? In reflecting on all of this, I find it makes a difference to think of the church in terms of its three major functions.

One function of the church revolves around the experience of presence. When I hear the word *church* now, I immediately think, "That is where I experience the presence of God." Through worship services, prayer, and Bible-study groups, and in countless other ways, the church provides ways for us to be with God. One elderly man was describing his feelings during a time of corporate prayer in his church. "I was afraid," he said, "to put out my hand, lest I touch God." This was his way of describing the immediacy of God's presence which we associate with the church at its best. Luke put it another way: "When they had prayed, the place in which they were gathered together was shaken; and they were all filled with the Holy Spirit" (Acts 4:31).

A second function of the church revolves around the experience of *mission*. Emil Brunner said, "A church exists by mission as fire exists by burning." We are not fulfilling our purpose as the people of God unless we are doing everything possible to share God's power and love with the world. We do this as individuals, learning from Jesus how to be men and women for others, loving neighbors, loving enemies, loving the members of our immediate family, loving those who have been left injured by the side of the road. We also do this through mission groups, moving out corporately into the world to witness for Christ with compassion and with a demand for social justice. One of the paradoxes of Christian life is that the more we give ourselves to others the more God is able to give himself to us. This is true of churches as well as individuals.

Some years ago I was on a busy street in Atlanta waiting for a bus. I noticed a prominent sign on a nearby church advertising a revival service for eight o'clock. It was then eight-thirty, so I slipped into the back of the church to see what was happening. The minister at that point was "preaching up a storm," using all the familiar words and phrases about salvation. There were four people in the congregation. Sadly I turned back to the busy street where so many anxious people and so many poor people were passing by. Somehow it seemed that the church was out of tune with the music of the streets, unaware of the opportunities for mission at its doorstep. I thought of a story Jesus told about a rich man. "At his gate lay a poor man named Lazarus, full of sores, who desired to be fed with what fell from the rich man's table" (Luke 16:20-21a). One of the functions of the church is to be on a mission of love to every Lazarus in the world.

The third function of the church revolves around the

experience of *community*. This is the discovery that has become so important to me. At a time in my life when I was very tired and under a great deal of stress, a friend invited me to go with him to his small mission church. In the love that was evident in that group I experienced a power of healing and hope which changed my life. I remained with the group for over a year, experiencing Christian community in a new way. Through my life in that group and in countless experiences I have had since then, I am now convinced that one of the main purposes of the church is to be the "extended family" for our life in Christ. My greatest experiences of God's presence and my richest opportunities to serve Christ in mission have been made possible by the church as community. I am just as involved in the organized church as I ever have been. I recognize the importance of the institutional structures, but things are different now because my heart is with the soul of the church, the community where I am nourished and equipped in unique ways for ministry to others.

A strange thing has happened in recent years. Life in an inner-city church can be very hectic at times, and I have always looked forward to the summer when I could get away from it all. In order to prepare myself for another busy year, I would put a lot of physical and emotional distance between myself and the church. I don't feel the same about summers now. It is good, of course, to have a rest and a change of pace, but now when I am away from the church I miss "the family" and look forward to the time when I will return home.

5
Preaching

The bishop who ordained me placed his hand on my head and said, "Take thou authority as an elder in the Church to preach the Word of God, and to administer the holy Sacraments in the congregation." In the ensuing years nothing in my ministry has brought me greater joy or consumed more of my time than the preparation and delivery of sermons. Enthusiasm for this phase of my ministry continues unabated!

A few years ago, while preaching in a church in Florida, I was distracted by a young woman in the congregation who repeatedly held up cards with words printed on them. Since I couldn't make out the words from where I was standing in the pulpit, I wondered what message she was trying to communicate to me. After the service, when she came forward to greet me, I asked her about it. She had grown up, she said, with the old-time religion where she could shout when she wanted to respond to the preacher. But in the modern church she knew this would not be accepted, so she had a set of cards printed with words she could hold up to express her feelings. As I shuffled through the cards I found words like *hallelujah* and *amen*. But I also found one expression which I had never heard in any old-time church I ever attended. It read "Go, man, go!"

That is exactly the way I have always felt about preaching. I am convinced God uses our preaching of the Word as an opportunity to make his immediate presence known, and I have developed a sacramental view of preaching in contrast to the lecture-hall approach which is so prevalent today. It has been shocking for me to discover how many persons think of the sermon as a kind of lecture or address about God and morality. In this view, the audience comes into a large room with a podium in the front and, after a few opening exercises, settles back to hear the sermon. The people go out judging the whole experience by whether they found the sermon entertaining or informative. Consequently, there are phrases in our language like "dull as a sermon," and we joke a great deal about people sleeping through the sermon. No wonder so many are turned off by preaching.

One of my theological students returned from conducting his last service in a student parish saying that an elderly woman had been crying after the sermon. When he commented about it, she replied, "It is because this is your last Sunday. You are leaving us." With appropriate modesty he replied, "You shouldn't cry. I'm sure they will send someone better to take my place." Whereupon she cried even more, and said, "Oh, that's what you all say, but every year it gets worse and worse."

Many persons feel this way about preaching because of their lecture-hall approach to the worship experience.

It is very different if we think of the sermon as a sacramental channel for God's presence. The minister's life, the sermon, and the gathering of the people are the outward and visible signs of God's inward and spiritual grace. The preaching event is not just an informative or entertaining public address, but a very special occasion which God uses to make his immediate presence known. "Through the activity of preaching," Karl Barth said, "God himself speaks."

It is important, in this connection, to note how the Reformation put the preaching of the Word back at the center of Christian worship. It was never the Reformers' intention to detract from the value of the Lord's Supper. What they wanted to do was put the preaching of the Word, along with the Eucharist, at the center of the worship experience as a way for God to impart his real presence. John Calvin, for example, had a view of preaching which is clearly sacramental in this sense. "The preaching of the word of God," he said, "is the word of God." The preaching of the Word does not merely tell us something about God and make us think about God. It brings us into an encounter with God. God himself as the living Word, who was from the beginning and through whom all things were created, God himself as this living Word is present to us. "The preaching of the word of God *is* the word of God."

This view of preaching excites me not only on Sunday morning, but also all during the weekly task of sermon preparation. Working with a biblical passage, letting the text determine the direction of the sermon, finding the right illustrations and the right phrases to reveal the truth in the text, preparing myself spiritually for the worship service are all exciting to me when I realize how God can use this sermon in the context of the worship service to make his presence known. For some persons this presence will mean healing, or forgiveness, or the rediscovery of hope. Others will hear a call to love more deeply, act more justly, or live with greater integrity. All during the week I look forward to the worship service in order to see what God will do in our midst with the preaching event.

In order to appreciate this particular view of preaching, it is helpful to think of what the preaching of Jesus must have meant to those who heard him. According to Mark's Gospel, "Jesus came preaching." The common people heard him gladly, following him wherever he went, so eager to hear him preach they left him little time to rest or be alone with his disciples. They went away saying they had never heard anything like this. His enemies were enraged because there was a power in his preaching which they could not understand or duplicate even though they were the official representatives of the religious establishment. The reason for all of this is that Jesus preached the good news about God in a way that made it possible for those who heard him to encounter God for themselves. If we follow the example of Jesus, every sermon will leave those who hear it in the presence of God.

A young woman wrote to me about how this had happened to her.

> I want you to know how much your sermons have meant to me in the last few months. When I came to Foundry my life had fallen apart—a messy divorce, unhappiness in my job, several medical problems, and a general feeling of hopelessness.
>
> Each week, during your sermon, I could feel something beginning to stir within me. I often found myself crying, but

they were not tears of sadness. I always went out feeling that my
hope had been rekindled. The sermon, "Love Can Fly on
Broken Wings," was especially helpful.

Now that I am feeling better about my life I wanted you to
know how God has used your preaching as a way of coming to
me. I can't explain it, but I know it has happened, and I am
grateful to God—and to you.

I have learned a great deal about preaching as a source
of presence from John Wesley, whose sermons changed
the course of history in the English-speaking world.
Early in my ministry I purchased a secondhand set of the
eight volumes of John Wesley's *Journal,* determined to
read them all the way through. At first I tried to read a
few pages each night before going to bed, but the
volumes are thick, the print is small, and the footnotes
numerous. The result was that I immediately went to
sleep, and I have since recommended these volumes to
friends suffering from insomnia!

Reading them when I was more alert, however, left me
with a profound appreciation for John Wesley and his
Spirit-filled preaching. Sermons in the Church of
England in his time had become lifeless talks or
addresses. But when John Wesley preached he expected
God to make his presence known, and he taught his
Methodist preachers to have the same expectation. In a
letter to a friend, he said, "Nor is it a little advantage as to
the next part of the service to hear a preacher whom you
know to live as he speaks, speaking the genuine gospel of
present salvation through faith, wrought in the heart by
the Holy Ghost. . . . And this you hear done in the most
clear, plain, simple, unaffected language, yet with an
earnestness becoming the importance of the subject and
with the demonstration of the Spirit." Demonstration of
the Holy Spirit is ultimately what preaching is all about.

I have learned over the years that preaching which demonstrates the Holy Spirit involves my total being. It is not something I can put in a compartment of my existence and bring out as needed. My physical and emotional condition, my prayer life, my relationships, my hobbies, my intellectual growth, the way I work and the things I do for fun all profoundly affect the way I preach.

After making her debut at the Metropolitan Opera, a young soprano talked about an important discovery she had made. She had found that her whole body, not just her voice, was the instrument for her singing. Then she talked about some of the things she was doing, such as jogging and dieting, to keep her physical being "tuned up" for making the best possible music. While listening to her, I understood in a new way the totality of the minister's involvement in the act of preaching. Our entire being is the instrument God uses to communicate his Word. I have had a struggle with this fact, because there are areas of my life I would like to enclose in thick concrete walls and keep separate for myself. But my preaching does not ring true until I knock down the walls and bring my total self into the preaching experience.

I have also learned that my preaching does not ring true unless it is deeply rooted in Scripture. It is not without reason that the Bible is often called the inspired Word of God. It is inspired, in the first place, because the books of the Bible describe certain unique events through which God has chosen to reveal himself in a decisive and definitive way. The supreme event for Christians is Jesus the Christ. Because of the uniqueness of this event in giving meaning to all levels of our existence, the Bible provides a unique source of guidance and inspiration from God. In the second place, those who wrote the Bible were inspired persons. This does not necessarily mean that they were infallible, but it does mean that their powers of thought and inspiration were far above the ordinary. The intensity of their faith in God made it possible for him to use them as channels for communicating his presence to others.

The importance of the Bible as history and the beauty of the Bible as literature are often emphasized. But the Bible is far more than history or literature. The value of the Bible as a guide to the good life is widely recognized, but the Bible is more than a guidebook on morality. As a record of the special acts of God written by inspired persons, the Bible can be read like any other book, but we soon discover that it is not like any other book. Because of its special nature, God is able to use the occasion of our reading of the Bible to reveal his immediate presence in life-giving and life-transforming ways.

The two men who walked with Jesus on the road to Emmaus made this discovery. "Did not our hearts burn within us while he talked to us on the road, while he opened to us the scriptures?" (Luke 24:32). An Ethiopian government official discovered this while reading a passage from Isaiah. When Philip interpreted the passage for him, the official became aware of the presence of the Spirit and requested immediate baptism (Acts 8:26-39). Augustine, Francis of Assisi, John Wesley, and countless others changed radically after encountering God through the reading of the Bible. "By the reading of Scripture," said Thomas Merton, "I am so renewed that all nature is renewed around me and within me. . . . The whole world is suddenly charged with the glory of God and I feel fire and music in the earth beneath my feet."

A sermon that has grown from biblical seed can be filled with this same glory. This does not mean working up a good idea for a sermon and then adding Bible passages to give it flavor. Ralph Waldo Emerson noticed a curious building in the process of construction in New Hampshire. When he had the opportunity, he asked a workman about the architect. "There isn't any architect," the man replied. "We're just building the building. Next week a man is coming up from Boston to put some architecture into it." On several occasions I have built a sermon and put some Bible into it afterward, but I always regretted it later. My best preaching has always been biblical preaching, working with a text and living with a text until the sermon literally grows out of it.

The excitement generated by God's presence in the preaching event has been an important part of my ministry from the beginning. But the bishop's charge at my ordination also included responsibility for Holy Communion. This is now the place where some of the most revolutionary changes are occurring in my life because of my growing awareness of the real presence of Christ here in the sacrament of the Eucharist. Until recently there has been what one scholar calls "a deplorable depreciation of the sacraments among nearly all the churches of contemporary Protestantism." This is reflected in the experience of many ministers who report that attendance invariably drops on Communion Sundays. But this situation has been changing in recent years as more of us discover the power of this wondrous meal as a source of sustenance for our souls and bodies.

The first three Gospels all agree that on the day before his death, Jesus sent two of his disciples into Jerusalem to make preparations for the traditional Passover meal. In the evening he gathered with the disciples in a simply furnished upper room. During the meal he took bread, blessed it, broke it, and distributed it to the disciples, saying, "Take, eat; this is my body." He took a cup of wine, gave thanks and gave it to them. As they drank it, he said, "This is my blood of the covenant, which is poured out for many" (Matt. 26:26-28).

These words clearly refer to the sacrificial death of Jesus, the death which gives life to others by opening up a new and living way to God. But they also refer to the possibility of our sharing in his life, taking his life into ourselves, experiencing in our own lives the power generated by his sacrificial death. In the sixth chapter of John's Gospel Jesus talks about this. "I am the living bread which came down from heaven," he said. "If any one eats of this bread, he will live for ever; and the bread which I shall give for the life of the world is my flesh" (6:51). Just as Nicodemus had taken the words *born again* in a literal sense, some of those with Jesus took his words about eating his flesh literally and asked, "How can this man give us his flesh to eat?" (6:52).

The discourse which follows shows how eating the flesh of Jesus and drinking his blood means becoming identified with him in his essential nature through the sacrament. "He who eats my flesh and drinks my blood abides in me, and I in him" (6:56). By eating the bread and drinking the wine of the Eucharist, we symbolize our desire to identify with Christ and receive eternal life from him. "As the living Father sent me, and I live because of the Father, so he who eats me will live because of me. . . . he who eats this bread will live for ever" (John 6:57-58).

The Christian community has never been able to agree on *how* Christ becomes present through the bread and wine, but many of us agree that it is real presence. By opening ourselves at the center of our being to receive this real presence we are healed and nourished by the power and love of God. This is not something we can fully explain, but it is something we know with increasing certainty.

It is difficult for us to find words to describe what it is like to receive new life through this real presence of Christ in the sacrament. Elsie Karo, our television producer, had an experience after surgery which reflects my own experience with the sacrament.

When thinking about the blood of Christ as it is presented in Communion, I could not help thinking of the modern practice of giving blood by transfusion. While one doesn't drink it, the blood is definitely taken into the body in a life giving way.

After recent surgery I had a vivid experience of this type of life-receiving from a blood transfusion. All day in recovery my only conscious feeling was of an awful coldness—in the middle of summer. Nothing seemed to bring warmth to my body. I was inert and completely uninterested in anything going on about me. I finally was aware that there was a search going on for the proper kind of blood. There were tests. I was also aware of a timing of two hours which seemed to be the time taken for the careful dripping of this blood into my veins.

Suddenly I felt warmth pour over me right out to my fingertips and to the ends of my toes. I seemed to come up from the bottom of the sea. I felt like smiling, greeting someone. I opened my eyes. The first thing I did was to find a clock—this seemed to relate me to my own world. I was amazed that it was nearly midnight and I was elated to think I was alive and warm and happy. Then I saw the doctor and couldn't help joking with him about keeping such awful hours. Surely he should be home by now. I heard him say, "Now I can go home." So everything was all right.

Later I felt that I'd give anything I owned to find that stranger whose blood had brought this warmth—this life, itself, to me. Now I walk the streets grateful to some unknown person whose very blood flows in my veins and contributes to my daily joy. This is a debt I can never repay.

Surely, Christ chose a marvelous symbol of himself when he suggested that his friends remember him with the wine which stood for the life-giving quality of his own blood.

In recent years this transfusion or infusion of Christ into my being through the Eucharist has become vital to my existence. To put it another way, I have discovered that my inner being needs this soul food just as my physical body needs physical food to survive. I am receiving Communion at least twice a week now, and I am also giving much more time and attention to the words in my ordination vow about distributing the sacraments, because I want to share my experience of the real presence of Christ with my community.

"Take thou authority as an elder in the Church to preach the Word of God, and to administer the holy Sacraments in the congregation." I could not know at the time the bishop spoke these words over me how much of my life would be invested in these two things, but my enthusiasm for both continues to grow. A magazine once described my preaching as "preaching on tiptoe." This phrase came from a friend who sat behind me during a worship service. He said, "Do you realize that you are always up on your toes when you are preaching?" Another friend, after reading the article, asked me, "What does it mean to preach on tiptoe?" The best answer I can give is that it means preaching (and receiving the sacrament!) with the full expectation that God will come and make his presence known.

6
Television

Our television series on "The Life and Teaching of Jesus" had been on the air for several months in Indianapolis when the station took us off one Saturday in order to show the state basketball tournament. The people of Indiana love their basketball, so the station management was surprised when the telephone switchboard lit up with protest calls. They still talk about one angry man who said to the operator: "Where in the hell is the teachings of Jesus?" Then, before an explanation could be given, he continued, "Get that damn basketball game off the air and put Jesus on."

I never met that man, but I would like to. He represents for me the vast number of persons in our nation who are hungry for God. He is also a reminder of the effectiveness of television as a medium for communicating authentic spirituality.

When we went on the air with that first series on "The Life and Teaching of Jesus," I never dreamed the program would continue to appear on television every week for more than twenty years. Now, after investing a major portion of my life here, I am more convinced than ever of the value of this medium, certain that if the apostle Paul had the opportunity to preach today, he would use television to share the unsearchable riches of Christ with the world.

From the beginning Christianity has been an evangelistic faith, committed to the task of sharing God's good news with the whole world. Jesus sent the first disciples out to preach the gospel in fields where the harvest was plentiful. "Go therefore and make disciples of all nations," he said. "And you shall be my witnesses in Jerusalem and in all Judea and Samaria and to the end of the earth" (Matt. 28:19; Acts 1:8). The early church took this seriously, even to the point of suffering martyrdom when necessary. Now, more than ever, the need is great and the opportunities are available for us to witness for Christ.

There are many ways of doing this, but proclamation and teaching (the *kerygma* and *didachē* of the New Testament) are still among the most effective. Television offers unlimited possibilities for both. I have been impressed with the penetrating power of television and astounded by the numbers of persons it touches. Our program reaches into homes, hospitals, prisons, military installations, retirement homes, and many unexpected places. We received a letter, for example, from a fire department whose members gather to watch the program and complain if a fire interrupts their viewing. Religious programs ordinarily receive low ratings, but even low ratings mean that thousands of persons are tuned in, many of whom never attend church or make any other effort to focus their attention on God.

Even more impressive than the wide coverage of television is its power to precipitate genuine religious experiences. The same series on the life of Jesus which caused the angry Indianapolis viewer to protest brought in the following letter from the wife of a physician:

> I thought I was a Christian but when I started watching you a year or so ago, I realized you had something I didn't have. I decided I wanted that more than anything else in the whole world.
>
> I could never find enough words to tell you what I feel right now. The tears of relief and release gushed forth from my soul today as you talked about the Gospel of John and I realized that *now* I know what you're talking about! *God* loves *me! Even me!* And his love is perfect and eternal. I could go on and on. . . . I feel a compelling urgency to love others now as he loves me.

Imagine being born again while watching a television program! Her letter and others like it have impressed me with the way God can use television as an instrument of grace.

It all began for me when I joined the faculty of The American University in Washington, D.C. Members of the local council of churches, the university, and Channel 7 (the ABC station in Washington) had been talking about the possibility of initiating a college-credit course in religion. After agreeing to work on the project I decided "The Life and Teaching of Jesus" would be the best possible subject for the first series. But how to present it on television? Ours was to be the first college-credit religion course ever offered on a commercial television station, so there were no models to follow. We wanted to make the program as spiritually authentic and intellectually appealing as possible, but we also wanted it to be good television. To attain these high goals has been difficult because television production is enormously expensive. Even with the station donating the public service time to the university for educational purposes, there are still large production costs. Now, after more than twenty years, the financial problem is still with us, but we have been able to pull together art reproductions, film footage, recorded music, artifacts from the Holy Land, and other visual resources to illuminate the message of the Bible. The two "Emmys" we have won from the local chapter of the National Academy of Television Arts and Sciences mean a great deal to me because they represent the recognition of what we have done by the industry itself.

The first sign that we were moving in the right direction came in an unexpected way. After the first few shows had aired, I announced that I would be at the Washington Cathedral on a certain Saturday afternoon to meet anyone who would like to talk about the program. When I arrived at the Cathedral on the announced date I found that special police had been called to direct the traffic. At that moment I knew we had a winner! Over the years since then I have compiled many program ideas which I would like to try, but we have kept our same basic format for the "Bible Telecast."

Every year we select a theme such as "The Life and Teaching of Jesus," "An Introduction to the New Testament," "The Sermon on the Mount," "Love and Marriage," "The Presence of God," "Through Death to Life," or "Where Your Treasure Is." Working through the summer, I choose and research the biblical passages which will help us develop the theme. A study guide is written, artwork is collected, and musical selections are screened. The taping of each series begins early in the fall, and from that time on producing a weekly television program is like running a dairy farm. The cows are there and have to be milked. The air time is there every week and has to be filled. Many talented persons have helped us with production through the years, but Elsie Karo and Audree Bauman have been the ones who have held things together from the beginning. Each week I meet with Elsie and share with her the ideas and insights arising out of my work with the biblical text. As the producer, she then pulls together the kind of material which will give the program on-the-air appeal. Audree is the coordinator, bringing all the pieces of the program and all the people involved into a coherent whole.

The officials of Channel 7 in Washington have not only given us outstanding directors through the years, but they have also provided the technical and moral support which have made the program possible. Heavy criticism has been directed at television for contributing to the deterioration of cultural and aesthetic standards, but I have found many dedicated persons in the industry who are eager to serve the community in creative ways when given the opportunity.

But that's the problem! The church hasn't given them the opportunity. In the area of religion nearly all programming is cast in the mold of the "electronic church." This is valuable to many persons, but there is a need for alternatives, especially programs that are intellectually appealing and spiritually authentic. By intellectually appealing I mean helping the viewer search for the truth with an eager and open mind. Our program, for example, would not interest the person whose car passed me on the highway proudly displaying the bumper sticker, "God said it. I believe it. That settles it." By spiritually authentic I mean conveying religious truth in a way which encourages viewers to seek affirmation of their own experience through the inner presence of the Holy Spirit. "It is the Spirit himself bearing witness with our spirit that we are children of God" (Rom. 8:16).

This is what has impressed me most during my years on television. This life-transforming Spirit of God can be communicated and shared through this medium with countless persons, many of whom are not formally religious in any way. Hearing the Word has the effect of strengthening the individual's relationship with God by evoking the Holy Spirit within. One person said to me,

> For many years I have been feeling restless and empty. My life didn't seem to be going anywhere. I had an affair which ended up hurting everyone involved. I was drinking too much. Watching your program over the past few months has made it clear to me that God is the only solution to my problems. Your program on "The One Thing Needful" was especially helpful because I realized that I had no place in my life for the only important thing. I still have times of restlessness and depression, but God is in the picture now and that makes all the difference.

A woman wrote about a similar experience.

> I'm sure your program on "The Pearl of Great Price" was put on the air just for me! I stopped going to church several years ago and didn't realize how much I missed God until the recent death of my father. I needed God then but didn't know how to find him. One illustration you used in talking about the pearl was especially helpful. You quoted a mother whose son had made a terrible mess out of his life. She said to him, "Son, you have put God out of the center of your life, and this is the cause of all your trouble." I knew immediately that these words were spoken just for me. Thank you for helping me find God again.

Another viewer writes about freedom.

> Your message of freedom in Jesus Christ has been a special blessing to me as I am one of those who grew up in a legalistic

church and really wound up, before giving up religion, a
self-loathing hypocrite. About five years ago I accidentally
tuned in your program and for days couldn't get your words
out of my mind that "God loves me, he accepts me, and all I
have to do is accept him." Well—I accepted him, finally, and
praise God! My life is a whole new ball game!

Many persons speak about moving into faith out of a position of doubt.

Thank you for the good news you have conveyed to me. I was
in a situation of non-belief and trying to live by reason alone. I
believe God spoke to me through your lectures and discussions. I no longer feel that "foxhole" religion is invalid but
rather that God uses those suffering/dying situations to unite
us with the Son's Spirit, who is one with the Father, "Through
Death to Life" gave me an appreciation for the entire life
process, including death and aging. "New Life in the New
Testament" opened my eyes to the contemporary message to
be found in the Bible, particularly the power and excitement of
the Spirit of Christ as witnessed by Paul and the early
Christians.

Others who began as doubters do not yet feel this
comfortable with the biblical message. While reading the
following poignant letter, I found myself feeling grateful
for the persistence with which God seeks the lost and the
lonely.

I have been watching your TV program since you began. I
rather enjoy the program, but often wonder what would
happen if you ever had an honest agnostic in your group?
One time you asked the question of the class, "What do you
think or feel when you think of God?" I thought and realized
that when I think of God my first reaction is one of fear. Then
logic comes to my rescue and I realize that no one really knows
if there is a God. No one can prove it one way or another.
I have lived a good many years, but I still recall how bitterly
unhappy my childhood was because of the cruel unkind
treatment I received at the hands of professed Christian people.

As a young adult I learned early to dissemble. I went to church and went through the motions. After I retired from business I stopped altogether.

Now when I run into a person who is very devout and sure I get across the road and go in the opposite direction as fast as my legs and years permit.

I shall continue to watch and listen and I wish you well, but I do not get any message nor can I find any real logic in the Bible.

The fact that he and many others like him "will continue to watch" kindles my enthusiasm for television and my desire to keep this channel of communication open. This is why we have created a nonprofit organization called Bauman Bible Telecasts. Gifted and dedicated persons are sharing their knowledge and experience on the staff and board of trustees to provide a supporting structure for this ministry. As a result, we have been able to provide video tapes to other television stations and to the Armed Forces overseas network. Films are in continuous circulation to hundreds of churches for Bible-study groups, and to prisons and retirement homes. Audio cassettes, filmstrips, and detailed study guides are also available. A radio version of the program is prepared each week, and there are special services planned for the handicapped. The purpose of the organization is very simple—to share the timeless Word of God using modern methods of communication.

Unfortunately, a television ministry is very expensive and money is always a problem. I have wished so often that the church was more involved in television, offering more alternatives to the current programs, but I know that the main problem is the expense involved. As a public service program, we have never appealed for funds on the air. However, we are creating a group of supporters who provide the financial resources necessary for our continued existence. When persons ask what they can do to help, I am quick to remind them of the motto of every college student when writing to parents: "When you care enough to send the very best, send money!" I do not know what the answer to all of this is for the church as a whole, but I do know that television is one of the most effective ways of communicating God's Word in the modern world and deserves our financial support.

On one occasion a young man who was serving as an apprentice on the technical crew asked me, "If you had ten seconds to tell a person what is really important in life, what would you say?" The striking thing about the incident was that we were in our final countdown before going on the air and I literally had ten seconds. Without time to think about it, I replied, "To find God, and having found him, to love him."

Reflecting on this later, I thought about how typical it was of television where split-second timing is so crucial and where the ability to react to the unexpected is so essential. Through the years we have had hollowed-out Easter eggs pop like hand grenades under the heat of the lights, clocks stop in the middle of a program, props fall over at just the wrong time, and misleading time cues given when there was no chance to recover. There are also the bloopers. The one which I would give the most to have back occurred during a program on the kingdom of God when I talked about obedience to the will of God as the way to live in the kingdom. My last sentence was blurted out in the panic of running out of time just before going off the air: "The most important thing in life is to live in joyful disobedience to the will of God!" On another occasion, still fondly remembered by engineers at the station, a camera caught on fire during a program, but we shouldn't have been surprised. The topic for that day was the coming of the Holy Spirit.

One of the images frequently used by Jesus in his teaching was the sowing of seed. Among other things, he was telling us that if we will be faithful in the sowing of the seed, God will give the growth. This has had special meaning for me since visiting the village in Switzerland from which my grandparents emigrated to the United States. I found out that "Bauman" originally meant the "man who sows the seed." On the family coat-of-arms a farmer with a sash full of golden seed is scattering it over the waiting earth. For over twenty years I have experienced the joy of sowing the seed of God's Word on television. I have no way of knowing where most of the seed lands, but I know that God's life in the seed will give it growth.

7
Confrontation

Learning how to confront social evil and oppression has been the most difficult part of my ministry. Because of a deep-seated emotional need to be liked, I avoided this kind of confrontation for many years. When my conscience and circumstances forced me to take a stand, I was unable to cope with the stress and my health broke down. Now, after years of struggling with this, I have learned a great deal about the prophetic dimension of Christian discipleship. But I still do not enjoy it.

The first major crisis came with the racial integration of our church. That this was so is ironic because at Foundry Church we are very proud of our close association with Abraham Lincoln. He attended our church often while he was in the White House and on one occasion paid one hundred and fifty dollars to become a Life Director of the Foreign Missionary Society of the

Methodist Episcopal Church. The certificate he received is on display in our chapel.

But our Lincoln connection did not prevent us from being a segregated congregation as late as 1964 when I arrived on the scene as minister. Even though the church was located in a predominantly black neighborhood, there were no black members. Although we did not turn blacks away from our worship service, some of our members made them feel unwelcome. As one member said to me, "I don't like going down to Sunday school and rubbing up against niggers."

It would be hypocritical for me to be judgmental toward others on this issue, because I had been a member of Foundry twenty years earlier and had done nothing about the situation. During the Second World War, I was stationed briefly with the Navy in Washington. While attending worship at Foundry, I was so impressed with the alto soloist that I joined the choir and married her. Audree and I feel especially close to the Foundry community because we met there, were married there, and eighteen years after our wedding came back to minister there. But we had raised no voice of protest about the segregation.

I would like to be able to say that the change which has occurred in the church is the result of daring prophetic sermons I preached on the subject. Unfortunately, I did not have the courage to confront the issue in such a direct way. Instead, I quietly let it be known that I was very unhappy with the situation and hoped that there were black persons in the neighborhood who would want to join the church. Soon afterward, a black family came to me seeking membership. I joyfully received them, naïvely unaware of the hornet's nest I was stirring up by doing so.

It is important that I do not give a false impression of our congregation. The majority of members were supportive of what I was doing and wanted Foundry to be an inclusive church. But there were a few persons who were struggling with this issue and felt very threatened. Emotionally, I needed to be liked by everyone, but that was impossible in such a situation. Anxiety, fear, anger, and hostility all surfaced quickly in a few of our members, and we suffered a great deal in the next few years. I received threatening letters and phone calls. Some members withheld their financial support and others withdrew their membership. One woman told me that when there were six blacks in the choir, she was leaving the church. A year later she kept her promise.

Matters reached crisis proportions when I received a call from a United States senator's office asking for the use of our building for a subcommittee hearing on racial violence. A hundred black young people from the ghettos of New York, Philadelphia, and Washington had been invited to attend. It seemed like a good opportunity for our church to become involved, so I made arrangements for the meeting. Unfortunately, the speaker scheduled for the first morning failed to appear and the young people became so angry they took over the church for several hours, refusing to let any white persons in and threatening to burn the building down. The story made the front page of the evening papers and precipitated a crisis for our congregation. A church board meeting had already been scheduled for that evening to discuss the whole issue. Several members arrived with newspapers under one arm and the church's *Book of Discipline* under the other, resolved to put an end to all this. It was a heated session and I felt like another minister who had suffered a heart attack shortly after finding himself in a similar situation. The leading layman of the church called on him in the hospital and said, "At the board meeting last night a resolution was introduced expressing a desire for your speedy recovery. It passed 43-37."

Even though our congregation was similarly split on many of the specific issues arising out of our predicament, we learned how to love one another in a new way as a result of our struggle. Most of those who opposed integration were good people, torn between Christian conscience and emotional patterns deeply rooted in their childhood. Change was painful, but there were many times when we felt the presence of God's Spirit in healing ways as we moved through this period of growth together.

On one Sunday morning, early in the process when emotions were especially high, I announced that I would be joining one of the controversial civil rights marches scheduled to pass in front of the church that afternoon. I made it clear that if anyone wished to join me I would be pleased, but I did not apply any pressure. I simply wanted to keep the congregation informed. About twenty persons came to the event, one of them a prominent leader in the church who felt very uneasy about integration. His participation was particularly moving because he was in the last months of the same illness which killed Lou Gehrig, and it was extremely difficult for him to walk. After telling him how grateful I was for his coming, I kept asking along the route of march if he didn't want me to call a taxi for him. But he insisted on walking the whole way, saying, "I want to march with my young pastor to show everyone that I support him." That was one of the most healing gifts of grace I have ever received.

It took several years, but we have now experienced the joy of being an inclusive church. The event which made us realize how far we had come together was the assassination of Martin Luther King, Jr. He and I had been in graduate school together, studying for our doctoral degrees under the same major professor. There is no way to describe my feelings on the day he was killed, especially after the riots broke out in the area around our church and brought the tragedy close to home. Looking out of the church window, I thought the whole city was going up in flames. By this time we had started a preschool program for poverty-level families in the neighborhood, and I was especially worried about what was happening to those families. Having sent the church staff home, I remained with the children whose parents had been unable to get through to pick them up. One of my vivid memories of the worst hours of the rioting is reading stories to several small black children, all of us frightened by the smoke and sirens outside in the streets.

The next Sunday we came to church with soldiers in riot gear lining the streets. It was Palm Sunday, and many soldiers had placed palm branches in the netting of their helmets. During the worship service we thought about the Roman soldiers in Jerusalem on that first Palm Sunday when Jesus entered the city only a few days before his sacrificial death. I remembered the words in Bernard Shaw's play about Joan of Arc, "Must then a Christ perish in every generation to save those who have no imagination?" As a congregation we thought about how far we had come down the road together on this issue, and we realized in a new way how important it had become to identify with Christ in breaking down the walls of hostility and estrangement.

Part of the price I paid for all this was the deterioration of my health which forced me to deal with my inability to handle confrontation. The solution came partly on an intellectual level and partly on an emotional level.

Intellectually, I experienced a major breakthrough when I realized that the prophetic ministry of Jesus was motivated by love. This insight came to me one hot summer day while sitting in the shade of an olive tree near the temple area in old Jerusalem. My New Testament was open to the incident in which Jesus confronted the dishonest money changers and merchants there in the temple during the last week of his life. I thought about the anger and hatred directed at him as a result. His action was both a challenge and threat to the religious leaders, challenging their authority and threatening their economic security. The Gospels tell us how they immediately made plans to destroy him.

I asked myself why Jesus had done this. Somehow the answers I had previously learned, such as the desire of Jesus to fulfill Old Testament prophecy, did not seem adequate. Then I began to picture the scene. Many humble poor people regularly came to Jerusalem to worship in the temple. Since this was the season of Passover there would be more worshipers than usual. The opportunity to praise God in his holy temple was a highlight in their lives and many of them had been looking forward to it for many months. But what happened when they arrived at the temple? Their own religious leaders were "ripping them off," cheating them of their hard-earned money and robbing them of the anticipated joy of their religious pilgrimage. Suddenly I realized that when Jesus made the whip of cords and moved in on the situation he was motivated by his love for these people who were unable to help themselves. The anger of Jesus was rooted in compassion, and the confrontation with social evil was motivated by love.

This insight has been very helpful to me intellectually. Compassion has always been easier for me than confrontation, but now I see that they belong together. By keeping my attention focused on the victims, those being hurt and exploited, it is much easier for me to confront social evil.

Emotionally, I have also made progress, partly by learning to recognize and express my feelings more honestly, partly through discovering new sources of healing. The progress I have made became obvious to me when I recently became embroiled in an angry confrontation on the issue of gay rights.

The whole thing started when I presented a television program and preached a sermon on "The Gay Life" as part of a series on love and marriage. As time for the TV taping approached I worked hard to prepare myself, covering the books on a long reading list and talking with numerous individuals—straights and gays, psychologists and psychiatrists, ministers and members of their congregations, men and women, young and old, Christians and Jews. I prayed and worked with the biblical passages on this topic. Then I presented the TV program and preached the sermon, emphasizing how the Spirit of Christ will enable us to express compassion and acceptance toward the homosexuals among us.

The intensity of the anger I encountered took me by surprise. The deep primal feelings many of us have on this subject have been so repressed that when we are confronted with them they break out like a pent-up storm. Some people actually wept in their fury, others called me names and became abusive. We went through another period of losing church members and financial support because of disagreement with me. Long letters continue to arrive, usually filled with biblical quotations "proving" that I am wrong. Many of the letters are unsigned. Most difficult to handle, however, has been the embarrassment of some of my friends who still love me but obviously feel I have made a mistake by speaking out on this issue. Comparisons with the earlier civil rights movement are inevitable. It is not surprising gay rights advocates are linking arms these days and singing, "We shall overcome."

The thing that impressed me most, however, and moved me deeply was the discovery of the incredible amount of suffering experienced by homosexuals in the past and present. For centuries the church refused to serve them Holy Communion. They were often stripped, castrated, marched through the streets, and executed. In Hitler's Germany they were exterminated by the thousands in the furnaces and gas chambers. And in our own country, gay persons have been disowned by their families, ridiculed and rejected by society, and made the object of cruel jokes. They have been barred from jobs and housing, often living in loneliness and seeking companionship in sordid places and in dangerous ways. How many young people are there who lie awake at night, terrified by their confused feelings about themselves with no place to turn for help? Is this one of the reasons for the alarming increase in adolescent suicide?

The following anecdotes are from incidents reported by Dr. Howard Brown in his book *Familiar Faces, Hidden Lives.*

One young man told his parents he was a homosexual. His mother said, "Son, I have made only one mistake in my life." "What is it?" he asked. "I should have had an abortion when I was pregnant with you," she replied.

From that time she spoke to her friends as if her son were dead.

A high-school boy told his parents he was gay. On his graduation day his father gave him his graduation gift—an envelope with a one-way train ticket and twenty-five dollars. "Start packing," he said. He drove the boy to the station in total silence and said to him as he got out of the car, "I never want to hear from you again."

I would like to believe that these are exceptional situations. They are not. It has become clear to me that homosexuals are among the most ridiculed and rejected persons of our society, as they have been for centuries. It is also clear that Jesus came to minister to the ridiculed and rejected. He ministered to them so completely that he became identified with them and was ultimately crucified "outside the walls" as one of the ridiculed and rejected himself. He came to bring God's love to them, to tell them that they are loved, that they are accepted. I am convinced that those of us who are in the church, the Body of Christ, are called to offer this same Christlike love to those in our present society who are ridiculed and rejected because of their homosexuality.

Part of the reason for the uncertainty many of us are feeling on this matter is that we are facing the issue on a level which is not discussed in the Bible. I cannot find any examples in the Bible of the lifelong homosexual condition which we now call "constitutional homosexuality." Furthermore, there is no mention of the possibility of a permanent, committed relationship of love existing between two persons of the same sex. This is a very different thing from the promiscuous relationship to which homosexuals are often driven by their rejection from society, relationships which are so destructive to the individuals involved and to the structures of family and community life. The biblical writers do condemn promiscuity, as well as homosexual acts which are related to violence, idolatry, and lust, but it is not the homosexual condition that is condemned. It is the expression of homosexual (and heterosexual!) desires in violent and exploitative ways that is forbidden.

But what if it is true that many persons are homosexual by nature and have no intention of using their sexuality to exploit others? Should they be condemned along with the others? What about those who believe they are born this way? The majority of homosexuals with whom I have spoken are convinced that this is a condition of their nature and not something they acquired. As one older man wrote me, "There is no 'cause' for it. It is inborn, same as the color of eyes or hair. You learn to conceal, cover up and 'act' at an early age. But it is so lonesome!"

It is difficult to refute this conviction that so many homosexuals have about themselves when there is so little reliable evidence to the contrary. In search of some light on this subject, I read many psychological studies only to find members of the medical profession in wide disagreement with one another. The American Psychiatric Association has removed homosexuality from the category of mental illness, although not without a heated debate which continues in the profession. Everyone seems to agree, however, that even if this is an acquired characteristic, the forging of our sexual orientation occurs at a very early age, thus raising questions about the individual's responsibility for his or her condition.

The first thing many persons think of when the subject of homosexuality is mentioned is the molesting of children. This stereotype is especially unjust, because the vast majority of people who abuse children sexually are heterosexual. If we are going to condemn a whole class of people for this crime, then those of us who are straight must carry the burden. Actually all responsible persons, both gay and straight, condemn every form of child abuse and support rigid laws to protect children. Persons with emotional difficulties that focus on the young should never be permitted to inflict their pathology on children. Condemning homosexuals for this problem, however, is not only unjustified, but diverts attention from the emotionally ill persons who constitute the real danger.

Many questions remain unanswered, but some things are clear. There is absolutely no justification, for example, in denying homosexual persons their basic human and civil rights because of their sexual orientation. At its best the American political system has always defended the individual's rights in such areas as housing, employment, and education. Many times this defense has been a costly one! It will be tragic if we have to go through a bitter civil rights struggle to establish the rights of homosexuals in our society, but if such a struggle is necessary it will be waged and it will be won by those who stand with Jefferson, Lincoln, and countless others who believe in the soundness and greatness of the American dream.

I am also convinced that God is expecting the redemptive community of the church to include homosexuals. Even while we continue to learn more about homosexuality and the implications of this particular life-style, we welcome homosexuals into the community of Christ. We love them as persons. We stand beside them and share the burden of pain which society has laid upon them. We listen to them and learn from them. To those who are in greatest pain, we follow the example of

Jesus and make ourselves most available to them. With the ridiculed and rejected, we share the ridiculed and rejected Christ who becomes Lord and Savior of all. In this way we grow together into the wholeness of life which God offers to all who love him and accept his presence as the source of life.

A medical doctor who spent most of his life providing good medical care for the poor was a homosexual who "came out" and suffered terribly because of it. Talking about it on one occasion, he said that because of the ridicule and rejection he experienced in the church he became an agnostic. When he died recently of a heart attack, he was still an agnostic. The church drove him away.

Another homosexual man wrote a letter from a federal penitentiary to a priest who had befriended him. He said, "If I could have found some years ago the acceptance and the advice that you have given, I probably would never have ended up here in prison. I wanted to enter the priesthood as a young man but the rejection and ridicule I was offered by my church led to my estrangement and embitterment. My sexuality is not something I asked for, it is something I grew up with, something I have always had. All I ask is your prayers and your love."

On one occasion Jesus spoke in a completely nonjudgmental way about eunuchs "who have been so from birth" (Matt. 19:12). This reference to a situation similar to constitutional homosexuality is important, because in the time of Jesus such persons were excluded from the religious community. But the first group of outcasts called into the early church by the action of the Holy Spirit is represented by the Ethiopian eunuch in the eighth chapter of Acts. The eunuch accepted

Christ, received baptism by water and the Spirit, and became a full member of Christ's people. In this way the Holy Spirit led the new Christian community to include those who previously had been excluded for sexual reasons. Can we do less than this today and remain faithful to the same Holy Spirit who is our life and our hope?

8
Feelings

As I mentioned earlier, part of the price I paid for learning how to confront social injustice was the deterioration of my health. Part of the reward I have received is the growing awareness of God's presence as the source of all health and wholeness of life. Looking back over the process through which this awareness has come to me, I realize how essential it has been for me to learn how to recognize and deal with my true feelings.

First, I suffered from a series of gastrointestinal problems. This went on for a considerable period of time, robbing me of the pleasure of eating because I knew that eating would lead to distress and pain. If only I had known then what I know now about the gastrointestinal system as a trigger point for stress-induced illness. Assuming the problem was physical, I went to many doctors for seemingly endless tests and diagnostic studies, many of which were more distressing than the illness! The doctors could find nothing wrong, but this was little comfort because the problems persisted.

Then I developed the additional problem of chronic fatigue. No matter how early I went to bed or how long I slept, I woke up tired and remained tired throughout the day. At times in my study I would have to lie on the floor for an hour in order to get the strength to sit at my desk and work. This led to another round of tests and the diagnosis—hypoglycemia. I felt relieved that it wasn't all "in my head." Furthermore, hypoglycemia, low blood sugar, was definitely the in-disease at the time, and I knew several people who had it.

Slender to begin with, I lost weight on the high protein diet which is part of the treatment. Soon I was looking like a fugitive from a concentration camp. I still had gastrointestinal problems. I was still tired.

At this point Audree called a man she had worked for during our student days in Boston, the director of the New England Deaconess Hospital. Arrangements were soon made for me to spend a week at the Joslin Clinic where the medical staff specialized in blood sugar problems. During that week of rigorous diagnostic tests I can vividly remember sitting with blood sample needles in my arms, working on a sermon I was scheduled to preach the following Sunday on the sufferings of Job. Seldom has my preaching been more authentic! At the end of the week a wise and patient doctor talked with me about my situation. He had come into the room with my medical records under his arm, shaking his head. I expected the worst, but he said, "We see ministers like you in here all the time. There is nothing physically wrong with you, but you will continue to have problems until you learn to deal with the stress and tension of your work." After discussing this at length, he gave me some mild medication and sent me home.

This experience was a gift of grace because it introduced me to a vital unexplored area of my life. Looking back now, I realize that the spiritual experiences I was having couldn't develop further until I had dealt with the repressed feelings which were blocking the movement of God's Spirit within me. But how to unblock them? The next major breakthrough occurred during an encounter experience at Kirkridge Retreat Center in the mountains of Pennsylvania.

The event had been advertised as an opportunity for clergy couples to get to know themselves better and thereby strengthen their ministry to others. Audree and I went, not knowing that getting to know ourselves included expressing our feelings while lying on a mat in the center of a circle of perfect strangers. Neither Audree nor I had ever done anything like this and I couldn't believe it when Audree, a very private person, was the first one in the group to volunteer. When I asked her about it later, she said she knew that if she didn't go first and get it over with she would never have the courage to go through with it.

When my turn came, I was shocked and embarrassed because I started to cry almost at once and I couldn't stop the tears. After all, grown men don't cry. Ministers don't cry! But I was crying. Tears of joy and sorrow and relief were flowing as I began to release the pressure of a lifetime of repressed feelings. Later the same day I found myself releasing tension in another unexpected way. A young minister's wife who had repressed her feelings of resentment toward her father was finding it difficult to express them. She had mentioned earlier how good she had felt on one occasion when she had thrown an egg at her husband in a moment of anger. I told her that I had always had a fantasy about throwing eggs at people, and that I would be glad to pretend I was her father and let her throw eggs at me, if she would let me throw eggs at her. A short time later as I stood in the midst of flying eggs I knew that I had entered a new phase of my life. My feelings could no longer be ignored.

Unfortunately, I did not have the opportunity to follow up the Kirkridge experience, and it took several years of reading and searching before I began to understand what was happening to me and how closely related it was to my experience as a child. My mother's parents had a very unhappy marriage which ended in separation while she was still a child. Her father simply abandoned her, moving to a distant part of the country and never contacting her. She never recovered from the devastating effects of this rejection. Her mother was a cold and rigid person, incapable of giving or receiving love. She died shortly after her husband left her and my mother was taken in by relatives. The end result for my mother was a pathological need for love and acceptance along with the inability to receive it when it was offered. During my teen-age years she suffered an emotional breakdown which focused on delusions of persecution. Not only was she certain that no one loved her, but also she was just as sure that they were out to get her. She worked very hard at the tasks of parenthood, loving her husband and children to the best of her ability, but she could never break the chains of her emotional heritage. On more than one occasion she attempted suicide after suggesting that she would be doing my sister and me a favor by taking us with her. Long periods of hospitalization followed each attempt.

As I began to examine my own emotions, I realized that what I had absorbed from her all through my childhood is that being liked and accepted by others is the most important thing in life. Therefore, I related to others on the basis of what I thought they would like for me to be and say and do, and not on the basis of my own true feelings. I was a slave to the desires and opinions of others without even knowing it. This included repressing anger and other feelings which might cause others to dislike me. Repressing the anger was especially destructive because such repression is one of the primary causes of depression.

It is ironic that the need to be liked can cause us to do good things for the wrong reasons. For example, I have always disciplined myself and worked very hard, first at school and then in my profession, as a way of winning the approval of others. Because of this I have accomplished a lot, but I have also missed a great deal of joy. I agree with the man who said, "If I had it to do over, I would pick more daisies."

The desire to win the approval of others has also caused me to live by the rules. A friend once said to me, "You are the most duty-bound person I have ever known." At the time I didn't understand what she was saying. I needed to hear what Zorba the Greek said to his friend: "The trouble with you, boss, is that you don't know how to dance."

These insights have helped liberate me from slavery to this need to be liked by others. But insight alone is not enough. Many of my emotional hang-ups are so deep-seated that it has taken a lot of prayer and a lot of practice to heal the memories and put my life on a new course. This is why the growth group which I joined has contributed so much to my life.

For years after my opening experience at Kirkridge, I felt the need for a therapy group or growth group where

I could learn to deal with my feelings, but nothing felt right until I learned of a group which Elizabeth O'Connor of The Church of The Saviour was starting. Elizabeth combines group leadership skills with the kind of patience and love that are so essential for an authentic growth experience. I was very glad when she accepted me as a member of the group, but when I let it be known around our church, many persons were very upset. One member of our staff said, "My God, if Dr. Bauman can't get it together, what hope is there for the rest of us!" A few years ago this attempt to "pedestal me" would have been very threatening, but this time it merely confirmed the value of the decision I had made.

To my surprise, I became angry during the very first meeting of the group and learned some helpful things about myself in the process. Since then, every meeting has produced some revelation or experience which has contributed to my growth. The first time we gathered we entered into a simple covenant with one other to hold in confidence everything shared in the group and to give the weekly time of meeting a high priority in our schedule. We further agreed to listen carefully to what other persons in the group were saying and then to express our feelings as honestly and directly as possible. The major emphasis was to be upon feelings rather than ideas.

Seldom at a loss for words, I plunged in and began to share what I was feeling. One of the eight persons in the group who had known me before couldn't believe that I would be willing to become vulnerable in this way. Earlier in the evening when he found out that I was to be part of the group he had looked at me in amazement and said, "Extraordinary!" I told the group that this evoked all-too-familiar pedestal feelings in me, feelings of isolation and loneliness. Many people pedestal the minister of a large church, especially a minister who appears regularly on radio and television. I had been taught, I said, as part of my seminary training that ministers are supposed to be friendly with everyone but friends of no one. I talked about how I had no one except Audree with whom I could share my deepest thoughts and feelings and about how difficult this emotional isolation was for me in the midst of my busy schedule. Then I sat back and waited for the strokes I felt I deserved.

But the members of the group did not take the bait. One woman said she couldn't understand how anyone could possibly live in a community for more than a year and not have at least two or three trustworthy and understanding friends. A man in the group said he felt my whole presentation had been an indirect plea for the group to pedestal me. Another quickly agreed, pointing out how I had let everyone know how busy and important I was.

Inwardly reeling under this feedback, I started to feel hurt and angry. They just didn't understand me. They didn't care. But then it began to dawn on me that everything they were saying was true! I began to see how my unconscious need to be liked was causing me to play all kinds of games in my relationship with others. I was appalled when I realized how I had been living. The pain of the revelation continued for many days but along with it came a liberating feeling that an emotional logjam was breaking up and that a burden was somehow being lifted from my shoulders.

With each new group experience my feeling of liberation has grown. This has been directly related to my ability and willingness to recognize my true feelings and deal with them appropriately, although dealing with them appropriately has turned out to be a learning experience in itself. Fortunately, I passed quickly through the letting-it-all-hang-out phase which is so common in emotional therapy. I learned that the ecstasy of my newfound freedom did not give me the right to afflict everyone around me with my raw feelings. I was able to be much more honest and direct in many of my relationships, but I also learned that direct confrontation was not always appropriate. The important thing was to recognize what was happening with my feelings and to avoid repressing them. I often say to myself now, "I'm not playing that old game anymore." Then I decide whether to express my feelings directly in the situation of the moment, to share them later with group members or other trusted friends, or to work them out in other ways such as jogging or music.

I have also learned how important it is to break the chain of destructive feelings which are handed down from one generation to the next. I never knew any of my grandparents because they all died long before I was born. The only material legacy I have received from any of them is one page of a recently discovered letter my mother's mother had written to her. At the top are the words, "Don't bother to read this. It isn't worth your time." This was a wrenching discovery for me, because I had often heard my mother express feelings like that about her own accomplishments. It was material evidence of the way my grandmother's unresolved emotional conflicts and deep feelings of inferiority had determined the shape of my mother's life. My mother, in turn, has handed on to me and my sister a heavy burden of destructive feelings. Unless I am willing to make the effort to break the chain, this burden will be handed on to my children. The emotional pain of parents is "visited upon the children, even to the third and fourth generation," until someone has the courage to strike out in new directions. Someone must confront Pharaoh with the demand for freedom to leave the old life of slavery and move toward the promised land of health and wholeness.

For me the freedom is still a new experience and I have a lot of wilderness ahead of me. But the things I have learned so far have strengthened my spiritual life and my ministry to others. Spiritually, I feel as though I am giving God something authentic to work with when I struggle to recognize true feelings and deal with them honestly. In many ways I feel like the prophet Jeremiah who spoke about a process of breaking down and building up that was going on in his life. But this is so much better than playing games with God and allowing repressed feelings to block the movement of his Spirit within me.

Working with my feelings has also strengthened my ministry to others. I have always tried very hard to be present to others and to go out of my way to help them. Recently I discovered that a lot of this was not only a way of trying to get people to like me, but also a way of running away from my own feelings and burying my true self. Whenever anyone started to get close to me, I quickly turned the conversation back toward them. I also told myself it was selfish and contrary to the Spirit of Christ to spend time thinking about myself. But by doing this I had nothing real to offer the other person in a relationship. All they had to work with was an image I was projecting and not my real self. Adjusting to a new pattern of ministry is difficult after a lifetime of building and projecting an image, but I have found that offering another person more of my authentic self is one of the most loving things I can do.

All of this has given me a new appreciation for Paul's freedom letter to the Galatians. "For freedom Christ has set us free," he says. "Stand fast therefore, and do not submit again to a yoke of slavery" (5:1). Both Paul and the Galatians had their own kinds of slavery from which they were liberated by God's presence in Christ. Mine has been in the form of bondage to unrecognized and unresolved feelings, and I find the taste of freedom exhilarating.

A hundred years ago a group of slaves had been promised emancipation on a certain date. They were so eager not to miss a single moment of that great day that they went up into the mountains so they could see the first rays of the rising sun. They all went, young and old, men and women, the feeble and the strong. I now have the same feeling they had at the moment when they first saw the sun and began to shout and sing, "We're free! We're free! Praise God! We're free."

9
Healing

Not a few eyebrows were raised in surprise when it was announced that Foundry Church would begin holding healing services every Sunday evening. The historic old church had been established during the War of 1812 by the wealthy owner of a Georgetown foundry out of gratitude for "the protection of divine providence" during the British invasion of Washington. It has been marked through the years by distinguished preaching and by dedicated service to the community. But spiritual healing? The whole idea seemed out of place in a church that has always avoided fanaticism. Furthermore, this was a time (the 1960s) when the emphasis in religion was not on inner healing but on caring for the poor and fighting for social justice at the barricades in the streets.

My own anxiety level was raised when an anonymous person called the church office and asked, "When is that

television fellow going to start laying hands on people?"
This was the image we wanted to avoid, but how to do so?
How could we establish a ministry of healing on the
integrity of the New Testament teaching without getting
ourselves involved in fanaticism and exploitation. Even
today, after years spent creating a sound biblical ministry
of spiritual healing, I still find it difficult to convince
people that we are not talking about the kind of
exploitative faith healing so often associated with the
church.

My own interest in this subject was partly motivated by
my personal need for healing, but there was more to it
than this. For many years I had wondered about the
mandate of Jesus to the disciples to preach the gospel *and
heal the sick*. Why had the modern church largely ignored
the second half of this imperative, preaching the gospel
faithfully through the years, but no longer existing as a
community of healing? How could we ignore not only the
example and teaching of Jesus, but also the words of Paul
about "gifts of healing" and other direct statements on
the subject throughout the New Testament?

"Is any among you sick?" asks James. "Let him call for
the elders of the church, and let them pray over him,
anointing him with oil in the name of the Lord; and the
prayer of faith will save the sick man, and the Lord will
raise him up; and if he has committed sins, he will be
forgiven. Therefore confess your sins to one another,
and pray for one another, that you may be healed. The
prayer of a righteous man has great power in its effects"
(James 5:14-16).

I soon found some others who were raising questions
similar to my own, and I suggested that we form a weekly
study group to share our ideas. This initial group
consisted of a medical doctor, a pastoral psychologist,

two clergymen, and several laypersons. At first our attention focused on the experience of one of the group members who had been fighting a successful battle against cancer for years by combining spiritual healing with the best medical therapy available. I was quickly convinced that the things she had learned should be shared with others beyond our small group.

We also spent a lot of time talking about Jesus. Any careful reading of the healing miracles in the Gospels makes it clear that Jesus had insight into the nature of healing that modern medicine has yet to attain. His growing consciousness and knowledge of the power of God, together with his deep compassion, made it possible for him to call forth the faith necessary for healing. He never claimed the healing power for himself, but said to those who had become whole, "Your faith has made you well." He was able to relate himself to persons in such a creative way that they gained the trust and confidence necessary to receive the healing power of God's Spirit within their own spirit. In such typical cases as the demoniac of Gerasa (Mark 5:1-20), the paralytic who was let down through the roof (Mark 2:1-12), the epileptic boy (Mark 9:14-29), and blind Bartimaeus (Mark 10:46-52), the power of Jesus called forth this expectant trust in those who needed to be healed. Furthermore, many of those who had been with Jesus were soon healing the sick in a similar way. The Acts of the Apostles contains clear evidence that the same healing power which had been present in Jesus was present in members of the early Christian community.

These biblical studies kindled our enthusiasm for bringing spiritual healing to our own church, but we still needed a practical way of relating all this to our own experience. The answer came to us when we became involved in a study of psychosomatic medicine. Since then this has been an essential part of my understanding of the nature and purpose of spiritual healing.

We have already seen that the word *psychosomatic* is made up of the two Greek words meaning soul *(psyche)* and body *(soma)*. It reminds us of the profound effect the inner condition of our being has on the health of our body. A direct relationship has been established between our inner condition and many physical complaints such as arthritis, high blood pressure, ulcers, migraine headaches, skin disease, and cancer. Repressed emotions like fear, anger, and guilt can have a devastating effect on our physical well-being.

Early researchers in this field, for example, were impressed with the large incidence of diabetes in persons who had experienced a prolonged period of grief. They discovered that when a crisis occurs, such as the death of someone we love, the body pours increased amounts of sugar into the blood to enable us to cope with the crisis. In most persons the blood-sugar level returns to normal when the crisis is passed, but in some cases the grief continues longer than usual. The bereaved person, unable to relinquish the one who has died, experiences continued sorrow and inner pain. During this prolonged period the blood-sugar level remains abnormally high and in some cases a diabetic condition develops. Treatment of diabetes ordinarily includes a special diet and insulin therapy but in some cases it would be incomplete and ineffective without dealing with the emotional state which contributed to the onset of the illness.

When Dr. Viktor Frankl, the prominent psychotherapist, lectured on healing at Foundry Church, he told us about a Jewish woman who was suffering from a severe case of spastic colon. She emphasized that she was not a practicing Jew, but she did notice that she suffered most after eating pork. Barium X-rays revealed no physiological cause for the complaint. When doctors then told her they were putting pork in the barium (actually they were not), the X-rays clearly revealed the spastic action of the colon. The next day when they repeated the test, telling her they were not putting pork in the barium (actually they were), the colon performed normally. With a twinkle in his eye, Dr. Frankl concluded that we now have X-ray proof of the existence of the human conscience.

Shortly after our healing ministry began at Foundry, I received a letter from a minister's wife further illustrating the relationship between the *psyche* and the *soma*. For many years she had suffered from periods of excruciating back pain during which she resorted to medication, physical therapy, bed rest, and back braces, all in vain.

> When moving to a new parish several months later I sought out a new doctor, driven to the point where I felt I could stand the pain no longer. The doctor said, "Have you noticed what it is that brings this on from time to time?" I answered, "Yes, whenever my minister husband and I have a difference of opinion." I gave him the happening of that very day.
>
> The doctor said, "I could send you to the Lahey Clinic in Boston for examination and tests but I want to try something else first. When differences arise between yourself and your husband, just say under your breath, 'What the hell!' and forget it."
>
> I thanked him, and walked the four blocks back to the parsonage saying to myself, "Is it possible that I have brought this burden, this pain, on myself all these years? Did it take a visit to a new doctor who didn't even know me to find the answer to my problem? O God, can you forgive me for my shortsightedness? I was always so sure I was right."

> I walked with lighter step. I felt like taking wings. I was a new creature. The minister got a new wife that day. How do I know? I have never had a backache since I left that doctor's office—and that was in 1938!

"What the hell" is an unusual medical prescription, but it worked in her case because it relieved the pain-producing tension in her back caused by her anger and frustration.

One of the most dramatic developments in psychosomatic medicine is occurring in the field of cancer research. We are discovering that cancer is not just a physical illness to be treated with such physical means as surgery, drugs, and radiation. Attention now is being focused on the patient's physical *and emotional* condition. Among other things, statistics have shown that many persons who develop cancer have experienced a significant loss, such as the death of a spouse, six to eighteen months prior to the onset of the illness. Research is now being conducted on how such a loss, often accompanied by feelings of hopelessness, represses the ability of the body's immune system to destroy the abnormal cells often present in our organism. If preliminary findings are confirmed, many cancer patients would benefit from meditation, counseling, and other methods of improving their emotional state, thereby reversing the downward spiral of the body's immune system. No reputable therapist is suggesting that our emotional condition is the sole cause of cancer nor that we should ignore physical forms of therapy. But it is becoming more obvious that cancer treatment must involve the whole person.

Our study group spent a considerable amount of time talking about research in psychosomatic medicine because it provided a clue to the nature of spiritual healing. We even found a statement in the writings of the apostle Paul which gave us the handle for which we had been searching. In his first letter to the Thessalonians, Paul wrote, "May your spirit *[pneuma]* and soul *[psyche]* and body *[soma]* be kept sound and blameless" (5:23). If the condition of our soul has a profound effect on the condition of our body, then strengthening our soul will improve our physical health. The most effective way of doing this is through our spirit, the center of the soul, the innermost part of our being where the Spirit of God is released within us. "When we cry, 'Abba! Father!' it is the Spirit himself bearing witness with our spirit that we are children of God" (Rom. 8:15*b*-16). Spiritual healing focuses on this innermost part of our being, the spirit in each of us where God's Spirit, the ultimate source of all healing, is released within us. It recognizes the value of physical medicine, but insists that we focus our attention on the source of healing at the place where that source is most directly available to us. We are made whole by learning how to be present to the Spirit of God at this spiritual center of our own being. Consequently, the purpose of a ministry of spiritual healing is to create a climate which helps persons move toward health and wholeness of life by experiencing and receiving God's Spirit in their spirit.

As we talked about this in our study group we concluded that every activity in the church which deepens our relationship with God has a healing effect. Every worship service can be a healing service and every study session or committee meeting a therapy session. In this broad sense, the church becomes a healing community when it helps individuals recognize and accept the presence of God within. But the need for specific healing in so many lives and the modern church's neglect of this ministry means that in many parishes we need to give it a special emphasis.

Our study group disbanded with the decision to launch a ministry of spiritual healing in our church, but we soon discovered that some kind of continuing support group is essential. Planning, coordination, spiritual replenishment, and mutual support are all necessary for those providing leadership in this demanding type of ministry. Through the years our support group has been able to provide regular healing worship services, study classes, meditation classes, intercessory prayer groups, personal counseling and visitation, special workshops, and retreats.

The worship service is the centerpiece of our ministry of healing. More relaxed and informal than our Sunday morning services, the weekly healing service usually includes a meditation on some passage of Scripture related to healing, and silence for prayer and meditation. The main emphasis, however, is on Holy Communion and the laying on of hands. The sacrament of Holy Communion is the ideal foundation for a healing service because of the way it makes the real presence of Christ available to us. Many times this takes on special meaning in the healing service because of the expressed needs of those who come for healing with hope and expectation.

The laying on of hands is a New Testament practice which we approached with a great deal of caution, wanting to avoid the bitter disappointment and the emotional confusion which sometimes accompany this practice. We have experienced great value on three levels when offering the laying on of hands in the context of a worship service in a supportive Christ-centered community. First, there is the therapeutic value of a healing touch. It is striking to note how often Jesus touched those to whom he was bringing healing. In our world today where there is so much loneliness and so much exploitation there can be great healing power in the touch of a caring person. Some nursing schools are emphasizing that the way in which a nurse touches a patient can make a difference in the process of healing. It is not surprising that the touch of a caring person in a worship setting can be therapeutic.

Second, there is sacramental value in the laying on of hands. It is not a sacrament in any formal sense, but the rite includes outward and visible signs of an inward and spiritual grace. It is an occasion which God can use to make his presence known in special ways. When offered within the community of faith it can be helpful and effective even when the person administering the rite does not claim any special gift of healing, just as the value of Holy Communion does not depend on the quality of the minister's life.

Third, there is a possible charismatic value in the laying on of hands. *Charismatic* means grace gifted. We have discovered that when a church faithfully develops its resources of spiritual healing, the gracious God calls forth the special healing gifts of certain individuals. These are the "gifts of healing" which the apostle Paul includes among the gifts of the Holy Spirit (I Cor. 12:9), always given for the common good to the members of the faith community. There is no doubt that certain individuals in every congregation possess an unusual ability to evoke the healing power of God and to transmit it with unusual effectiveness. After several years of experience, I now have a physical sensation of heat in my hands and arms when laying on hands in the worship service. Scientific experimentation has produced photographic evidence of the power emanating from the hands of gifted healers. There is much that we do not understand about this, but we do know that many persons can benefit from this gift of the Holy Spirit.

At the weekly service those of us who will be providing leadership first lay hands on one another. Then others are invited to come forward to kneel at the altar rail. We lay hands on each individual's head and say a brief prayer asking for God to help us be open to his presence. Then we remain silent for a minute or so, resting in this presence. Finally, we offer a brief prayer of thanksgiving. Many persons have told us how the laying on of hands, especially over a period of time, has deepened their relationship with God and been instrumental in their healing.

In addition to the worship service, we have provided an introductory class on spiritual healing which usually meets during the hour before the service. There has also been a strong emphasis on prayer and meditation. Classes are offered at various times during the week and intercession groups pray each day for those on our lengthy prayer list. Even before these activities began, our church's interest in healing was expressed through the establishment of a pastoral counseling center under the direction of a highly qualified pastoral psychologist. The counseling center is an integral part of our health ministry, providing counseling, group therapy, and referral service whenever needed. From the beginning we have recognized the value of medicine and psychiatry, in addition to spiritual resources, in dealing with specific health problems.

God, in his great goodness, has provided many healing resources which we use in our times of need. The greatest of these is the power of his own presence with us and within us. In our relationship with God we learn how to draw upon this power in such a way that illness which might occur is prevented, and illnesses which do occur are healed. We have also discovered that healing can take place without a cure. While a specific illness may not be fully cured, the person can become more of a whole person and experience the healing of the self at a deeper level. It is not without reason that the English words *health, whole,* and *holy* all come from the same root! A letter we received expressing gratitude for this deeper healing contains feelings typical of so many.

> It is with great joy that I can thank you for your intercessory prayers and laying on of hands on my behalf. The operation, the chemotherapy, and two minor operations are over. So are many tests. It was a long siege but the final outcome was never in doubt in my mind.
>
> Knowing your strict, loving disciplines, I was able to rest in the healing hands of our Lord. I was too weak to pray, but my faith and trust were somehow being fanned to a white healing heat.
>
> It was also interesting to note that the doctors all made the correct decisions, over and over again. Drugs were hardly used at all, aside from the chemotherapy, because pain and side effects were minimal. My body has responded and become stronger, and I feel healing taking place at deeper levels of my being.
>
> God bless you all for your selfless devotion, and be encouraged. The Holy Spirit listens intently to what you ask!

We still have a lot to learn in our congregation and a long way to go in developing this ministry. All of us who have assumed positions of leadership are "wounded healers," in continuous need of the healing power of God in our own lives. But I feel that a ministry of spiritual healing is like leaven in the life of a parish. The power that it releases affects our life together on every level. Because of this way in which it can release and nourish the experience of God's presence, the community of Christ was in the beginning, and can be today, a genuine community of healing.

10
Marriage

It was early on Christmas Eve in 1946. The poinsettia-filled sanctuary of Foundry Church was bathed in candlelight. The sounds of Handel's *Messiah* could be heard in the distance as the choir rehearsed downstairs, preparing for a midnight performance. When I looked at the star on top of the sanctuary Christmas tree it was shining with a special brightness. This was the night Audree would become my wife.

From a practical point of view, Christmas Eve is not a good time to be married, especially for a minister and his wife. It is such a busy time in the church and the family that we never have the opportunity to celebrate our anniversary. But from a theological point of view, it is an excellent time. Christmas is the season of Emmanuel, "God's presence with us." It is a celebration of God's becoming flesh to dwell among us full of grace and truth,

110

fully identifying with us in our real humanity. Standing at the altar on our wedding night, with the spirit of the season all around us, we were asking God to bless our marriage with the incarnational love of his Christmas presence.

A Christmas wedding was also appropriate for us because a year earlier, while still in the Navy, I attended a performance of *Messiah* at Foundry and heard Audree sing the alto solos. When I found out she was single, I joined the choir. We began to spend a great deal of time together and within a few months were talking about marriage. Plans to wait until I had completed college and seminary were quickly changed because the pain of separation was too great. We decided we would go through these years of preparation together, joining the many other married couples who were attending college in those postwar years.

When we married, I was nineteen years old. We were together while I went through college, seminary, and graduate school. Together we raised three children. Together we have ministered on campuses and in parishes. Together we have written books and developed a television ministry. After all these years she is more than ever my best friend, the person whose company I enjoy most. The shape of our relationship is ever changing, but the covenant we have made with each other grows stronger. Neither of us has ever had a sexual relationship with anyone else. We fully intend to stay married to each other "until death us do part." Happiness, for both of us, is growing old together.

But I must confess, as I look around, that I am confused by some of the new attitudes toward sexuality and by the so-called "new rules of marriage" in our contemporary life. Has the enduring quality of our relationship been a special blessing for which we should be grateful? Or have we been missing something? So many persons are having affairs, changing marriage partners, and going to bed for one night stands. Is it because they are looking for what Audree and I have already found in a permanent marriage relationship? Or is it because they have found something better? I do not have the answer to these questions, but I do know there are times when the changing attitude toward love and marriage makes me feel hopelessly out of step with the world around me.

As a counselor, I have been through the pain of affairs, love triangles, separations, and divorce with so many persons that it is difficult for me to be objective. I have shared the anxiety, confusion, and fear of the children of divorce. I have talked with schoolteachers who tell me that the majority of their students are from broken homes. Sometimes I wonder why we are so afraid of the atomic bomb falling on America. Something worse is already happening to us with this disintegration of marriage and family life. The unraveling of our society from within is not as dramatic as the bomb, but it is just as deadly.

Part of my confusion is caused by the ease with which we ignore the direct teaching of the Bible on this subject. In the second chapter of Genesis, for example, there is a statement about God's ideal intention for marriage that has had a profound effect on human history. The author insists, in contrast to our modern attitude toward marriage, that every true marriage has an "ontic" quality about it, which simply means that it is rooted in the nature of being itself. From the beginning God has created us male and female so that the wholeness which he intends for us might be experienced through a permanent life-enhancing marriage union.

When the Pharisees asked Jesus about divorce, he based his answer on the idea of marriage as an order of creation, quoting from this same passage in Genesis (Matt. 19). God, who from the beginning made us male and female, intended for those who marry to enter into a permanent one-flesh union. "What therefore God has joined together, let no man put asunder." This bond, which is given as an order of creation, is even stronger than the bond which joins us to father and mother. Closely related to this is the idea that the remarriage of divorced persons actually constitutes adultery, based on the assumption that a marriage once entered into continues to exist, and that even though a divorce occurs, it cannot affect the foundation of the marriage in being itself. Since the original marriage continues to exist, entrance into a new marriage becomes an act of adultery!

It is important to point out that Jesus offers this teaching as the ideal intention of God for our human life and not as an absolute law. He clearly recognized the reality of our human weakness and imperfections which cause us to fall short of God's intention in so many areas of our existence, and a part of his good news is that God comes to us even in our fallen state with forgiveness and the possibility of a new life. There is no escaping the fact that a marriage union may deteriorate to a point where the values of life would be diminished and threatened through the continuation of the relationship. Hatred, cruelty, and even physical violence may be present. When every possible effort to redeem such a marriage has failed, then divorce may become the lesser of evils. Divorce is always a failure to achieve the ideal intention of God, but under some circumstances it becomes the most loving alternative, and in this sense may be said to be in keeping with the spirit of Jesus, who left us only one absolute law, the law of *agape* love. Agape is the kind of Christlike love through which we say to another person, "How can I give of myself in order that you might become the person God created you to be?" rather than "What can I get out of you for myself?" It is love that is *for* the other.

I recognize the inevitability and necessity of divorce as an act of *agape* love in many situations. I am always eager to help divorced persons discover ways in which the resurrection power of God can transform pain and guilt into new life and new hope. I also fully believe that the marriage covenant represents a relationship between persons and not some kind of inhuman bondage to the idea of fidelity. But I also have a strong feeling that those of us who are part of the Christian community need to put a greater emphasis on permanence as God's ideal intention for marriage and provide practical ways for persons to move toward that ideal.

"Moving toward the ideal" is a good way to describe Christian marriage. In actual practice it is more of a process than an achievement. There is always more to learn. There are always growing edges. There are many mountains to climb together in sickness and in health. And there are always surprises.

I have been surprised, for example, to find myself struggling with the closed nature of our marriage. If by open marriage is meant one in which the interaction between the partners expands their freedom to be themselves and enhances the personal growth of each, then ours has been an open marriage. But if open marriage also includes the freedom of each partner to develop relationships with members of the opposite sex, then ours has been closed. I am not talking about sexual relationships. Even those who first popularized the term "open marriage" are no longer advocating sex outside of marriage. I am talking about husband and wife developing friendships with members of both sexes so that the marriage does not need to carry the full weight of each partner's emotional and spiritual needs. The danger of a closed marriage is that when either person finds someone outside the marriage who can meet needs not being met in the marriage, he or she may be taken by surprise and begin losing control.

But are the risks of an open marriage even greater? I am sure this is why ours has remained so closed. A close relationship with a member of the opposite sex very often leads to a desire for sexual consummation, and in our present permissive society it is very easy to give in to this desire. When I was discussing this with a group of young adults recently, their response was, "What's wrong with a roll in the hay between friends?" I am convinced that a roll in the hay between friends outside of marriage violates the marriage covenant, usually involves a great deal of deception, and always ends up hurting someone. Moreover, it is unusually easy at the time to deceive ourselves into believing that we are acting responsibly and that our situation is an exception.

Again, the biblical teaching on this subject is very straightforward. The Hebrew and Greek words for adultery used in the Bible mean unfaithfulness to the marriage vows, the violation of the covenant a man and woman have made with each other in the presence of God. In the Old Testament it is viewed as a serious sin. Not only is it strictly forbidden in both versions of the Ten Commandments, but Leviticus prescribes the death penalty as its punishment! (See Exod. 20:14; Deut. 5:18; Lev. 20:10.) In the Sermon on the Mount Jesus internalizes this Old Testament teaching by insisting that the desire to commit adultery is as evil and destructive in the sight of God as the act itself (Matt. 5:27-30). It is clear from the Greek idiom used here that he is not talking about the involuntary awakening of sexual desire, but looking at someone with the deliberate intention of using the person to satisfy lustful desires. It is not so much the momentary impulse as the will which is involved. Harboring the desire, dwelling on it, deliberately looking at another in a lustful way is the evil Jesus is talking about. One of the many reasons for this strong biblical condemnation of adultery is that it harms the interior life of the ones committing it and inevitably results in the exploitation of others.

There are other implications in the teaching of Jesus about adultery. On the one hand, he expands the definition of adultery so that it is not limited to sexual activity outside the marriage. The almost universally accepted modern definition of marital infidelity focuses on physical intercourse, but there are many emotional and spiritual ways of being unfaithful to our husband or wife. On the other hand, Jesus implies that the physical union between two persons is not to be taken lightly. It is not just a roll in the hay. Sexual intercourse is an act of the whole self which affects the whole self, involving our attitude toward ourselves, toward other persons, and, ultimately, toward God. It can either contribute to our wholeness of life or it can be a hollow parody of marriage which undermines our inner integrity and leaves behind a deep-seated sense of anger and frustration.

On my first trip to the Holy Land I remember meeting the Bethlehem leather worker to whom the Bedouins brought the first fragments of the Dead Sea Scrolls. We sat in his little shop, drinking Turkish coffee and talking about how his decision to take these strange scrolls to

scholars in Jerusalem had added a whole new dimension
to biblical studies. But he confessed that when he first
paid the Bedouins a small amount for the scrolls, he fully
intended to use them in his shop to repair shoe soles! The
picture of the uniquely valuable Dead Sea Scrolls being
used in shoes comes to me when I think of the way we
often drag the priceless gift of our sexuality through the
dirt of casual and exploitative relationships.

Because deep friendship between members of the
opposite sex often leads to a desire for sexual union, the
risks of open marriage are very great. Audree and I have
not been willing to take those risks. Fortunately, the
emotional burden this places upon our marriage has
been somewhat relieved by our recent involvement in
separate growth groups. In these groups we have found
nourishing friendships outside of our marriage and a
supportive environment for testing our feelings and
expressing our needs. We both look upon participation
in our groups as a major step toward the goal of creating
a healthy openness in our marriage.

Along with all these factors in our marriage there is
one other which has reinforced our unwillingness to risk
undermining our relationship with each other. Having
worked a great deal with the children of divorce, we have
become very conscious of a child's need for a secure and
loving family environment. Because our own children
are so important to us, we have been unwilling to take
risks which might threaten the stability and security of
our home environment.

There was never any question in our minds that we
wanted children, but we had a difficult time getting
started. After eight childless years and many medical
examinations, we went to visit the hospital director for
whom Audree had been working. He helped us begin the

process of moving toward adoption. Audree immediately became pregnant and nine months later our Deborah was born! Eleven months after that Kathleen was born! I fired off a telegram to the hospital director and said, "You helped us get this started. How do we turn it off?" I also remember having trouble with some of my seminary friends who insisted that I give back the one-hundred dollar prize I had just been awarded for an essay on "The Christian Ethics of Birth Control." Fortunately, Mark waited six years before being born!

Our children have always been one of the greatest sources of joy in my life, but I have deliberately avoided violating their privacy and integrity by talking about them in books and sermons. I learned a valuable lesson in this connection early in my ministry when Mark was still very young. His Sunday school teacher had spent a great deal of time explaining to the children that Mark's daddy was the minister of the church. The next morning Mark crawled into bed with Audree and me and said, "I sure do like cuddling with my minister." When I used this as a sermon illustration the following Sunday, many parishioners teased Mark about it, and I resolved never again to subject my children to public humiliation by invading their privacy in this way.

When Ann Landers asked parents whether they would have children if they had it to do over again, the majority of those responding to her question said they would not. Our children have never given us any reason to feel this way, but a great investment of self is involved in the raising of children and there are inevitable times of stress and uncertainty. Even Mary, the mother of Jesus, had problems. "Son," she said on one occasion, "why have you treated us so? Behold, your father and I have been looking for you anxiously" (Luke 2:48). The healthy home is one in which feelings like these can be dealt with openly and honestly, where there is good communication taking place and where *agape* love is the common ground. These are things which Audree and I have wanted for our family.

Now that the children are grown, we are learning the difficult process of relinquishment. One by one they are leaving home. The empty-nest phase of our marriage has given me time to discover a new dimension in my attitude toward Audree. I have never thought of myself as a male chauvinist, especially where she is concerned. I have tried to be very sensitive to her wholeness and independence as a person and to her rights as a woman. Recently I have been appalled at my blindness to the unspoken and unrecognized assumptions in a closed marriage of our generation. The woman has a certain subordinate place in the marriage. She may question her husband's judgment but not his ultimate authority. If the husband's work is transferred to another city, the wife automatically pulls up her roots and goes with him. She was created to be his helper and her fulfillment is found in the reflected glory from her husband. It is not without reason that the apostle Paul, who had a great deal to learn about this, discusses husband-wife relationships and master-slave relationships in the same breath!

One by one, these hidden assumptions of masculine superiority are being revealed to me. I remember, for example, how my eyes were opened when I received my honorary degrees. What an ego trip it is to be awarded an honorary doctorate! The recipient stands in front of an assembled multitude while a glowing list of his or her virtues and achievements is read by the president of the university. I can remember the luncheons, dinners, and other activities all designed to emphasize my greatness.

The first time all this happened Audree accompanied me, and I assumed she enjoyed it as much as I did. Later, when another university offered me a degree, I shared my elation with Audree. I was shocked to discover that while she was glad for me, she preferred not to accompany me to the ceremony. Thinking back, I realized how she had been treated as an appendage the first time, entertained in a condescending way, and ignored as a person. I went on the second ego trip alone and saw the same thing happening to other wives.

It is a small thing, perhaps, but this has become a symbol for me of the unexplored territory in many marriages and has increased my desire for Audree to be recognized as a full partner in every dimension of my ministry and as a person who deserves to be honored in her own right.

Meanwhile I continue to work gratefully with other revelations, painful as they are at times, which contribute to our mutual growth, and I struggle with my confusion about the changing attitudes toward marriage in our society. But many of my recent experiences have strengthened my conviction that the depth and permanence of the commitment (covenant) is the secret ingredient which makes a marriage so potentially enriching. All husbands and wives have an opportunity to move quickly from the in-love phase of their relationship to the loving phase. The permanent commitment provides the context within which they can move through this difficult transition in a life-enhancing way. The marriage isn't over when they discover they are not in love the way they were before. It is just beginning! This enduring quality of marriage as an order of creation, grounded in being itself, is what marriage is all about.

A beautiful young woman, a recent honors graduate of an outstanding university, was talking with me about her plans for the future, including marriage. "The idea," she said, "that the person I choose now for a partner will be the right person for me for the rest of my life is sheer insanity." Is it sheer insanity? Or is it one of God's greatest gifts to us in our search for wholeness?

11
Prayer

An affirming awareness of the presence of God came to me one summer day while I was walking and meditating on the Mount of Transfiguration in Galilee. In a more general sense this experience confirmed the direction my faith journey had been taking in recent years. More specifically, it verified the value of the major changes which had been occurring in my prayer relationship with God.

One of the exciting things about God is the way he often arrests our attention and reveals his presence when we least expect it. We may be busily engaged in some project or activity, not thinking about God at all, when suddenly we become aware of his power or love working in our lives. One man reported having an overpowering experience of the Holy Spirit while opening a can of soup to prepare his children's lunch. There is no doubt that God is full of surprises.

But it is also clear that those of us who earnestly desire to know God need more than these surprises. It becomes very important to us to spend as much time as possible giving attention to God and making an effort to communicate directly with him. This means earnestly directing our minds to God, talking to God, paying attention to him, expecting him, waiting for him, listening to him. In other words, it means learning how to pray and taking time to pray.

Prayer has been an important part of my life as far back as I can remember. In my childhood "saying my prayers" before bed was a regular part of my daily routine. I can also recall my frustration during my first visit to a hospital. When placed on the operating table for a tonsillectomy I was very frightened and kept trying to pray, but the doctor repeatedly asked me questions, wanting me to talk so he could tell when the anesthetic had taken effect. Many years later, as an adult, I can remember awakening in the recovery room after surgery and finding myself praying (was it the Spirit praying in me?) for a small child who was crying in the bed next to mine. Through the years there have been times when I wondered: Has prayer been important to me because it is the most direct way to experience the presence of God, or is it the other way around? Has the presence of God been the thread that has held my life together because I have prayed?

The major changes which have been occurring in my prayer life began when some of my friends became enthusiastic about Transcendental Meditation. In a very disciplined way they were setting aside twenty minutes every morning and twenty minutes every evening to center down and repeat their Sanskrit prayer word *(mantra)*. It was obvious from talking with them that they were more relaxed and more enthusiastic about life because of their meditation.

As a result of this observation I started asking groups of church people all over the country how many of them spent at least forty minutes a day in prayer. I was careful to phrase the question so that they would understand that I did not mean devotional reading or reading about prayer, but actually praying or meditating. It soon became obvious to me that very few of us in the Christian tradition have a regular, disciplined prayer life. Very few of us are faithful in giving our undivided attention to God. I felt very strongly that the time had come for me to do something about this in my own life.

Then God surprised me again. I "accidently" discovered a form of contemplative prayer that was just right for me, similar in some ways to Transcendental Meditation, but deeply rooted in the Christian tradition. Based on the example and teaching of Jesus, this way of being present to God surfaces again and again in Christian devotional literature such as the fourteenth-century *Cloud of Unknowing* and the works of St. John of the Cross. The surprising thing is that this came to my attention while I was casually listening to some audio cassettes in search of sermon illustrations!

One of the cassettes included a talk by a Trappist monk on the subject of centering prayer. The things he was saying rang so true for me that I wrote to the monastery asking for more information. Since then I have listened to more cassettes, read several books on the subject, worked under spiritual directors who are experienced in this form of prayer, and gone on retreats at the monastery, St. Joseph's Abbey in Massachusetts. Some of the monks in this Trappist community have found a new

way of packaging this ancient Christian form of prayer so
that those of us who are living active lives in the world can
regularly experience God's presence at the center of our
being.

Centering prayer is sometimes described as an
effortless kind of prayer, but that does not mean it just
happens. It has taken me several years to learn how to
quiet my intellect and emotions enough to be present to
God at the center of my being. Twenty minutes, twice a
day, are devoted to centering in this way. As in
Transcendental Meditation, a prayer word is used in this
type of prayer, but in at least two ways it differs radically
from a mantra. In the first place, the word chosen is a
Christ-centered word rather than a meaningless combination of syllables. The word which I have found most
helpful is *Abba*, the title Jesus used to address God in the
intimacy of prayer (Mark 14:36). Paul also refers to this
word in two of his letters. "God has sent the Spirit of his
Son into our hearts, crying, 'Abba! Father!'" (Gal. 4:6).
"When we cry, 'Abba! Father!' it is the Spirit himself
bearing witness with our spirit that we are children of
God" (Rom. 8:15*b*-16). There are, of course, many other
Christ-centered words which might be used, but this one
is especially helpful to me because it is so closely
associated with Jesus and the New Testament tradition.

The prayer word in centering prayer differs from the
mantra, in the second place, in the way in which it is used.
Instead of continuously repeating it in a chantlike
rhythm, we use the word only when needed as a way of
returning to the presence of God. Our attention is
focused on God and not on the word. But because our
minds and emotions are so active we easily become
distracted. Whenever this happens, we return to God's
presence by the use of the prayer word, not wasting time

in anger or frustration because of the distraction. We simply return in this gentle way, as often as necessary.

One reason this kind of centering prayer has been so helpful to me is that it affirms my growing conviction that the essence of prayer is listening to God. This is something I have known intellectually for some time, but now, more than ever, it is determining the shape and direction of my prayer life.

Ordinarily, prayer begins with our talking to God. Jesus made this clear in his teaching: "Ask, and it will be given you; seek, and you will find; knock, and it will be opened to you. . . . If you then, who are evil, know how to give good gifts to your children, how much more will your Father who is in heaven give good things to those who ask him!" (Matt. 7:7, 11). The English word *prayer* actually means to ask or beg for something. On one occasion the disciples came to Jesus with the request, "Lord, teach us to pray." He responded with the Lord's Prayer, a model prayer given to beginners who were asking for instruction, and it shows us what things to request of God (Matt. 6:9-13; Luke 11:1-4).

It is clear, however, from the experience of those who spend much time in prayer, that as we mature in our prayer life we will spend less time talking to God and more time listening to him. Prayer, at its best, is listening to God, being present to him, seeking to learn his will for our lives, trying to identify with the movement of his life within us. It is a matter of being with him in order to hear very clearly what he is saying to us so that we can abandon ourselves to him.

Charles de Foucauld, one of the masters of prayer, wrote a paraphrase of the Lord's Prayer which is actually a prayer of abandonment. After years of growth in the life of prayer, he no longer used the Lord's Prayer to ask

things of God, but rather as a way of abandoning himself
to God.

Father,

I abandon myself into your hands;
do with me what you will.
Whatever you may do, I thank you:
I am ready for all, I accept all.
Let only your will be done in me,
and in all your creatures—
I wish no more than this, O Lord.

Into your hands I commend my soul;
I offer it to you with all the love of my heart,
for I love you Lord,
and so need to give myself,
to surrender myself into your hands,
without reserve,
and with boundless confidence,

for you are my Father.

This is the kind of experience I had on the Mount of
Transfiguration which affirmed the direction my prayer
life had been taking since I began using centering prayer.
The summit of Mount Tabor is a quiet and peaceful
place rising above the Sea of Galilee and the surrounding
fertile plains. The fact that tourist buses cannot ascend
the narrow winding road partly explains the peace on the
top of the mountain, but there is also the reflected glory
of the fullness of God's presence which Peter, James, and
John experienced there long ago (Luke 9:28-43).

The transfiguration marked a turning point in the life
and ministry of Jesus. Up to this point he had moved
about in Galilee, preaching, teaching, healing, and
training his disciples. But the pressure from his enemies
had grown to such a point that he was forced to make a

decision. Should he retreat, or wait for the confrontation in Galilee, or move to Jerusalem and face his enemies there? Under the pressure of making this critical decision, Jesus went up on the mountain to abandon himself to God. While he was praying, Jesus was so transfigured by the power of God's presence that "the appearance of his countenance was altered, and his raiment became dazzling white" (Luke 9:29). The cloud which surrounded him was the *Shekinah*, the ancient symbol of divine presence (the cloud of unknowing). The voice was the *bath qôl*, literally the voice of God.

It was a beautiful summer afternoon when I visited Mount Tabor. A steady breeze kept the flowers and the trees dancing in the sunlight. After a refreshing drink at the small monastery, I went out to sit on an old stone wall and live my way into the story of the transfiguration. Feeling more and more in tune with the spirit of the place and with the event which had occurred there, I suddenly *knew* that the essence of prayer and of all Christian life is total listening and abandonment to God. It was an unforgettable moment of insight and confirmation. Because centering prayer had been helping me move in this direction, I resolved to let it provide more and more of the basic structure for my practice of prayer.

I was very reluctant to leave the Mount of Transfiguration as that summer afternoon drew to a close, but I realized this feeling was also part of the story. Peter had wanted to build some booths and remain in the cloud of unknowing on the top of the mountain. But Jesus took him and the others down into the valley where an epileptic boy and his father were both in need of God's healing power. As I thought about this, I realized that one of the most striking things about the life of Jesus is the vital balance he maintained between the inward journey and the outward journey. The inward journey is the journey to the center of our own being where we make a direct connection with God's Spirit within us. The outward journey is the journey of work and ministry in which we make a connection with persons in the world around us. Both are essential. Without the inward journey we tend to become lifeless and ineffective. Without the outward journey we tend to become stagnant and self-centered. In Jesus we see the kind of vital balance which is so essential for our own lives.

There is no question that centering prayer has strengthened me for the many forms of my own outward journey to others, including regular intercessions. By going down to the center of my being, I am able to connect with other persons through the God who is the ground of all being. Making myself available to God for others in this way is one of the most creative expressions of love and one of the most effective forms of intercessory prayer. Through trial and error I have found that one of the best times for me to offer this intercession is in the morning immediately after a period of centering prayer.

In addition to setting aside specific times of prayer, I also find myself increasingly intrigued by the apostle Paul's idea of "prayer without ceasing." "Rejoice always," he wrote to his friends. "Pray constantly, give thanks in all circumstances; for this is the will of God in Christ Jesus for you" (I Thess. 5:16-18). It is obvious from his letters that he practiced what he preached. "Without ceasing I mention you always in my prayers." "We are bound to give thanks to God always for you. . . . To this end we always pray for you" (Rom. 1:9; II Thess. 1:3-11).

Prayer without ceasing obviously does not mean withdrawing from life in order to spend all our time thinking about God. It means the conversion of life itself, with all its obligations, distractions, and responsibilities into conversation with God. It is the gradual transformation of the continuous monologue all of us carry on with ourselves into a dialogue with God. It is being with God everywhere under every circumstance.

But I do not believe this desirable goal of unceasing prayer can be accomplished and sustained unless we are willing to set aside regular times to focus our attention directly on God. In this regard it has become popular in some circles to say that prayer is not a matter of leaving whatever we are doing to be with God, but a matter of being with God in whatever we are doing. For me it is not an either/or situation. In order to be with God in whatever I am doing I need to have regular times when I leave whatever I am doing to be with God.

Regular times spent in centering prayer have convinced me that the only treasure ultimately worth seeking is the presence of God at the center of my own being. The power of this presence not only gives meaning to my own existence but also strengthens me in all my relationships with others. There are so many persons and so many things in the world around me in which I am eager to invest myself. But until I find God at the center there is nothing to give. I agree with Rabindranath Tagore, the Indian poet, who said it very simply:

> You wander restlessly from forest
>   to forest while the Reality
>   is within your own dwelling. . . .
> Go where you will—
>   to Benares or to Mathura;
>
> until you have found God
> in your own soul, the whole world
> will seem meaningless to you.

12
Hope

The news director at our television station recently stopped me in the hall outside his office and asked, "Do you see any hope at all?"

Having known him for several years, I was surprised at the despair in his voice when he asked the question because he is basically a life-affirming person. But living with the news every day, he had become extremely discouraged about the future. Looking for someone who could give him a word of encouragement, he asked again, "Do you see any hope?"

Reflecting later on the encounter, I realized that the feelings his despairing question evoked in me were similar to those I experienced teaching a college course on the writings of Albert Camus. This contemporary French writer believed that life is ultimately absurd and that the question of suicide is the most urgent one we face

in an absurd world. He compared us with the legendary
Sisyphus, doomed forever to push a huge boulder up a
steep hill, knowing that at the very moment the boulder
was about to reach the top, it would slip and roll to the
bottom, and he would have to start all over again. The
best we can expect of ourselves in such a hopeless
situation is an act of courage enabling us to continue the
struggle. I was in Paris at the time of Camus' death and
was surprised at the deep grief expressed by so many
persons. When I inquired about it, I was told that he had
expressed so well their view of life, and now his absurd
death, in a sports car crash while he was still so young,
proved that he was right. Life is absurd.

It is true that Camus had a gift for describing a vital
force at work in the midst of life, speaking on one
occasion for example of "an invincible summer in the
midst of his winter." But I generally come away from
encounters with his writing feeling the absence of God's
grace. And without God's grace, there is no hope. In one
of his stories Camus talks about the doves (symbolizing
the Holy Spirit?) circling above the gray clouds of
Amsterdam with no place to land. If the Holy Spirit
cannot come to us, then our life is gray and hopeless.

But the good news of Christian experience is that God
cares, that his Spirit comes, that he reveals his love for us
through Jesus Christ. This means that life is not absurd,
that it has meaning and a future toward which we move
with hope and expectation even when the outward signs
are very discouraging. Such a viewpoint is illustrated in a
letter from a third-century Christian named Cyprian to a
friend.

> This seems a cheerful world, Donatus, when I view it from
> this fair garden under the shadow of these vines. But if I
> climbed some great mountain and looked out over the wide

> lands, you know very well what I would see. Brigands on the
> high roads, pirates on the seas. . . . under all roofs misery
> and selfishness. It is really a bad world, Donatus, an
> incredibly bad world. Yet in the midst of it I have found a
> quiet and holy people. They have discovered a joy which is a
> thousand times better than any pleasure. . . . They are
> despised and persecuted but they have overcome the world.
> These people, Donatus, are the Christians—and I am one of
> them.

Because I am also "one of them" I continue to live with
hope in an incredibly bad world. The source of my hope
is God's presence, fully and decisively revealed through
Jesus Christ. Because I know that I can trust God with my
own life and with the life of the world, my whole
existence is open toward the future.

In recent years I have found the continual renewal of
my hope becoming more closely related to the resurrection of Jesus. "Blessed be the God and Father of our Lord
Jesus Christ! By his great mercy we have been born anew
to a living hope through the resurrection of Jesus Christ
from the dead" (I Pet. 1:3). These words express my own
feelings exactly. The ultimate source of my living hope is
the presence of God's mercy in the resurrection.

According to the New Testament the mood of the
disciples on the eve of the resurrection was one of
shocked disbelief and bitter disappointment. At first they
could not bring themselves to believe that it had all ended
this way. God had let them down. Then an utterly
unbelievable thing happened. Early in the morning on
the first day of the week they discovered the empty tomb,
and before the day was over they knew that Jesus was
alive! Refusing to trust their own senses at first, Peter and
John ran to the tomb to see for themselves. Thomas

would not believe until he had an opportunity to touch Jesus. But before long they all knew that it was incredibly true. Their Lord had risen from the dead!

At the center of John's Gospel, precisely at the turning point between the two major sections, Jesus reveals a vital part of the inner meaning of this resurrection event. "The hour has come for the Son of man to be glorified," he said. "Truly, truly, I say to you, unless a grain of wheat falls into the earth and dies, it remains alone; but if it dies, it bears much fruit" (12:23-24). The immediate intent of this statement is obvious, though the disciples missed it at the time. Jesus is saying that his own death is a necessary stage in his glorification. Just as the grain of wheat must die if there is to be new growth, so he must die in order to become the risen and triumphant Lord.

But this same principle is telling us something vital about our own lives and about the possibility of living with hope on every level of our existence. The loving God who reveals his presence through Jesus Christ is a God of resurrection power. Everywhere and at all times he is acting through a process of death and resurrection to give us new wholeness of life. He is always working to transform death into life, sickness into health, sorrow into joy, and despair into hope. As I experience this resurrection process at work within me and around me, I can identify with it and move into the future with expectation. This applies to my daily dying, to the death of my physical body, and to the dying institutions and structures in the world around me.

As for daily dying, it is not difficult to identify with the apostle Paul. "Why am I in peril every hour?" he asks. "I protest, brethren, by my pride in you which I have in Christ Jesus our Lord, I die every day!" (I Cor. 15:30-31).

When he wrote to his Corinthian friends about this daily dying, Paul was writing about something common to us all. A popular football coach declared, "Every time you lose, you die a little." When a former secretary of state left the government for private life, he said, "To leave positions of great responsibility and authority is to die a little." A man who spent his life working with orphan children watched them grow up and become independent. "Every time one leaves," he confessed, "I die a little."

Every day we suffer this pain of separation or loss in some form or other. It may come through the relinquishment of some harmful habit or thought pattern. It may come in the inevitable weakening of our faculties through the process of growing old. We may lose a friend or a member of the family. Retirement, divorce, bereavement, confession, and financial loss are all forms of dying which may strike us at any moment, sometimes without warning. But the good news of our Christian experience is that God's resurrection power enables us to move through this daily dying into wholeness of life. This does not mean that we look forward to these deaths or that we enjoy dying. But it does mean that we can face every experience of death with hope, looking forward to the new life made possible by the dying.

Many sensitive persons have struggled with the daily dying involved in human suffering. If God is good, how can we justify the fact of suffering in our existence, especially suffering which falls on the innocent, suffering which seems unjust, suffering that has no apparent purpose? We can easily identify with Teresa of Avila who was riding in a carriage across a pontoon bridge. Suddenly the bridge collapsed. Wading out of the water, she complained, "O God, one more ill on top of the others." God said, "This is the way I treat my friends." Teresa replied, "And that is why you have so few of them!" Even God's friends suffer in ways that are beyond our understanding. In a Christopher Fry drama, Barabbas, the thief who was released at the time of the crucifixion, cries out in his own anguish, "Why can't God make himself plain?"

Instead of making himself plain, God makes himself present as resurrection power. If we use our suffering as an opportunity to trust God, throwing ourselves more completely upon his mercy, then his resurrection presence is released in and through our lives. This is the way the apostle Paul dealt with the thorn in the flesh which was not removed even when he prayed repeatedly about it. God answered him, "My grace is sufficient for you, for my power is made perfect in weakness" (II Cor. 12:9). Paul concludes that for the sake of Christ he will be "content with weaknesses, insults, hardships, persecutions, and calamities; for when I am weak, then I am strong" (II Cor. 12:10). In his weakness he was strong because he was ready to accept God's grace and resurrection power. When we are strong, then we are usually weak because we are trying to live on our own. But when we are weak, then we are strong because we can use the weakness as an opportunity to live in and through the power of God.

I have often wondered in this connection about the change that occurred in Rembrandt's life after 1642 when his dearly loved wife, Saskia, died. Prior to this time he had been popular and successful, but there was much in his work that was superficial. Then, following Saskia's untimely death, he went into a period of deep mourning and did not paint at all. One of the first paintings he produced after this was the famous *The Night Watch,* followed by numerous other paintings of great power, many of them on religious themes. It is hard to be certain about these things, but the suffering he experienced in his wife's dying may have been the turning point. I have been unable to verify this, but while viewing *The Night Watch* in Amsterdam I was told that Rembrandt had later painted a self-portrait with the words underneath, "When I am weak, then I am strong."

No matter how much we say about our daily dying, however, the death of our physical body is the real problem for many of us. The apostle Paul called death "the last enemy to be destroyed." It is an enemy because it comes to assault and terminate our life and everything our life means to us. Or so it seems. Is there any hope that we will live again?

The New Testament answer to this question is crystal clear. The God who gives us life here on earth will give us life after death. Moreover, the God who has given every form of life here on earth an appropriate body can be trusted to provide us with a spiritual body for the next life (I Cor. 15:35-56). When the physical body returns to the earth, God "clothes us" in a new body appropriate for our continuing life with him. "It is sown a physical body, it is raised a spiritual body. If there is a physical body, there is also a spiritual body" (I Cor. 15:44).

One day when John Quincy Adams was eighty years of age, a friend met him on the streets of Boston. "How is John Quincy Adams?" the friend inquired. "John Quincy Adams himself is very well, thank you. But the house he lives in is sadly dilapidated. It is tottering on its foundations. The walls are badly shattered, and the roof is worn. The building trembles with every wind, and I think John Quincy Adams will have to move out of it before long. But he himself is very well." With the passing of the years, the house we live in, our physical body, begins to show signs of wear and tear. Eventually we move out of it and it is destroyed. But God's resurrection power makes it possible for us to continue to live in a new house, "a building from God, a house not made with hands, eternal in the heavens" (II Cor. 5:1). What reason do we have to suppose that any such spiritual body will be forthcoming to replace our present physical body? Anticipating this question Paul replies, "He who has prepared us for this very thing is God, who has given us the Spirit as a guarantee" (II Cor. 5:5).

As I grow older, all of this is becoming more important to me, both the daily dying and the death of the body. It is just as important to me as ever to live fully into the present moment, but in each present moment I am conscious of moving toward an unending future with God. This awareness makes me more eager than ever to begin new adventures and to continue growing, knowing that the creative element in every experience will live on as part of my true self for the rest of this life and into the next.

This has motivated me, for example, not only to break new ground in several areas of my ministry but also to start taking piano lessons. A music lover all my life, I have always been frustrated because I didn't know how to make music myself. There comes a time when the spoken word is inadequate, and we find ourselves wanting to express our feelings with the sound of music. The "morning stars sang together" when they were created,

Miriam sang and danced after crossing the Red Sea, David played his harp and composed psalms, and the angels sang a Gloria to celebrate the birth of Jesus. When I become aware of the presence of God, I feel like praising him "with trumpet sound . . . with lute and harp! . . . with timbrel and dance . . . with strings and pipe! . . . with loud clashing cymbals!" (Ps. 150). Some of my friends were surprised that I would subject myself to the humiliation of becoming an adult beginner at the piano, but it didn't even occur to me to think of the lessons in this way because of the joy of venturing into a beautiful new world.

This same eagerness to learn and grow has also opened up a promising new area in my spiritual life. During the past few years I have visited several monastic communities, hungering for their structured life of worship and contemplation as an antidote for my often-fragmented existence in a downtown parish. To my surprise, the result of my brief retreats into monasticism has been a return to the world with a growing desire to become an "active contemplative." Jesus, after all, did not leave the world to live in a monastic community like the Essenes, but gave constant attention to God while living a very active life in the world. In this sense he took a contemplative stance toward all of life, including the demands of his servant ministry to others as well as opportunities for solitude. A large part of my present joy is rooted in the exploration and discovery of what this kind of active contemplation can mean for my own life and ministry.

Excitement about the future, along with an eagerness to continue learning and growing, is one of the legacies from my father for which I am grateful. He has always had an adventurous spirit, a desire to do new things, to meet new people, and to make new friends. Even after he retired he enrolled in cooking classes and auto mechanics workshops and became increasingly involved in neighborhood and community affairs. I have been grateful for this model of the open-ended life that moves into each present moment and into the future with affirmation and expectation.

It is important to emphasize that this hope we experience as individual Christians also applies to God's world. At times it is difficult to believe this. A nuclear war, possible at any moment, would be over in a matter of minutes with resulting desolation beyond the power of the human mind to comprehend. Even if the bombs don't fall, massive starvation with accompanying political and economic revolution may bring the same results. It is easy to be pessimistic about the world's future. Recently one prominent minister, preaching from the Washington Cathedral pulpit, read a passage from Romans 8 in which Paul talks about the greatness of God and how nothing can separate us from the love of God. Then he said to the congregation, "I hope you will memorize this and keep it with you. You will find it comforting in five years when the darkness falls." He did not stop to explain what he meant. He did not need to.

But even if the worst is true, God is still God. The Christian community knows that God is Lord of history, that he will ultimately win the victory over evil, that nothing human persons can do will ultimately thwart his creative purpose for the world. This means, first of all, that we have *something to look forward to*. Even in the worst of times we know there is a future in which God will work out his purpose for the world he has created. This is why the biblical writers put a strong emphasis on eschatology, the teaching about the consummation of God's purpose in the "end time." In the second place, our Christian hope means that we have *something worth waiting for*. One of the things we discover about life is that God's time is not always our time. We find out that waiting may be required of us and that waiting can be one of the genuine signs of our faith. We learn patience, knowing that "not yet" can be a creative word from God for our life in the world. Finally, our Christian hope means that we have *something to do*.

Our hope encourages us to move into the world and work with all our strength to identify with the movement of God's life into the future. This means standing with Jesus to preach good news to the poor, to proclaim release to the captives, and to set at liberty those who are oppressed. It means marching with Martin Luther King until we are free at last. It means creating something beautiful for God with Mother Teresa by sharing Christ with the homeless and the dying. We move into the world, ministering to others as if the future depends entirely on us, knowing that, in the end, it depends entirely on God. This is our hope.

Because of this, the story of any human life, at any given point in time, is an unfinished story. I feel that I am a work-in-progress and that my life has changed profoundly in the process of writing about it. I am no longer the same person I was when I started to describe my faith journey! Furthermore, we do not know what undiscovered country lies ahead of us, what joys and sorrows await us, and what companions we will meet along the way. But we do know that God can be trusted.

In my own unfinished story the thread that has held my life together this far, God's presence, continues to hold.

When I think about how his gracious presence has guided me and protected me in the past and enabled me to find meaning for my life, I know that the future is secure and that I can look forward to it with great expectations.

> Through many dangers, toils, and snares,
>   I have already come;
> 'Tis grace hath brought me safe thus far,
>   And grace will lead me home.

I not only preach on tiptoe. I live on tiptoe.

With Sincere appreciation
To Sec. of State
James C Kirkpatrick
June 6 1976

Lois Roper Beard.

From Sunrise
to
Sunset

First Printing
COPYRIGHT 1971

BY

LOIS ROPER BEARD

PRINTED IN SPRINGFIELD, MO.
MIDWEST LITHO AND PUBLISHING CO.

THIS BOOK IS FOR MY FRIENDS

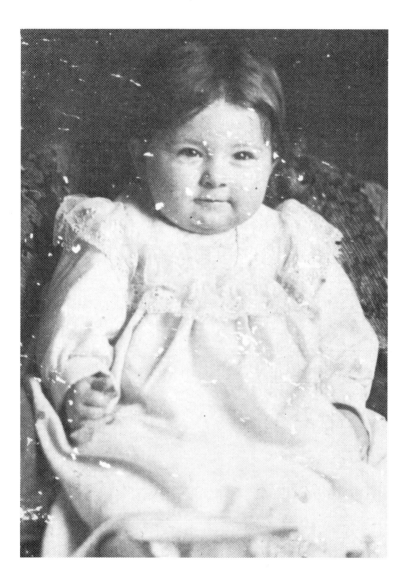

at Sunrise

From Sunrise to Sunset

Words do not describe the beauty of a sunrise over the sparkling waters of the Osage Fork on a clear April morning.

It was a morning made to order in 1905 when the second daughter, a tiny butterball with dark ringlets arrived soon after sunrise, after an all night of waiting, in the home of Miles and Ella Roper.

Bathed by the kind hands of Aunt Jane, a neighbor, who pinned the umbilical band and the soft flannel diaper and put on the soft white nightgown with the dainty brier stitches all around the sleeves and collar.

Warmed and fed I was contented when I was laid beside Mother in the big bed in the parlor where Dad, my older sister, big brothers and the neighbors came to see me and loved me.

It was a busy morning. Aunt Jane built a fire under the kettle early to get the family wash started. But when Papa rode up all breathless and excited Aunt Jane changed her apron and grabbed Uncle Bob's Sunday hat as her bonnet was already in to soak. Uncle Bob saddled Old Daisy and the two rode off under whip.

A neighbor called Uncle Dr. John on the call bell. After my arrival, and Mother was made comfortable, Blanche, the hired girl, said: "Oh! this is the day for the little turkeys to hatch." Sure enough when she went to see there was a whole nest full of the little gray fluffy fellows.

Blanche and Papa made a pen out of the wagon sideboards under the big wild cherry tree above the garden. With a cloth string they tied one leg of the old mother turkey hen to the tree to keep her close by. Their first feed was clabber cheese with black pepper and some green onion tips.

1

Those little turkeys grew so fast they were flying over the wagon sideboards when Mother was able to walk out to see them.

It was planting time. No one had much time for me, but as long as I was fed and changed I was happy. The summer passed quickly and harvest was in sight. But, the rains began, thunders rolled and so did the big river. After several days of continuous rains the floods came and washed the corn, which was waiting to be harvested, down the river.

The hard work of summer was for naught and one of the hardest winters lay ahead. But, with faith in God, the farmers pressed on. They were ready for another planting come springtime 1906.

During the winter when clouds were darkest, Papa said to Mamma "We are going to sell this farm and move to the ridge. I had rather burn up in drought years than to be flooded out every other year." Four years on the Hicks place, two crops were washed away.

The farm was sold. They learned the Warren place was for sale since Mr. Warren's death. Dad looked the place over. He made an offer and the family accepted it. But, the Warrens could not move until the first of the next year so the little three room house on Grandpa's east forty was our home while we waited. I was almost two years old when we moved to that farm.

I had learned that a smile brings love and kindness. I loved our new neighbors. One old couple called me their "Doll Baby". I can see Uncle Frank, so straight and tall, as he came to meet us when we sisters walked down to their house. He would pick me up an say: "This walk is too much for the little short legs of my Doll Baby."

I grew up to be my Daddy's tomboy. I followed him wherever he went. He seemed to want me with him as I wanted to be. I was happy when he started to the west side of the farm in the wagon if he would stop out front of the house to call "Dump come go along to help me through the gates". I felt important sitting in the spring seat when he would hand me the lines to drive through. If he was driving

2

the mules he would have me open the gate while he drove through.

Many hours we sat together in the crib shucking corn. Papa would tell tales of his childhood and the shucks would fly. When it was feed time he would carry the shucks across the driveway to the shuck bin to be fed later to the calves. I would climb out of the sliding crib door, which was about two feet from the floor, and wait for Papa to put eight big ears of corn on my arm to feed Old John the saddle horse, while he would feed the other horses. Then we took the nubbins to the old barn to feed the milk cows. In winter we also gave each a cup of bran in her feed box along with her share of nubbins. I learned to milk before I was old enough to go to school.

There were never any growing pains in my life for I was ever ready to see the rosy side of things. There was always someone to love me and call me their "little girl".

Two weeks before my fifth birthday my new baby sister was born. She was so pretty with big blue eyes and blond hair. Not one bit like me for my eyes were little and black. Most folks said they sparkled with laughter.

Vera had a difficult time getting started. She cried a lot as babies do with the colic. Mother was so tired all the time from so much care of the baby so I hunted for excuses to go to Uncle Charley and Aunt Annas. They were so kind and good to me.

The night Vera was born Mother let me go over there to stay all night. I had never spent the night away from her and the Indermuehle family went all out to keep me happy. But I never thought of being homesick. Bobby and Jessie were so sweet to me but Alfred was special. He would sit me on his shoulders, hold my feet around his neck and carry me all over the place. We would go down to the branch to look for crayfish or over to the playhouse to build furniture of big, flat rocks covered with moss.

When night came, and we must go to the house, after supper Alfred would get down on his hands and knees and let me ride his back like a horse. He would run, buck and kick but I would squeal and hang on. When he got tired and stopped to rest, I would kick him in the belly and make him keep going.

I had no resentment or jealousy toward my beautiful baby sister. Thanks to those wonderful neighbors who filled my life with the love I craved.

I was heartbroken when these neighbors moved away. I missed each one but I really grieved for Alfred. Why, I would have danced a jig on the ridgeroll of our big barn if I thought it would please him.

Time changes things. With the Indermuehle playmates gone and Lee was too big to play in the playhouse any more. Edith and I moved it from the four big oak trees across the branch to the Ben Davis apple trees in the orchard. We wanted to be close to the house now that we played alone.

Jim Parlett, a kind bachelor, lived in the little house where we used to live. He came to our house often at night. While the boys finished the chores he would churn for Mother. I would sit on his lap as he churned with that old dasher and sang some lonesome tunes, such as, "Redwing" or "The Indian Love Call".

After Mother took up the butter she would fill a bucket with buttermilk for him. Sometimes she would put a nice ball of fresh butter in for his hot cakes or biscuits for breakfast.

We girls usually polished a pan of apples, we brought from the cellar, and popped a pan of corn. Sometimes Lee would crack a panful of walnuts. We sat around the fire and enjoyed the fiddle music Jim and Lanna played while Edith would second with them on the organ.

Lanna and Jim thought it was cute when they taught me to waltz and do the two-step. They would take turns holding my hands to show me the steps while the other one played.

We all loved music. Not all of us could play but we could all sing. Each one could sing a part so we had a quartet. I sang the lead, Edith alto, Lanna tenor and Lee sang the bass. We liked the latest popular hits, but hymns were our favorites.

When I was ten our schoolteacher, Mr. Long, came to our house most every evening. He boarded with Uncle Tom and Aunt Mary Ann, but he enjoyed coming to our house to sing with us. One night we were singing a new song, one we all liked, "Beautiful Beckoning Hands". I was standing in my usual place reading the words from the book on the organ. I had not yet memorized the words of the song and I made a mistake. I was so embarrassed but when I looked up into the kind eyes of my beloved teacher he was smiling and I knew everything was all right.

The young folk of the community knew they were always welcome at our house. Often times the group was there. We would sing and sing. Mother was always asked to sing awhile. She would roll down the organ stool as far as it would go and try the chords, F, G and C. Love songs, Folk songs and Ballards, we enjoyed them all, but Mother always finished with "Little Brown Jug" or "Home Sweet Home".

Papa had a beautiful voice but he seldom sang with the group. He would however sing to me when we worked outside together. One of his favorites was "The Dying Cowboy". Following are the lines in part:

"Oh! bury me not on the lone prairies
These words came low and murnfully
From the pallid lips of a youth who lay
on his dying bed at close of day.
Oh! bury me not on the lone prairie
Where the wild Coyotes will howl over me
In a narrow grave just six by three.
Oh! bury me not on the lone prairie."

The minor chords made the song even more lonesome sounding. I often wondered at night about that poor dying cowboy.

Decoration Day

Decoration Day, May 30, was a special day. We looked forward to meeting with neighbors at the little country graveyard to remember our loved ones. Decoration Day, 1912, is stamped on my memory as a day my older sister and I did some fast growing up.

It was early in the morning of May 29 when my little sister was born. Mother's delicate health during the past winter, when she had a long battle with pneumonia, caused much concern. We were all happy because Mother and the baby came through her birth in good condition.

Why Lanna ever selected that afternoon to break Old Billy to ride I'll never know. He and Lee and two neighbor boys, Dick and Karl, put the riding bridle on the pretty black horse and led him out on the east side of the barn. They put the saddle on him and tightened up the girth. Lanna mounted. The boys gave him the reins and the two were off. Around the barn they came. Old Billy made a big lunge or two and headed straight for the big locust tree. Its limbs drooped almost to the ground. Lanna was a good rider but he didn't last the second trip around those limbs.

Lanna came out of the ordeal in fair condition with only a sprained ankle. Lucky for him that Aunt Sarah had come to check on Mother and the baby for she knew just what to do. In fact, Aunt Sarah always knew what to do. She put some apple cider vinegar in a pan to heat and put brown paper bags to soak in the vinegar. After she put the vinegar soaked brown paper on his ankle Lanna felt better.

Edith and I were already wondering how we would manage everything the next day. We were seven and nine but we proved equal to the task. Now with Lanna's crippled foot we had an added problem. He was to provide the music for a short program and drill at the graveyard on the morrow.

Everything worked out all right however. Aunt Sarah helped us cook some that afternoon and promised to take enough bread for us. That helped so much for we couldn't go to the store and buy a loaf of bread in those days. Aunt Sarah's light bread was always tops. She used ever-lasting yeast.

We cleaned the wash tub and lined it with a small tablecloth. The old hen and dressing, the stack of pies and a cake . . . Edith was an expert cake baker . . almost filled the tub. We left a portion on the small table by Mother's bedside for her dinner.

We got along fine getting everyone dressed and ready to go until we came to Lanna's tie. After so many tries we gave up and Mother raised herself up on one elbow and tied it for him. We girls were worried that the effort was too much for her.

About eleven o'clock all the neighbors were gathered. The little girls were all dressed up in their "Sunday best" with flowers from their yards ready for the drill. Lanna stood near the gate with one crutch under his arm and played several old Civil War songs on his cornet. Uncle Jasper stepped to the head of the waiting line with the flags and Lanna played "Tenting Tonight" as we followed to each old soldier's grave to place our flowers and flags.

It was a day mixed with sadness and joy as we remembered the tears and heartaches of the past. When we returned from our march to the gate the tablecloths were being spread in preparation for the dinner on the ground. With good neighbor fellowship the dinner was a special treat. We lingered long around that spread of good food.

After eating, groups made a tour of the little silent city and talked of loved ones who had "out stripped us". The children were happy picking the ripe wild strawberries that grew in sheltered places over the graveyard.

When we returned home Mother and the baby were fine and Mother was proud of her big girls when Papa told her how well we did with the dinner and cared for our little sister Vera.

Vernace was the best baby. She was always smiling. She learned early to coo and try to talk when we older ones talked to her. It was fun when she learned to hold our fingers and pull herself up.

Everyone shared the work around the place and years passed swiftly. I always liked to set the old hens, watch the turkey hens to their nest and pull weeds in the garden. I never did like to hoe. Sometimes the weeds would get ahead of us around the tansy bed and the two rows of grape vines. But, when I started a job I stayed with it until it was finished. The big white grapes that ripened early were ample reward for the hot job.

Wash day was never blue Monday if Mother decided to wash at the spring. The spring water was soft and made the white clothes whiter and the colored ones brighter. Sometimes when the men took their dinner to the old place Mother would announce "We will go to the spring and do the washing." I would make several trips with the little wagon to haul the tub, board, long black kettle and the clothes down the path while Mother and Edith put the house to order. The old chair to set the tub on was in the spring house.

There were usually enough fallen limbs under the old walnut trees to get a good fire going. After the water heated the first tub of white clothes were soon rubbed through and put in to boil. I kept the fire going and punched the clothes down once in awhile. I played with the little girls while Mother and Edith took turns at the tub and board.

We would boil some eggs in a can by the kettle and Mother would let me broil strips of bacon on a long forked stick over the coals. With some cornbread and green onions we had a dinner fit for a King.

The shallow pool of clear, cool water behind the spring house was just right for Vera to play in while Vernace would sit in the little wagon and laugh and play.

Lanna Joins The Army

We were a happy family. There was nothing to mar that happiness for a time but when things changed, it seemed the bottom just dropped out. Lanna was the jolly one, always kind and loving to his little sisters. He said he had "itchy feet". Before we realized he was grown up, he was gone. It made no difference how far he went, we always knew he would get homesick enough to return.

Lee was like the Rock-of-Gibraltar to Dad. He was always there to share the farm load. We though our family was complete with two grown brothers and four little sisters. Not so, for on September 30, 1916, our little brother Lloyd was born. He was soon the pride and joy of us all. With blond hair and big blue eyes and the sweetest personality everyone loved the little fellow.

Lanna came home when the baby brother was six weeks old. When he returned to his work in Springfield it seemed Mother was so sad. I didn't quite understand why. But a few days later a letter came telling us that Lanna had enlisted in the army. On December 16, 1916 with angry war clouds boiling on the horizon it was evident that our American boys would soon be sent to the battle-front. So true, for it was only a few months until Lanna was writing from old Ft. Moultre in Charleston, South Carolina. He expected to go to the front lines in France with the first old regular troops when the States declared war. It was almost three years before we saw that kind hearted brother again. A lot of sadness filled our home. There were many tears shed. The winter of 1918-1919 brought the most dreadful influenza and also the black measles to our community. When we three younger girls took the measles we were so sick. But time spent in a darkened room to protect our eyes and the usual home remedies . . . plenty of alternate hot and cold lemonade to drink . . we soon broke out and began to get better.

When little brother Lloyd took them everything was

different. Nothing was effective, they just wouldn't break out. Before anyone knew it, he had double pneumonia. It was at eleven o'clock the morning of February 1, 1919, when this precious little one looked up at Dad, raised his hand to Dad's cheek and went to sleep for the last time.

Late in the evening, after the burial services for little brother, we were all doing our usual chores. Mother was left alone at the house. The telephone rang. She thought it was only a neighbor calling but it was a long distance call from Lanna. He had arrived in the States the evening of February 1 after thirteen months in France. Knowing our oldest brother was safe again on the homeland somewhat softened our sadness.

Lanna returned to Ft. Moultree at Charleston. We counted the days until he would come home. It was July 1 when he arrived for his first furlow. What a joyous month with a host of unforgetable memories.

The old organ was showing signs of wear. Lanna insisted we buy a new piano. It was wonderful for we bought a Gulbranson Player with a whole lot of rolls to play. The only effort it took to have good music was pumping the pedals.

Edith or Lanna could play the songs we liked to sing as well as they could play them on the organ. We seldom went to bed without singing awhile.

We sometimes walked to singing at the Baptist Church. We would sing on our way home, the old barber shop numbers such as: "Silver Threads Among the Gold", "When You and I Were Young Maggie", "Seeing Nellie Home" and many others.

Aunt Lou and the boys would listen from the porch or their bedroom window. They would call out to us when we were in front of their house to tell how they were enjoying the singing.

The month passed all too soon. Lanna was to leave Lebanon by train at 11 o'clock on Sunday night to return to the Fort at Charleston.

The Tri-County Singing Convention met on Saturday and Sunday at the Happy Home Church. We all went and what a wonderful time. Lanna was the life of any singing. He could direct a song like nobody else could. Folk sang without trying when he was the leader.

I still wore my hair in long curls with a big ribbon. But to my big brother I was a grown up lady. When the young folk each had a "beau" for thetrip to the train to see Lanna off, I went along and had my first date. Lanna promised me he would see to it that Dad and Mother didn't scold me. That date led to several months of steady dating.

When Fred and I went places together folk were shocked for everyone thought I was still too young to have "a feller". Fred was so attentive to me. He would lift my curls, ever so tenderly, as he helped me on with my coat.

"Cloudless Day"

13

Life has been blessed for me with an abundance of friends. I have especially treasured the friendship of older folk. As a child, when unpleasant things happened at home, I would wend my way down the path to Uncle Pate and Aunt Nan's house, thinking seriously about my heartaches. But, after I had told them all about it, and was assured of their love and understanding, I soon forgot my disappointment and returned home in a joyful mood.

When their oldest daughter was left a widow, with four little girls to raise, the dear old couple opened their heart and home to them. When they came to live with their grandparents we girls soon became inseparable friends. They yet call me their fifth sister.

Although Aunt Caroline and Uncle Jasper lived more than two miles from our house, I often walked over there and spent the weekend. Their granddaughters, Lola, Jessie and Jennie, who lived close by, would come down to play with me. But most of all I looked forward to the evenings around the crackling fire in the fireplace when we would pop corn in the wire popper over the fire or roast apples in the hot ashes on the hearth.

It was a wonderful weekend when Aunt Caroline taught me how to crochet. She gave me the spool of thread and the Hair pin lace I had learned to make. But I had no crochet hook. Several weeks later I found a nickel in the road as I was going to the mail box. I went to Aunt Sally's that very afternoon and bought her crochet hook. I made yards and yards of lace with that hook.

Aunt Sally was old and had no home. She lived several years with Granny. I always appreciated those two dear little old ladies. When Granny wasn't feeling well, many times Papa would have me go over and stay all night with them. The family who lived in the other part of the house were good to Granny but she wanted me to be there too. So the path through the field was worn deep where we walked it each day.

We had fun, Della, Oval, Clarence, Lawrence, Roy and I. We would stop by the persimmon tree and eat the delicious ripe persimmons. When the blackhaws were at their

15

best we were sure to come home with visible signs of eating them.

When snow drifts were deep the boys went ahead and kicked the path to make it easy for we girls to walk. What blessing can be greater than the love of childhood friends?

I did my first cooking for Uncle Tom while Aunt Sarah and Beulah were gone to Oklahoma to be with Susie in her illness and grief after the death of her baby son. Uncle Tom was so kind and patient. He would eat anything I tried to cook and brag on it like it was good. I made fried apple, dried apple pies. Oh my! I had the crust so rich they almost fell apart, but still they were perfect according to Uncle Tom.

Life was not all work and no play. The Morgan community was noted for its lively group of young folk. They were also noted for their singing and the ball team held an enviable record.

The girls went to all the games for moral support. Sunday afternoon games in the "Old Phillip's Field" was the gathering place for both old and young.

The two big Maxwell trucks that Fred and Levi (the stock buyers) owned were always ready when there was a game away from home on Saturday or a singing convention to go to on Sunday.

The Morgan Singers made any Singing Convention one to be remembered. With several good leaders, and all parts well done, they put life in the fast timed songs. The older folk were ever ready to assist or support anything the young folk ask for.

Harvest Time

Harvest time was the longest work season of the year. From the beginning of oats harvest, the last of June, until threshing, which usually lasted until September, there was no let up.

We always hoped to finish the oats cutting by July 4. With four horses to the binder the work was much faster than with three. It was difficult to drive four and handle the binder so Edith rode one horse, and did a good job of driving, while Lee rode the binder.

Papa and I did all the shocking. He was wonderful to praise me when I did my work well. He always told me how to set up a shock of grain and said I did the job better than most men did for the shocks stood up well.

Words are not adequate to describe the beauty of a ripening field of wheat when a gentle breeze waves the tall, golden grain. The wheat harvest was lots of hard work but it was our best cash crop, especially during war time.

Sometimes when Papa hauled a load of wheat to market, to the Silver Lake Mill, in Phillipsburg, Mother went along and bought material for new dresses at McMenus General Store for we girls. That was enough to cause us to forget how tired we were at the end of a long day of harvest. Even the tedious work of pulling the cockle plants out of the young wheat before it headed.

The hay harvest came between wheat cutting and threshing. Haying was more fun. When the barn loft was filled the rest was put into shocks and pulled to the stack. It was then pitched to the stacker. Sometimes we used rope lines and rode the shocks instead of riding the horse. It was my duty to finish the raking before I got to pull in shocks.

I was happy when I hooked the old mare, usually the one we drove to the buggy, to the rake and started raking. I always sang as I raked.

One fear in hot summer time was getting that dark tan. We kept a pair of long cotton ribbed knit stockings and cut the toes off. We then made a hole for our thumb. These were pulled high and pinned to the shoulder of our dress. A split bonnet helped but the wind and sun got our faces browned however much we tried to prevent it. Our night cream? It was very effective and worked wonders.

We would crush a few big fragrant leaves of Tansy and let it soak all day in a jar of thick clabber milk, then smooth it on our face before going to bed. Oh yes! When it dried it didn't rub off much.

That little old hut was a mansion to me.

There's No Place Like Home

"For lo the winter is past. The rain is over and gone. The flowers appear on the earth. The time of the singing of birds is come. The voices of the Turtle Dove is heard in our land."

Springtime is here again with its nostalgic memories. The words of the old song, "Down by the Old Mill Stream" float through the air as I go about my work each day and relive memories of that springtime in 1923 when Cole and I met, fell in love and began plans for our future life.

After seven months of courtship, Easter Sunday, April 1, 1923 was set for our wedding day. With the help of his sister, Edna, and some good neighbors, Georgia, Chloda and their mother, Mrs. Howell, the old log house in the Orla community was made livable again. It was papered, painted and shined like a new one even though oldtimers told us it had been built 97 years.

We received a few wedding gifts but showers were unheard of. I remember the shiny new copper bottom tea-kettle from his sister Georgia, a kerosene lamp from Kate. Mother gave us another lamp so we could have light in the kitchen and the front room at the sametime. We also received a butter dish, a sugar shell, butter knife, one small kettle, a lovely jelly knife and a new broom.

One of the brothers divided his seed potatoes with us. One sister gave us bean, tomato and cucumber seed. It all helped and we did appreciate it.

While Cole was gone to town Edna and I washed the windows. There were two in each room. I had three used window blinds. Edna and I put them up. Cole said the three worked fine for we didn't need one behind the cook stove. It was on the south and sometimes that summer it would get so hot I couldn't see much need to build a fire to bake the bread.

Cole surely thought I would be a big eater for he took wheat to the mill at Orla and had 500 pounds of flour put away upstairs on a table he had made to put it on. He had cut strips of tin and tacked them around the underside all around the edge to keep mice from going up the table legs and eating holes in the flour sacks.

Cole attended a farm sale and bought a dining table and the cutest little four cap cook stove which was so small it stood on bricks. He made a cook table with shelves across the top to store supplies and one underneath for pots and pans. It was covered all over with the prettiest oilcloth with little bunches of cherries on it.

On that cold, snowy Easter day, at 4 p.m., we stood in front of the double windows in the parlor of my old home and solemnly repeated the marriage vows before a group of relatives and close friends. The Reverend Fred McClanahan was the minister.

After the wedding supper at the home of my parents and the infare dinner at the home of his parents, we began getting our furniture into our little home with no thought of diamonds or honeymoon trip.

Cole went to town alone in the wagon to buy the necessary things to complete our housekeeping equipment. The total cost was $52.50, which included everything we had to have, even to a milk bucket.

Cole had also butchered two big hogs and had the hams, shoulders and bacon all smoked, wrapped in paper, then tied in clean flour sacks hanging in the smokehouse. The lard was rendered and put upstairs with the flour and 132 quarts of canned fruit. He had early garden planted and five old hens setting.

With my 12 Rhode Island hens, a sow, cow, yearling heifer and two mules to go with his two sows, two cows, two heifers, a team of mares, a mule and 20 sheep we thought we had a grand start.

We did work hard to raise a crop but we enjoyed working together as we were accomplishing something worthwhile. We made a good payment on the mortgage as well as the interest on our home that fall.

Many times my kiddishness caused much embarrassment. Like the time Cole picked a mess of greens. I didn't know there was anything other than Lamb's Quarter, Sour Dock and Mustard. When he brought the greens in there was some Polk and something that looked like Canadian Thistle. I dumped them all over the fence into the hog pen and politely told him I was not going to cook them for they would kill us both.

My brother Lee had always said: "Maw, that kid will never know how to do anything but clean the safe and make a bed." Lee was out buying feeder pigs one day and came by to see us. He was the first one of my family to visit us. He found me down in the field driving three horses to the disk. He said: "You go cook dinner and I'll disk awhile for you." We were planting corn and I was drisking ahead of the planter.

It was about 11 o'clock. I quickly put a fire in my little stove, then ran out to the smokehouse and cut some big slices of ham. Then down to the garden and gathered lettuce, radishes and onions. I opened a can of peaches and made a pan of cornbread. Lee had worked up an appetite and the ham and red gravy, with the tender lettuce, onions and radishes sure hit the spot. Although he didn't say a word, I knew he was more than a little surprised.

When dinner was over I said: "Lee, come see my little chickens." We had a fine bunch then. Each old hen had her own coop but they all ate in the feeder coop which was a long, low slat covered pen where I put the ground corn and rolled oats. The little chickens could go through the cracks to eat but the old hens just ran around the coop clucking.

When I called, one old hen brought her babies from the glade, another from the branch and another from the gooseberry bushes. Lee just stood there chewing his tobacco and looked shocked. When he went home he said to Mamma: "Well, my gosh Maw, that kid can beat you raising chickens and she sure can cook." What he didn't know was that I had a good teacher, a good provider and helper both with the chickens and the cooking.

One day when Cole was plowing corn I saw him tie his team to the fence and come walking very fast around the hill. He came to the door and said: "Mother (imagine him

23

calling me Mother when I still had long curls when I un-braided my hair and let it down) come with me a minute. There's the finest school of Spring Millets over there in the creek." I got my bonnet and went, even though I didn't know what we could do about it. Cole took somehooks, he called them grabbs, and we slipped up so easy and peeped over the bank. Sure enough, there they were in that clear, cool water.

He worked quietly, dropped the hooks in just in front of a big one, jerked, and out came the prettiest fish I had ever seen. He kept on until he got six. He cut a forked stick and put one prong through the fishes gills then out through their mouth and we went carrying them to the house.

I thought, now isn't this great, just go to the other side of the field, drop a little old hook in the water, no bait, no waiting for them to bite or anything, and come back with these.

Cole helped me get them ready to fry and were they ever good. Fresh from the creek, rolled in homemade corn meal, fried in hot hog lard, we thought they were fit for a king. We learned we had two more than we could eat so the next day we only caught four. But we did have fish for several days. There was one great big one that looked dif-ferent. He was very alert and evasive but one day Cole got him. He called it a Hog Mollie.

After that week's experience I became Cole's fishing buddy. Anytime he came in to ask if I would go to the river or creek with him I would lay aside whatever work I had to go along. It was a thrill the time I caught my first fish. We had driven over the Howell Eddy. Cole got my Pawpaw pole ready first, baited my hook with a nice big worm, spit on it, and threw it out in the still water. Before he even had his pole near ready, I got a bite. When it started to run I was so excited when Cole said jerk, I landed that poor little perch high on a Sycamore limb.

The next Spring was a cold, late, wet season. We had so many days when it was too wet to work. This is enough to give any farmer the blues. Clyde was staying with us that Spring. One morning after breakfast and chores were done, Cole said: "How about going fishing since we can't plow today?" Like any fourteen year old boy Clyde was ready for that. So while they watered the team, harnessed and hooked them to the buggy, I fried the young squirrel they had killed the evening before and boiled some eggs. I had biscuits left from breakfast and a few cookies. We were soon ready and took off to "Old Bartley Pond" for the day. This was a natural body of water, near the river, on the Uncle John Massey farm.

The water was high and muddy. We were not disappointed when we had "fisherman's luck" but we did enjoy the day and forgot for a time about the work we were unable to get done at home.

We received our mail at the Orla Post Office. Sometimes it would be two weeks old. I looked forward to reading all the news and helpful hints in the weekly Kansas City Star.

One time my brother Lanna and his wife Florine wrote to tell us they were coming to see us. We had about a week to get ready for them after we received their letter. We wanted our log house to look its best and it did need to be pinted. We were busy with field work but we decided to try to get it done. When we came in at evening time I would start beating and sifting white sand rocks while Cole fed the hogs and milked the cow. We worked as long as we had daylight. We completed the front and south side that week. Both chinked and pinted.

Then the ceiling paper in the kitchen was our biggest problem. The mice had eaten some holes in it so we decided to redo it by lamp light. We made flour paste and worked late that night to finish putting the paper up. The next morning that floor looked like some dignitary had visited us for it was covered with confetti. I looked at that ceiling and thought the whole mouse family had moved in.

I studied all day what we could put in the paste to keep the mice from eating it. I went over to Mrs. Nunns that afternoon and asked her. She gave me a string of real hot peppers and told me to cut them up fine in the paste. We did and I'll tell you the next night that paper didn't get any holes in it.

When our company came I pust my best foot first and my dinner turned out passable. You see, we couldn't go to the store and buy anything prepared, not even a loaf of bread. I had not tried to make light bread, and I thought many times my biscuits would be the death of me. I was teased so much about them. I'll admit, they did resemble little rocks sometimes.

Cole was a good judge of weight and value of calves. I could usually out guess him on hogs. When we had a veal calf or two to sell he could haul several in the wagon to the market in Lebanon as easy as two.Hewould buy enough from neighbors to make a load.

About a year and a half after we were married Cole was taking a load of real good calves to market. We had two, he bought two from Mr. Howell and one each from Mr. Nunn and Mr. Savage. He was ready to go before daybreak. When he told me goodby he said: "I believe I will buy a dozen steel traps if I make good on the calves." They would cost $3.50. I said: "That would buy me a new dress. I haven't had one since we have been married." I had been asked to sing in the Christmas program at the Morgan Baptist Church and I so much hoped for a new dress.

The calves sold for a good profit. Cole went to The Farm Supply to buy the traps. They were up to $3.75 and he almost came home without them. But he thought of how we could use some extra dollars so he bought them. Early the next day we went in search of the best dens along the branch and creek. There were so many good places it was difficult to choose the best ones to set the twelve traps.

When Cole run the trap line the next morning, he was so happy because he had caught two big short striped skunks. They sold for $2.00 each so he had the traps paid for and a quarter over. The next several nights were also lucky. When Fred and Levi came the first of the buying season he sold out and made $11.50.

The country roads then were not made for cars. The buyers asked Cole if he would go to some of our close neighbors and buy their furs for them. Almost every family had a good hunting dog and the boys usually made their Christmas money catching furs. When Cole came home late the next night he had sacks of furs tied all over the saddle and he was walking leading Old Gips. I had the chores done and supper waiting. We took the lantern and worked several hours cleaning up those pelts and grading them ready for the buyers.

We figured the profit at a price we thought might be a little high, but knew there would still be a good days work even if we had to reduce the price. But, the market was strong, they said, and they didn't ask us to take less. The $80.00 fur money we made in December, 1925, because of those twelve steel traps, was a blessing to us that winter.

We paid the $58.50 semi-annual Federal loan payment and had some help with the taxes. Oh yes! I also got the new dress for the Christmas program.

Even though our house was old and small, it was a palace to Cole and I. The latch string was always outside. We gave friends our best and they returned. We attended church at Fairview. It seemed the ministers found nothing lacking in our hospitality for many visited in our home.

One time we were having a two weeks revival meeting. Brother Russel was the evangelist with Brother Walter Parker and Brother Charley Wood to help out. The Darrus Hokes, Dick Southards, Grant Jones, Elva Hough and others were the workers and pillars of that country church.

It was a wonderful meeting. I recall several who are now carrying on God's work who accepted Christ as their savior and were obedient to his commands during those two weeks.

We had a neighbor, Mr. Rue, who had been ill for a long time. We invited the folk from the church to our house for dinner, then we all went to Mr. Rue's house and had services for him.

Another time, when Walter was visiting us, we decided to go see Mr. Rue. We were going to ride the horses. Cole and I were both riding "Old Tony". Leslie, who was living with us then, was going to ride behind Walter on "Old

Gips". It was muddy so Leslie was wearing his four buckle overshoes. When he stepped in the stirrup and threw his leg over, the old mare switched her tail. Leslie's overshoe buckles were just right to catch that tail. Those three really put on a good show. Very calmly Walter would say: "Son, if you don't get her tail out of there she is sure going to pile us both." Poor Leslie kept hanging on by one foot while the old mare stepped around pretty lively. He finally got loose. It could have been a tragic thing but we have had many laughs about the show.

We were the only ones of our families or friends who still drove a team and buggy. We were both agreed that our debts must be paid first before we spent anything for our own pleasure.

One day we went to Hough Chapel to funeral services for a friend. It was a large crowd and we were not a little embarrassed for we were the only ones there driving a team.

The next week we went to my folks and Cole had Papa and Vera take him to town and he came back driving a 1926 Model T Ford Roadster. Oh! we were proud of that little car. We made a place for it in the driveway of the barn and believe me it was always put there.

We were looking forward to going home in style for Christmas. The family all came home driving shiny automobiles and could spent much time telling about the good points and advantages of each one. We always felt left out of their conversations. Our car had special curtains on rods that fit in the doors. They didn't have to be buttoned up after we got in. A special feature we had to be proud of. Cole would go out after dark and turn the lights on just to look at that pretty little car.

A real cold spell blew in one morning a few days before Christmas. Cole thought to drain the radiator. He turned the cockpit and hurried on with the chores. But, he didn't go back to check and see if the water all drained out.

Christmas morning the weather was much better and we had everything ready early. Cole took teakettles of hot water to fill up the car so it would start easy. We learned later to jack up a hind wheel before we cranked and it would start. When he raised the hood to pour the water in he was shook. He found the water had not drained out as he thought and the engine head was frozen and bursted. Well, we just did make it home in time for dinner for we had to get the team harnassed and go to the neighbors and borrow their buggy.

Our neighbors were wonderful. Always ready to help in any way. I shall remember always the butchering times and threshings. Both jobs lasted for days. But we had lots of fun helping each other.

Although there have been many mountains to climb there was always the green valley on the other side. Time passes swiftly. One day high in the sky we see flocks of wild geese as they wing their way homeward and we know that Summer, like our lives, is almost past. But, far in the distance one lone goose calls loud and long for its mate who has been lost in the travel. But it bravely flys on to finish the journey alone.

"Life seems so little when life is past.

And the memories of sorrow flee so fast.

And the woes which were bitter to you and
to me,

Shall vanish as raindrops which fall in the
sea.

And all that has hurt us,

Shall be made good.

The puzzles which hindered be understood.

And the long hard march through the
wilderness bare,

Seems but a day's journey when once we are
there."

ARTHUR COLEMAN BEARD
October 25, 1895 - November 15, 1960

33

Roper Cemetery

With many worthwhile projects waiting to be done there is no time for idleness. Small, neglected, country graveyards have long been a challenge to me.

When the first graves of pioneer families were made in a selected spot on the homestead they were the beginning of community cemeteries. They were small enough that the families kept them cared for like they did their door yard.

As time passed, and the number of graves increased, neighbors met on Memorial Day to have a general cleaning day. Many folk searched the river-bed for mussel shells. They cleaned them in lye water to make them white and covered the freshly raked mounds with the shells.

There are yet many cemeteries that are known by the name of the family who settled the farm.

In the mid-twenties, when the once a year clean-up was not sufficient, a neighbor and I met often at the cemetery. We discussed ways in which we might improve the appearance of it. We set out roses, iris and peonies. There were three bunches of bright pink peonies at my grandfather's grave that were put there before the turn of the century.

One day the neighbor's son, Bill, said: "If you ladies will do something about it, I will give $10.00 to start a fund to help clean up Roper Cemetery." We wrote some letters to folk away who we knew cared and received several dollars to add to the ten.

Members of the "Helping Hand" (a neighborhood club) discussed it and decided to meet for a work day. With hoes, ax, garden rakes and other small tools the members came one hundred percent strong. Uncle Henry Hilton brought his one horse wagon. The sprouts were thinned out, stumps burned, rocks and clumps of dirt hauled away. After several days of work, and many blistered hands, the cemetery took on a new appearance.

With the monetary gifts a new 18-inch hand push lawn-mower was made possible. At that time I was secretary-treasurer of the "Helping Hand Club" so it became my duty to keep a record of the money and pay the bills.

The work progressed. Everyone was proud of the progress made. The project increased and as money came in it was soon put in the bank in an account to pay all bills by check.

Through high and low times, dry or rainy seasons there has always been enough money to keep the cemetery in good shape since the beginning of the work. However, a few times the bank account has been almost as bare as Mother Hubbard's cupboard. There has been those who did more than their share and the work has continued.

Near the beginning of the year 1966, after much thought and plans, and upon the advice of a lawyer, it was decided to begin a Perpetual Care Fund for The Roper Cemetery. Three men were selected to serve on the board of trustees, with one to be elected each year. I continued to serve as secretary-treasurer.

The cooperation and response was far above expectation and the goal was surpassed in record time. With careful management, the interest on the fund, will now, throughout time, keep the cemetery cared for. It will be a community project of accomplishment that all may point to with pride.

There have been problems in the many years of service without compensation, but the knowledge of a job well done is ample reward for any disappointments.

In 1964 I completed a history and plot book of the cemetery which has been made available for all who desire.

Storm Clouds

As a knot appears unexpectedly in a thread so disappointment blocks the smoothness of life. If a few skillful strokes can untagle the skein, life continues evenly. But, if it cannot be corrected, then it must be quietly woven into the design. Thus the finished piece can still be beautiful, though not perfect as planned.

The great disappointment came to me on Tuesday morning at eleven o'clock, November 15, 1960, when the Master said, "Your mansion is completed, come on home" to my wonderful companion.

The storm clouds gathered after a bright and beautiful morning when we had laughed together. But the sun went down while yet it was day. The house was soon filled with friends and neighbors with outstretched hands willing to do whatever was possible to help lighten my load of sorrow.

After thirty-seven and one-half years of close companionship, with a guiding hand to steer the vessel, it seemed my island was far out to sea and I was so alone. I fully realized my aloneness when I entered the door of our home late Thursday evening. My minister cousin, who is nearer than a brother, placed his hand over mine and said: "My dear, it will take courage to go on now but you must and you will. Don't forget there is one who is ever beside you, who loves and cares for you. Trust in Him and He will show you the way."

Many times in the weeks and months that followed I was grateful for the faith and trust in a Supreme being. There were many problems but the way was made brighter by the kind deeds of thoughtful friends.

Those who had children were wonderful to share them with me. The four teenage girls who lived close by would often spend a night with me.

For several weeks twelve year old Darrel did his chores early so he could come by on his way to school and eat breakfast with me. They all learned to like hot tea because I drank it. We had many tea parties.

Life was much like a puzzle with the most important piece missing. But with each new day I found added courage to face problems alone. Many times when I faced a difficult task I would ask God for guidance and courage and promise Him to do my best. It was then I could fancy I heard Cole say, "Mother, you are doing fine."

One of the greatest lessons came to me late one evening. We had our first snow of the winter. The skies began to clear and the sun shone through. Like a compelling force the desire to take a walk over the fields as Cole and I had done so many times over the years, came over me. When I was tempted to go, that inner fear silently said "You can't". But I put on my boots, coat and scarf and started. Down through the barn lot and around the hill I walked a mile in the snow making the usual trip that we had so often walked hand in hand. As I returned the sun was going down in a blaze of beauty. I recalled the many times Cole had remarked, in almost the same spot, how he wished our sunset of life could be such.

Although my tears flowed, that walk proved to me that I could conquer fear and in spite of the knot in the thread that I could continue the pattern.

Cole's eminent personality was the rainbow of my life but I had been content to remain in its shadow. As time passed the pieces of the puzzle became more easy to put in place. I began driving the car part-way home after we were off the busy highways when Nadine was with me. Each day brought more courage and each time I tried to drive I did better.

Junior would come by on his way home from work in the evenings and put the car in the garage backward so if I decided to drive someplace I would not have to back out. One evening I asked if he had dehorned his little calves? We had always dehorned with Caustic Paste when they were small. Junior said he wasn't sure he knew how to do it. I said: "I'll be over in the morning to help you." About daylight I bravely started the car and drove over to their house.

38

There were some rough places in the road but I was beginning to be used to the rough spots in life. I made it fine. They followed me home to be sure that I made it back all right.

That family spent much of their time trying to help me in making adjustments. They were all so good to me.

Although I never thought of missing Sunday school and church that was the most difficult place to go. It made no difference who served at the communion table, to me Cole's chair was always empty. The kindness I received from those whom we had had Christian fellowship with each Lord's Day for so many years was overwhelming. We had each filled our place as teachers and leaders in the Washington Church. Our Saturday nights were set aside for lesson study together. Cole was rated tops in Bible teaching.

The Sunday School Class

Contrary to our pattern of promptness, Cole and I were late for Sunday School on the first Sunday morning in September, 1930. Classes were already in their places when we arrived.

Mrs. Alice and her class of small children were seated on the ground in the shade of the small oak trees in the North Church yard. She waved for me to come to her and asked if I would assist with her class that morning. When I accepted her teacher's book and began to read and explain, the children quieted down and became attentive. They became more eager to answer the questions. Several took my hand and ask if I would be back next Sunday?

After the prayer of dismissal, Mrs. Alice said: "Lois, I believe you would make a wonderful teacher for this class. I have about finished my usefulness in teaching them. Won't you please give it serious thought." I was sure I would appreciate the children and would learn much while doing my best to instruct them.

There was one problem. The road between our house and the church was some times impassable because of the high waters of Brush Creek. But I did accept the class with the understanding that she teach when it was impossible for us to get there.

It was several years before we had a high water bridge over the creek. Sometimes we would let most of the air out of the tires on the Model T. That would keep them from cutting down deep in the soft gravel. When we had crossed to the other side it took several minutes to pump up each tire with the hand pump.

It was a pleasure that I looked forward to each Lord's Day. To sit with the children on the moss covered ground, in the shade of the oak trees. A great challenge to prepare lessons to teach them to live as Jesus would have them live.

When winter winds made it necessary for the class to move inside, it was a problem to teach twelve to eighteen

40

active youngsters in a wee corner of the church without disturbing the other classes.

We talked Cole into making a couple of oak benches. The men put the wood on the north side of the wood house. We put the benches along the south wall, put a piece of old carpet on the dirt floor and some pictures on the wall. We had a real nice room in winter for our class to meet. Many Sundays we wore our coats and overshoes to keep warm but we appreciated being away from the other classes. We stayed there until the new wing was built on the north side of the church in 1934.

It was sad when that group of children were old enough to go to a higher class. But, there was another group ready. They too were soon attached to my heart strings. And so it has been over the years, each child has held a special place in my life.

I have given to them my best and the best has been returned a hundred fold. Two regrets I have. First, that I have not kept a record of all the children who have been a member of the class, which would no doubt reach hundreds. Second, that I did not record all the cute things they have said. Only a few I can recall, such as the time Paul, our minister, told me he planned to visit our class the following Sunday. I was giving instructions of how I wanted them to be when Ruthie said, "Lois, don't you think we should get Paul a gift when he visits us?" I said: "Yes, that would be fine Ruthie, but what would we get him?" Before anyone else could even think of an appropriate gift, Sherry, his own little girl said: "Well, he sure needs underware."

Our class moved several times over the years. But when the furnace room addition was built about the year 1950, a classroom was built on the south side, which has been our room since.

In 1965 when special recognition was given me for teaching the same class 35 years, there were 60 present who had been members of the class. There were several fathers and mothers whose sons and daughters had followed them.

Two are now in regular church attendance who were in the class on that first Sunday morning.

Our part of the Christmas program each year is a high-light of the evening. Since the children are small, I write our own program so that each one has a suitable part. The most remembered, outstanding, program was the one we gave in 1960. We named it "Home for Christmas." It was so real. I was grateful the lights were out except on the stage so I could not see the many tears that were shed in the   audience.

Some of our most outstanding Bible students have had their basic training in this class. For the past five years we have studied from colored illustrated Children's Bibles.

I am humbly grateful for the many years of service I have been permitted to give at Washington Church. Not only for the opportunity to teach so many children to follow the straight and narrow way, but also for the thirty years of directing the song service and the many special numbers in song that I have been able to give.

Because of the advice of Dr. Jake, our family physician, I went shopping in Springfield with Ada and Helen for a new organ. It had long been my deep desire to learn to play some musical instrument. It was another big decision to make. After four weeks with a rented one, I bought a double manuel Lowery Holiday. What a blessing that proved to be.

Even though my fingers were short, thick and stiff, with the help of the Pointer System, I soon began playing simple pieces. After a few lessons from Mrs. Elinor, who was a wonderful teacher, I was playing hymns. Many nights when I was unable to sleep I would spend time playing the organ. Sometimes I would play from two until four in the morning. It was the challenge I needed to fill wakeful hours.

More than a year passed. One day I went in to the Lebanon Rustic-Republican office. The editor asked me if I would help him write a feature article about my hometown, Morgan. I said: "Tom will you let me write it?" Why I ever thought I could do a thing like that I'll never know.

When I came home I began searching for information from old-timers, from abstracts, church and post office records. I put it all together with what I had in my memory. Emil Morris, the photographer for the paper, came out to take pictures. I wrote so much we had to divide it into two installments.

The response was so great I began writing about all the oldtime folk who had lived in the vicinity. With old pictures I had two more week's installments. I was so thrilled the way the articles were received I began thinking about others I could write.

That proved to be the turning point in my life. It seemed there was always another story ready to begin when I had finished one. I especially wanted to do those about oldtime personalities and places.

The first time I had a story ready to take to the paper office and none of my friends who drove with me could go that day, I knew I must make my decision to either sit home and wait for others or to go alone. My decision was made. But I want to assure you it did take courage to drive that car out and start to town alone.

When I opened the doors of the garage I started singing. I slid under the wheel and quietly bowed my head to thank God for his guidance and protection and to ask that he might keep his hand upon me as I went on this my first journey to the busy city alone.

I drove slowly and as carefully as I possibly could and sang ever so softly all the way to town. I parked in the M.F.A. parking lot and walked the four blocks to the paper office. Again I had conquered the fear that was almost overpowering.

The employees of the paper and radio station were so kind and thoughtful of me. I soon became a part of that one big family. Their praise and encouragement helped take away some of my timidness and gave me assurance in my own ability. I found myself looking forward with great anticipation to the days when I would take my feature article to the office.

Constructive criticism from the editor once in awhile was just what I needed. Tom was ever ready to point out mistakes and to help me with corrections. My first fan mail was exciting. I soon learned I had friends and admirers in all walks of life.

While thinking of those whom I wanted to write about, I thought of Uncle Sam and Aunt Sarah. A dear old couple who lived across the creek from us in our early days together. I went to ask them if I might do a story about their lives. After we had visited for awhile, when I went to leave, Aunt Sarah put her arms around me and kissed my cheek as she said. "Lois, you will never know how we missed you in this neighborhood when you moved away." There were tears in my eyes as I drove away from their home that day. It had not occurred to me that the friends we had made were not all because of Cole's wonderful personality.

Each article that I completed and had printed brought kind remarks. The old mill and the country store that were almost forgotten. The pioneer families who cleared the land of timers and rocks to make tillable fields. Those were the backbone of our country. The one room schoolhouse and the little church by the side of the road which had once been the hub of the community wheel. They too were almost forgotten. All made most interesting historic subjects that were well read and enjoyed.

With suggestions from friends I had no trouble finding material for stories each week. One day the editor asked if I would take an assignment? I felt both humble and proud. Proud because he thought I was good enough to do the article as he wanted it. Humble because of the opportunity to do something that would bring happiness to others.

Emil and I drove by his home to ask his wife to go along. We left town about noon with instructions from Tom to go by Brady's Post factory to get story material there.

That proved to be a pleasant experience for me for it gave me a first-hand chance to see and learn all about the process of making Penta treated fence post.

When we arrived in Plato, about 3 p.m., we were instructed to go to the barber for information. He proved to be a genius in memories of history about the town. In one hour Emil had taken several pictures and I made notes from the stories I heard. We bought some good apples and candy bars to eat on our way homeward. We had not taken time out to eat lunch.

When we returned to the newspaper office Tom said: "Now I want a full page on Plato." Whew! I thought . . . can I do it? My first time there, didn't know a soul, spent one hour there, then asked to write a full page.

It was late when I returned home that evening but I did not call it a day until I had sorted my notes and made others so that I would not leave anything out. I did enjoy writing that story and was justly proud when it only lacked a short space in one column filling that full page.

One day there was talk of having a get-together of the employees of the radio and paper and their families. It was Summer time and my big yard was the ideal place. I invited them all out for a picnic supper. What a good time everyone seemed to have with plenty of space to play. The children loved it. The yard was pretty. The roses were at their best and the garden was doing well. Everyone marveled at how I could keep things so ship-shape. Well, it was easy for I had sold "Old Prince" our garden horse and bought a Ro-To-Tiller. I had also bought a new gasoline powered lawn mower to replace the old hand push mower. Most all the families came, about forty in all. The party proved so successful everyone was ready for another one soon.

Pictures were the making of my stories. When Emil and his family went away from Lebanon for a better job I knew how much the pictures meant to my stories. Emil was great to take the pictures I needed. He was the best photographer I had ever known. We would be going along when he would see some subject to shoot. He would stop the car, be out and have the picture and back under the wheel to go before I realized what picture he had wanted to take.

Ron filled his place and did a good job until he received his call to service. And then Andy joined the staff at the printing office. For several years he and I have worked together. He is never too busy to go wherever I ask him to go. We have each added a great number to our list of friends because of our work together. Andy is the friend who brings the ray of sunshine on a dark day.

"The joy of being friends is just
A simple code of faith and trust.
A homey comradeship that stays
The threatened fear of darker days.
The kind of faith that brings to light
The good the beautiful and bright
And best and blest, and true and rare
Is having friends who love and care."

Some folk like to travel while others stay at home. I didn't know there were so many wonderful places to see until I was well past my half century mark.

After my most lonely year, 1961, I was adivsed to make a trip away from home. When I began to make plans neighbors came to offer help. Everything was in order when Nadine, Sonja, Glenna and Brad took me to the railroad station. Just before train time Kenneth rushed in from the florist shop with a lovely corsage from Hope, Harold and the children.

There were tears as I said good-by, but I was mistaken when I thought I would be lonely on the train. There were others just as I who were happy to find someone to visit with.

My friends, Grace and Perry, were waiting at the station for me when I arrived in Oklahoma City. We attended church at The First Christian on Sunday morning. That building was one of the first of many I was to see that would live long in my memory. The folk took me to several places of interest in the city. After a few days with them I went by bus to Comanche to spend some time with Pat, Frances, Andy and Richie.

Frances drove me over to Wichita Falls, Texas. I went by bus to Odessa to spend two weeks with my special cousins, Dave and Thelma. The Roper home was much like my own, with always a group of young folk playing the piano, singing and eating. I fit perfectly into the crowd. They included me in all their activities, even to helping on the radio program on Saturday afternoon.

I made a host of new friends while in Odessa. When I sang my last solo at the Sunday evening service at the church, and told them all good-by, I felt as though I was leaving friends I had known always.

That first trip was the beginning of many. Each year I have taken time out of my busy life to make at least one trip. To visit with friends and loved ones and to see another part of this wonderful world that I had only read about.

From the summit of the beautiful mountains around Denver, the mile high city, to the floor of Carlsbad Caverns,

I have enjoyed the breath-taking beauty of the most interesting places.

The day I was sixty I took my first plane ride as a gift from Mr. Wright and the gang. Gene was at the controls and pointed out many places of interest around Lebanon from the air.

I could write a volume about the many things I have learned in travel to other parts. But, there are still many others that I wish to see. If the Lord tarries, and it is His will, perhaps I may add more knowledge to my storehouse of memories.

Many times I pause to count my blessings. At the top of the list is good health. Until I was well past my three score years, I had never known serious illness. And then one day I became so sick that none of the home remedies I tried brought relief.

When I entered the hospital on Monday, January 19, 1970, still not knowing what had caused my all night of suffering I was soon aware of the true value of friends. Someone was always there ready to help when I needed them with a kind pat on my hand or a kiss on my cheek. The many, many cards, the flowers and gifts from friends far and near.

After four days of semi-consciousness, mail time became a bright spot in my day. I could not visualize the number of friends I have made in my lifetime. Because of letters and cards from friends, whom I had not seen or heard from for so long, I relived days of my childhood, my adolescent years and all the years that have followed with friends and changes the years have brought.

A few times my pillow was wet with tears of pain, but many times tears were close to overflowing because of the kind and thoughtful, loving deeds of friends.

From all walks of life the messages came. From both high and low estate, but all showed their love and concern for my well being.

Again and again I have said thank you Lord for the dedicated, consecrated folk of the medical profession, who are ever ready, however late the hour, to relieve pain and suffering and to stand by to give assurance that they are there if needed. For a wonderful hospital and its staff of workers who do not think of their patients as number one in one fourteen. But their tender look of compassion was true unspoken friendship. Again I say, thank you Lord for friends who care.

My three weeks in the hospital followed by the weeks of convalescing at home were only another of life's detours. But the beautiful scenery around the hill far over shadows the discomforts of the rocky road.

"The crooked path proves to be the best way.

We climbed the height by the zigzag path and
    wondered why until

We understood it was made zigzag
    To break the force of the hill

A road straight up would prove too steep
    For the traveler's feet to tread.

The thought was kind in its wise design
    Of a zigzag path instead.

It is often so in our daily life;
    We fail to understand

That the twisting way our feet must tread
    By love alone was planned.

Then murmur not at the winding way.

It is our Father's will

To lead us home by the zigzag path

To break the force of the hill.

              (From Sprigs in the Valley)

I soon resumed my daily walks, most usually to the top of the hill, there to watch the sun go down. One evening after a refreshing shower, the walk was especially pleasant. My mind returned to friends and loved ones of long ago as I looked over the familiar fields in all directions. All at once I faced the east and there on the blue cloud was the most perfect rainbow. Childhood days returned when we talked of the search for the pot of gold at the foot of the rainbow. While I stood thus, lost in thought, another rainbow appeared, high above the first one. It was then I thought of the many friends I had made in the years I have been alone.

The wonderful personality that for so many years had been the beautiful rainbow of my life while I was content to remain in its shadow. But when I looked again I understood the secret, the rainbow has no shadow, and the smile that brought love and kindness at sunrise did the same at high noon and evening time.

"The shadows lengthen. The shuttle must fly that the pattern may be completed ere the sun sets. For the end of the journey is near. But the twilight hour is the most beautiful time of all."